D0918549

LOVECHILD

LOVECHILD
A SELF-PORTRAIT

by

Mary Hanes

J. B. Lippincott Company
Philadelphia and New York

U.S. Library of Congress Cataloging in Publication Data

Hanes, Mary, birth date
  Lovechild.

  1. Unmarried mothers—Personal narratives.
I. Title.
HQ999.U6H3   301.42'7   71–39757
ISBN–0–397–00773–6

To Joseph and to James,
who's now my friend

Author's Note

This is a true and very personal story centered around having a child out of wedlock. Originally I planned to write it under my own name, but to protect the privacy of others I have taken a pseudonym and have changed all actual names, places and dates. I have also altered incidents, physical characteristics and familial facts to prevent identification.

I am not trying to speak for all unmarried mothers. I think my case may be more extreme than most. I do hope, however, to alleviate some of the loneliness and isolation those in my position may feel. Certainly my story should provide encouragement where it is needed: if my child and I—wacky, confused and ambivalent as I am—have made it thus far and are finding an increasing share of happiness and satisfaction, then surely others will too.

LOVECHILD

1

The deadline is only four hours away, so now I must telephone
volcanic little Stephen Turner to answer to those questions I
strategically omitted from our interview several weeks ago.

I have delayed getting these final bits of information because that
interview was so unpleasant. Turner is a hysterically vicious young
man. He erupted in anger all over his office again and again and
finally grabbed the telephone and, smiling at me triumphantly,
called the publisher of my newspaper and demanded that I be fired:
I did not know my place as a reporter, I asked too many questions.

Turner is a fool, and it is just his kind that I have come to fear. I
wince inside at the thought of hearing his whining voice. But
tomorrow the newspaper wants to run a profile of him along with
the announcement that he has been appointed to head yet another
charitable project to build old-age housing in Dryden.

I begin with a lie: "Mr. Turner, I understand you're committed to
giving most of the work to black construction companies."

"You're out of your mind," he shouts. "Those people aren't up to
doing the job. What do they want, anyway?"

And so it goes, a battle I am secretly winning until I ask what is to be the first of several personal questions: "You were married twice before your present wife?"

He sputters around for words. "You . . . you . . . you have your nerve!" he yells at last. "You—you have a child and you've never been married. I know all about you. You're nothing but a stupid—a stupid whore."

"I'm sorry to have upset you," I say, automatically slipping into my calm-mother voice, "but sometimes we must ask offensive questions, if we're to keep the record straight."

I hang up the telephone, put a piece of paper in my typewriter and am well into the third paragraph before I begin to cry. It is ridiculous; I must be premenstrual. I type another sentence or two, and then I have to get up and leave the city room.

In the bathroom, I cry freely. It is that kind of an easy hurt, but its deepness surprises me. It shows, I suppose, how long it has been since anyone used the fact that I am an unmarried mother in a hostile way, and inside I am no longer prepared to meet it. The pain leaps up in me from another time and much greater hurts, and I am afraid.

When I have stopped crying, my hands are still shaking. I want to get away. I walk back into the city room and tell the editor behind a pile of stories that I am going to lunch, at ten fifteen in the morning.

"I know," I answer his raised eyebrows. "Your boy Stephen Turner and I just had a run-in again. He called me a stupid whore."

"I knew you were stupid, but the whore's a surprise."

I try to laugh with him.

"Go back and finish my story," he says.

"I'm going to lunch now."

"Jesus, and you think we should hire more women!" He shakes his head good-naturedly. "O.K. Go to lunch now, and have one for me."

But I have little faith in alcohol. Physical activity and exercise are my great painkillers. In my time, I have vacuum-cleaned my house twice in a single night and scrubbed the shiny floor boards and wainscoting until my fingerpads were raw and my knees bruised. Now, I run in my high-heeled shoes six blocks across town to the YWCA and its ancient, overheated swimming pool.

I swim back and forth rapidly in the hot, stinging water, shooting my arms forward and away and kicking furiously at Turner, the

12

newspaper that exposed me to him, my child James and most of all at myself and what I feel. And it works, pretty much. Soon I am too tired to think of anything but the effort of swimming. I slow down and begin to take pleasure in the act of moving forward and then turning, weightlessly, slowly, under and up to start again, forward and on.

As I shower and wash my hair, I am planning how I will get even with Turner, how I will tell the facts and use his own bigoted words to let him hang himself in my story.

I dress, and as I give my locker key to the woman at the desk, she admires my shirt.

"I'm making myself a summer dress in that same shade of red," she confides. "I've never had one, a red dress I mean, but I think they do so much to—well, just sort of lift one's spirits up? Do you know what I mean?"

"Yes. You'll look nice in red," I say, feeling her sadness for a moment. I am sure she leaves the green dungeon walls of the locker room, which she has hung with pink tissue-paper roses, and goes home at night to the mustiness of her gray mother and gray father, and perhaps a Boston bulldog—who is glad to see her. She is 50, perhaps 60, and irrevocably chaste, an old maid who hesitates to open her mouth to any feeling, even the admiration of a color, lest her sorrow or her shame at being unchosen slip out on its coattails.

She is the kind of woman my parents used to ridicule interminably at the dinner table during the long nights of my early childhood. They picked old maids—as handy scapegoats—to dissect in their efforts to hide their own failures from themselves and from each other, and to postpone the quarrels that exploded through the apartment at night and brought my baby sister into my bed and arms.

My father, then almost forty, had been through three wives and a sizable inheritance. He was partially disabled by a bad back, recovery was slow, and his desire to support a fourth wife and two little girls was too slim to sustain an effort to get himself placed as an executive—the only kind of job he would consider. During that period, he saw no direction to his life other than in his annual trips east to his prep-school and college reunions.

My mother, bitter because she had thought she was marrying a rich man when she abandoned her chances of becoming an opera

13

singer, grew doubly bitter when, far from being supported by either wealth or honest work, she found herself, her husband and two daughters—not the longed-for sons—living on the charity of her middle-class father.

There were three old maids in the dingy Colton apartment building we lived in then. Cornelia Simpson, whose fiance had been killed in the war, was different from the others, for at least she had enjoyed "a promise of one." But she was laughable, clinging to a honey-colored poodle and venturing out of her black-veiled mother's apartment for only the briefest walks—to the hydrant and back. Of course, everyone knew that Adele McCarthy, who lived across the hall, slept in her underpants because she was afraid of any man, even her father, the judge. But the one who really shook the dining-room table was Mimi Fitzpatrick, a lacy, yellow old lady who wove from side to side as she walked. Old Mimi lived alone with a tall, skinny avocado tree, the symbolism of which escaped me, of course, at the age of six, but which my parents found uproariously funny.

I would sit at the table waiting for dessert and disobediently pinch the soft wax at the base of the candle flame when they were blinded by their laughter. I felt faintly hostile toward them and their mirth, which I could not share but had to endure because young ladies do not leave the table until everyone is finished.

The old maids were always nice to me, and especially good to my baby sister. At Christmas they gave us presents long before Santa Claus came; candies and paper dolls with real hair and, from Miss Fitzpatrick, a baby doll who wet his diaper when you gave him a bottle of water.

I adored the doll in his blue knit cap and jacket, but it concerned me that he had only smooth plastic between his chubby legs. What was even worse, the water came out of a small hole way up above the base of his spine.

I ran my hand across the top of my father's behind very carefully as he was sitting on the bathroom stool to clean his toenails after his shower. There was no hole there.

"Of course not. This is where I urinate," he said, and stood up to demonstrate the act for me by releasing a marvelous yellow jet into the toilet bowl. "The world is filled with prissy old maids who give little girls vulgar toys."

An old maid I would never be because I would die long before I

14

reached adulthood. By the time I was seven, I knew that to be a grownup was to be either a parent, a person trapped and drowning in a bitter sea of marriage, or one of those ludicrous creatures known as old maids.

I decided that, if I should happen to survive to maturity, I would become an Episcopalian nun. I knew there were such creatures, and they were acceptable because my grandmother took me to church with her each week and we put pennies in a mite box to help the nuns keep hookworms from crawling into the feet of little Puerto Rican children.

When I did survive to physical maturity, I had for a while the idea that something besides death would save me from spinsterhood or the terrors of marriage. Surely, I thought, the right man would come along, and when he proposed, panic would not grip my heart. Inside Mary was a sleeping beauty capable of trust, and his words would awaken her.

By the time I was twenty-four and met Ronald, I'd been through a good many right men and found only more panic. I'd begun to think I'd better do something about shaping my own life. Mostly as a joke, but not entirely, I'd talk about entering a convent. It was a pretty good line, followed by a pensive stare into my glass and then a wistful, "So, that means I'm giving up the sins of the flesh, lover." I'd let whoever he was think that just maybe I wasn't joking after all, that only his charms had whisked me back from the convent gate.

Eventually, of course, I escaped both pathetic old-maidhood and miserable marriage by becoming an unmarried mother. I got pregnant by accident, but certainly these conflicting dreads were strong factors in my decision to let the pregnancy run its normal course and to bring up the child on my own.

In any case, I have been quite a bit like the clerk in the Y locker room. I feel sympathy for her, and, as though my parents were watching or would care, I delight in expressing my admiration and enjoyment of her. So, I stand there for five minutes letting my red shirt go limp and my hair kink while I encourage her to go on talking about the effects of various colors on various moods.

"Well," she says at last, "since Daddy died, Mother felt that we shouldn't wear anything but the more conservative colors, you know, navy, oxford, maybe a little beige. But I do hope she'll let me get away with this red," she again confides.

15

"If she doesn't, tell her to get herself another daughter," I say, suddenly impatient.

I go back to the paper and jab out an appropriately vicious profile of Turner. It will be censored in places, but I don't give a damn. For underneath the business at hand, all I can think of is how much I want to be done with work, to get to James, to be comforted by the sight of his snarled yellow hair and blue eyes as he runs across the schoolroom to meet me.

James and I have come a long way together in the four and a half years since his conception. Today, most days are good days. He is discovering the joys of ants and Babar books and water pistols. He is in love with me and I with him. I have doubts and worries about us, but generally our relationship is erotic and happy. I have a job I enjoy, reporting on "urban affairs" in this small Southern city of Dryden. Some people say I was hired because, as an unwed mother and outcast of white society, I'd be acceptable to the resentful black community. I rather doubt this, and in any case I don't care. The winters are mild, the springs are fragrant, and in the summer even we inner-city residents can grow lettuce in our tiny back yards. And of course there is Joseph—deep, calm Joseph, who takes me to a peaceable kingdom and flows into me like a ballast of heavy honey. But it is so easy for the desolation of a few years ago to come back with a quick rush of fear that awakens all the old demons within me.

When James is in bed and the dishes are done, I sit on the couch beside Joseph. He is curled up in a circle of light to read one of his little Unitarian essays, which pass before my eyes like air when I try to read them.

I tell him about Stephen Turner.

"You must have done something right to get him so angry," he says. Sleepy and affectionate, he misses the point of my hurt. "Now that Mary's got a boyfriend and life is easier, she doesn't like to be reminded about being an unmarried mother," he teases, pulling me down onto his chest.

Immediately, I want to protect myself from such acknowledged vulnerability. "Life is no easier with you," I start to say, about to mention the meal I have just cooked and the dishes I have washed. But suddenly, I realize what he has been showing me in the months we've been together, that a big part of love is letting another take

16

pleasure in the knowledge that you love and need him. This is a gift I find hard to give, so I disguise it somewhat.

"Pretty confident, aren't you?" I ask, trying to make my voice sound cross, but the sparkle of his light gray eyes undermines me. "Damn confident," I say, unbuttoning his shirt and slipping my hand in to feel the wondrous flatness of his breasts and tiniest of nipples. "Wonder why?" I ask, hiding my face from him in the warmth of his skin.

2

I got pregnant in the summer of 1967. Since then society has become more tolerant. Today single people adopt children, and shelters for unwed mothers close for lack of business. In many states it is fairly easy to get an abortion. In 1967, if you were pregnant and unmarried, you were in trouble. With considerable difficulty you could get yourself certified emotionally incompetent and have a legal abortion. More often, you stood on a street corner with a pack of Kools in your hand and five hundred dollars in your shoe and waited for a voice you'd heard on the telephone to offer you a ride. If worst came to worst, you fled to a shelter and hid with girls who shared your shame.

That summer, when I was not working at my job on a Colton newspaper, in the evenings and on the long, hot, hazy weekends, I tutored black children in a southside neighborhood house. Some, in their early teens, I tried to teach to read. Others I tutored in what culture I'd picked up, so that when they went to their private schools on scholarships in the fall, they would not be so obviously "culturally deprived."

My efforts were inspired as much by a desire to escape a miserable

18

affair with a married man as by any belief that I might actually help the black race. I knew that the children I came in contact with would grow up no less hated, no less handicapped because of me, but the hours I spent in the basements of their churches were hours when I was safe from Ronald.

He refused to believe that after a year-long relationship I was through with him. At work he was polite, even cold, merely glaring at me occasionally across his desk, but he would wander into my apartment at dusk, his blond hair gray in the half light, with a bottle of gin under his long, stringy arm and the same old feeling of insignificance and helplessness inside. It eased his pain to beat against me, to beg, cajole, threaten. I stopped letting him in and I stayed home as little as possible.

But I had forgotten that he still had a key to my apartment, and one night when I rushed home to get some money, he was sitting on my couch drinking a martini. Two girls would soon be at a nearby bookstore waiting for me. It seemed easier and quicker to let him have me and be gone than to get pulled into a night of fighting. I could no longer feign desire. I lay back and felt sad and sick for him.

When I thought he was asleep, I pulled on my dress and started out of the apartment. But he was awake, and my apathy had wounded him, perhaps as I'd planned.

"You'll be sorry," his voice came distinctly through the darkness.

As the gears of my bicycle began to click, he said it again, standing in the doorway of the apartment house and wrapped in my bedspread: "You'll be sorry."

"Watch out," I said. "Here come the cops."

I didn't think about that night until three months later when I realized I was not ill but pregnant. I was overjoyed. And that joy persisted despite the troubles that followed.

At first I was just sleepy and out of sorts, but then a cold heaviness began to rise in me, filling me, swaying back and forth with me, often coming dangerously close to spilling. If it was an illness, it would be fatal, because I knew as it settled into my core that it was more powerful and purposeful than I could ever be. I lay on my bed, unable to go to work, and slept as though I had been drugged. In snatches of consciousness, I saw the yellow and green August days reeling past my window, and I was afraid.

I was too afraid even to call a doctor until one dawn when I awoke from a formless sort of dream to find I retained its feeling of warmth and belonging. I got out of bed and made some tea, and then, for the first time in a week, I got dressed. The floor was still swaying as I moved, but I was cheerful and confident that I could face whatever was happening to me.

As an adolescent, I'd felt that Dr. Browning was the only human being in the world who knew me well and still managed to care for me, despite my unworthiness. His office, with its many colored photographs of his small daughter, felt like home to me, and as I sat there, looking at him, I suddenly knew what I'd been unable to face in the preceding weeks. I smiled at him.

"I'm not sick, I just realized. I'm pregnant."

He was used to my imagination. He smiled back at me tolerantly. His reception room was filled with patients waiting to see him.

"I doubt it. You used your diaphragm?"

"Yes, but something must have gone wrong."

"Well, diaphragms are only 95, 98 percent effective, so it's not out of the question. How long has it been since you menstruated?"

"Two or three months. But that's not unusual for me. I've been very sleepy, and cold and terribly seasick. And I have to urinate every five minutes."

"Sounds good for a pregnancy," he said. "But I wouldn't worry. Let me see if Dr. Roy can fit you in this afternoon. No point in letting this worry drag on, and you're overdue for a Pap test anyway. Have him call me after he's seen you."

Dr. Browning did not handle gynecological problems himself, and he'd sent me to Dr. Roy several times before. Dr. Roy, in fact, had fitted me for the diaphragm I now knew had failed to do its job.

Dr. Roy's office was filled with pretty young matrons in pale summer dresses with lots of gold bracelets and rings on their hands. His was a fashionable practice and I felt very scruffy and disreputable in his waiting room. His nurse separated me from all the proper young women and took me into an examining room. I wrapped myself in the yards of paper toweling as she'd directed and sat shivering in the cool of the air conditioning until he came in.

As he peered into me, he said from between my knees that he'd enjoyed the article I'd had in last Sunday's paper. He'd even pulled it for his wife. Funny, he couldn't remember now what it had been about.

"I think we'll know for sure in about a month," he told me. "We'll see if some progesterone will bring you around." He started to leave.

"What will you know in another month? What do you think's wrong with me?"

"I think you're right, you've got an early pregnancy. But I wouldn't swear to it."

"You think? Don't you know?"

He looked irritated. "Do you want me to have my nurse run a test on you? Remember if it's negative, it could be wrong."

"Of course I want a test," I said, equally irritated.

"O.K. I'll see you in a month anyway. If the test is positive, I'd like to have you bring your husband with you for that first appointment. I'll answer his questions at the beginning."

"Dr. Roy, I'm not married," I said, surprised that he didn't remember such a fundamental thing about me. "I'm single."

He paused a minute in the doorway, and I thought he was going to say something, but he just shrugged his shoulders and left.

I gave the nurse a urine specimen.

"I should get a chance to do the test in about an hour," she said. "Why don't you wait downstairs in the coffee shop? You must be very nervous."

But I didn't want to sit in the smoky, crowded coffee shop. I crossed the street and walked along the banks of the river, across from the hospital, and then down toward Miss Seymour's School. I knew it was a very dramatic hour in my life, and I began describing it to myself: "As she walked along the river bank. . . ." This was an old trick of mine for lessening anxiety by escaping from the heart of the situation and making myself an observer.

As I neared Miss Seymour's, I saw a disheveled-looking workman staggering along the path toward me. One too many on a Friday afternoon. I smiled at him as he passed and he took off his cap to me. He was just the sort of man who'd worried Miss Seymour's School to the point where it had made a rule that no girl could walk along the river path. In order to circumvent its treacherous bushes, we had to walk on the main road, a good six blocks out of the way.

Several times in fits of depression and self-destruction, I'd deliberately plunged into the well-screened paths and strolled past the deserted benches and thickets. I'd hoped I'd be seen by one of the teachers I loved and be called in for a scolding. Any attention

21

was better than none. But I was neither seen nor attacked by the rapists who were said to hide in the rushes down by the stream.

For a minute I thought of going over to the school and trying to find one of the teachers to wait with me and help me plan what I was going to do if I were pregnant. But it was summer, and the school was deserted. Besides, no teacher had ever talked to me outside a classroom when I was a student. It seemed unlikely that any would remember me nine years after I had been graduated. And Miss Seymour's was such a pretentiously moral place. Sex was mentioned only in the rather veiled language of the biology textbooks distributed in our senior year.

I remembered the heavy smell of formaldehyde that hung in the biology laboratory, and how the smell lingered in my hair. I remembered the cold steaminess of the winter mornings at Miss Seymour's and marching warmly packed in a line of other girls, backs straight as military cadets, down the stone corridors to prayers and assembly. A half hour later, we'd burst out of the hall singing one of the school songs: "Arise, arise, the trumpet sounds . . . we bring our hearts, our youth, our zeal . . . our honor an untarnished shield . . . ." as we rushed off to our first class of the day.

I'd wanted so much to belong to that naïve and goodhearted female world of love and trust, of nice girls who grew up, left Miss Seymour's, made their debuts, and went to nice junior colleges until they married nice men, doctors or bankers. But I'd never quite made it. I had bad posture, and I was not nice. I had all sorts of horrible feelings inside me, and when my classmates were rushing off to have their cotillion dresses fitted, I was dragging my book bag sullenly downtown to see my psychiatrist. All this Miss Seymour's forgave, but what it could never understand was my hostility. I fought the school each and every day because I was afraid someone might discover that I loved its warm womb and wanted nothing more from life at that point than the security its strict rules gave me.

At graduation, on a green spring day, I sat in my white dress, in a line of other girls in white dresses, and knew that everyone could see my hangnails and pimples. Everyone knew I was not quite normal, and that I didn't quite fit in. When the ceremony was over, I was jubilant. I had made it, I had gotten through without anyone even suspecting that I cared about the school. But the asthma that I'd had since early childhood really betrayed me, flaring up so that I spent

22

the summer wheezing alone in my room, grieving about my loss, all the teachers, all my friends. Every other night on his way home, Dr. Browning would stop by, give me a shot and tell me life would be better in the fall, when I got away from my mother's unhappiness —far away, into Bennington in the Vermont hills. He was right. At Bennington, everyone seemed to be a misfit. I could breathe easily, and I found new teachers to love and new friends. I sat outdoors looking at the mountains and wrote a poem or read a little French each day. There was no one to tell me what to do or take care of me, and I began to realize that this was probably a good thing.

By the time I finished college and came home, both my parents were dead. I had become quite close to my sister, but she was just going east to Bennington herself. I got a little apartment and went to work as a reporter for a newspaper.

When I got back up to Dr. Roy's, I could tell by the look on his nurse's face that the test had revealed something quite serious. I was ushered into his office.

"Mary," he said, getting up to meet me as I entered, "your test was positive. You are pregnant."

I immediately burst into tears, perhaps because he expected them, but more likely because I was so moved by the news. Something good, a life, was growing inside me.

"Can you get married?" he asked, and I shook my head.

"What do you want to do?"

"Have a baby, become a mother," I said, crying all the harder. "I'm sorry I'm crying all over your office—I'm just so happy."

"There are alternatives, you know. Abortion—certainly you should think about that seriously. If you decide not to interrupt the pregnancy, you can put the baby up for adoption. Think about it; there's no rush. You have another month."

I spent the afternoon walking through the city and talking to my baby, whom I visualized as a little girl of perhaps four or five. I picked her up at kindergarten, and we walked home, shushing through the fallen leaves. We were working on an elaborate doll house together, one made out of wooden packing cases carefully refinished and wallpapered. I had made curtains for the windows and woven real rugs out of scraps of yarn.

When she asked me about her father, I told her that a woman

23

didn't have to be married to have a baby, and I was not married when I had her. If she wanted a father, it was up to her to pick out a man who would be her friend. Her blood father and I did not get along, and we thought it best to spare her from the bad feelings we had for each other.

When I got home, I sat by the window watching it get dark, and listening to the happy yelps of the next-door children as they ran back and forth in the alley in some wild and elaborate game. There would be plenty of time for me to plan. That night I just wanted to enjoy my happiness and pride at being honored by life.

In the days that followed, I became more practical. And I was not entirely pleased to be pregnant. There were flashes of apprehension; I would be an "unwed mother." In the past when I'd wondered what I would do if I ever became pregnant, I'd always decided that I'd have an abortion. Now, this alternative seemed unthinkable. What was inside me was the force of life itself, demanding that I clothe it in flesh and blood that it might be born. If I were to allow that force to be destroyed, I too would be destroyed in a most complete and frightening way.

And of course, I'd always wanted to have a child. It made me very sad to think of going through life childless. What I hadn't wanted was marriage, because that, for a woman, meant making someone else your primary source of happiness. You were completely dependent on your husband; and people, no matter how you might love them, were basically unreliable.

It would be embarrassing to be an "unwed mother," at least in the beginning. But so what? I'd brazen it out for a few months, until it became an accepted fact of my life. I certainly would not give away my own baby just to save myself a little embarrassment, or even a lot of ridicule. The child might be handicapped by not having a father, but I'd always known lots of men, and I was sure it would grow up loving some of them as I did.

The fact that I was pregnant should not require me to make too many changes in my life. I could continue living where I was; there was even a spare room for a baby. My job at the newspaper paid me $10,000 a year, and there was every reason to assume I would continue to get annual raises. I would not be rich with a second person to support, but many large families lived on half of what I made. I would ask for a leave of absence from the paper, just for the last two months of pregnancy and a month after the baby was born: I didn't want to be walking around with a giant belly, embarrassing everyone. I thought I had enough money saved to tide me over this period, especially if I began economizing right away, did some free-lance work, and took advantage of the health insurance provided by the paper.

As I thought about Ronald's role in all this, I became quite sentimental. I suddenly felt that he had loved me and that I'd probably loved him. I began to want to share my happiness with him and to wonder if he might not be pleased and proud of me. But at the same time, I knew very well that he would react with rage and selfishness. I knew I would have to coddle him along for days, until he found the courage to face up to the situation and help me. I didn't have that kind of strength anymore, because I needed to save all my energy for myself and my baby. I would involve him only in an emergency.

My sister and the few friends I had would understand my decision and encourage me, I decided, but I was just as glad that my parents were dead. My father had loved me deeply in his own way and had wanted for me all those intangibles which he'd been unable to find. It would have broken his heart to think that I too was unable to make a happy marriage. And my mother would have felt herself wronged by my pregnancy. In fact, she had always known in her almost psychic way that I'd get pregnant, and she'd made me promise to handle the pregnancy her way.

One afternoon the summer I was twelve, I was reading on the porch of our cottage at the lake when my mother came out to talk to me. She usually let me go my own way, so I knew she had something very serious on her mind when she sat down beside me.

"You're going to menstruate soon. That's something that happens to women once a month. Blood comes out of you because you're not having a baby."

Two or three years before, I'd spent a Saturday afternoon in the city library, giggling with a friend over books which described the reproductive process, so I knew all about menstruation, but somehow, I'd never figured on it happening to me, and my mother's words terrified me.

"Blood won't come out of me," I told her. "I'll hold it in."

"You can't; it just flows right out of you and you have to wear pads to absorb it."

"I'll hold it in until I get to the bathroom," I repeated. I was quite sure she was wrong, and that I could control it.

"Honestly, I really can't communicate with you at all. It's as though you weren't my own flesh and blood. Why are you so stubborn all the time? Other girls are close to their mothers, and other girls do not act the way you do."

I put the book up in front of my face and began to read again. I was reading *Of Human Bondage* and identifying with those parts of Philip's loneliness and misery that I understood.

My mother began to cry. "Everyone knows how awful you are to me, how you torment me and hate me. It's just not normal."

"I don't hate you, Mummy," I said, beginning to cry myself. "Leave me alone."

"All right, all right." She ran into the house. But, several minutes later she came back and grabbed my wrist, so that the book fell to the floor.

"Just promise me one thing," she said, tears tracking through her make-up. "When you get pregnant, don't go to some back-street butcher of an abortionist. Come to me or Fred Browning, and we'll—well, we'll handle it in a way that will cause us the least embarrassment."

"I'm not going to get pregnant," I said. After all, I knew what strange things you had to do to get pregnant. Ugh.

"Just promise me you'll do it my way? I just couldn't live through all the gossip, and if you went to one of those quacks, he'd probably kill you. There are all sorts of safe ways to get an abortion, just remember that."

"O.K., O.K. I promise," I said. "Now, leave me alone."

After she went back in the house, I picked up my book, but I couldn't read.

I'd certainly never tell my mother anything private. She used confidences the way my father used jokes—to entertain people. Fred Browning? That was a possibility; he was the handsome young doctor who'd just begun to take care of the family. But it was all ridiculous. I'd never get pregnant, unless my husband insisted that we do that thing. And if, by some disaster, I did get pregnant I

26

wouldn't go to any abortionist. I remembered all too well the story I'd read about a year ago in one of our baby-sitter's magazines: Fifteen-year-old Karen had died in the abortionist's office, while her boyfriend Chuckie waited in his car outside. The abortionist had taken her body out the back door in a laundry bag. At home he'd hacked it into small pieces. The climax approached when Chuckie was watching the abortionist's house and saw him come out with a brown paper bag. When Chuckie fished it out of the corner trash barrel, he found it contained Karen's hand, complete with his high-school ring, taped to fit her third finger.

When I took the magazine in horror to show my father, he ripped it up and gave me *An American Tragedy* to read instead. Needless to say, at the age of eleven I found the love magazine story much more comprehensible.

When I went back to see Dr. Roy he tried to talk me out of keeping the baby. At least, he said, I should remain flexible about keeping it or not. And—he'd taken the liberty of talking with Dr. Browning, and they both felt they could arrange legal abortion if I wanted to reconsider that. Fred had told him I'd been seeing a psychiatrist earlier in the year, and they both knew he was one who was fighting to liberalize state abortion laws and would recommend me for abortion without a second thought.

I shook my head; no, I wouldn't even consider it. I was shocked that Dr. Browning, who knew how I felt, would have conspired behind my back. I went over to his office and waited until his last patient left to confront him.

He was annoyed. "I simply felt that if you happened to change your mind, you should be able to have an abortion easily. That was all. Personally, I probably would advise you not to. You have enough ideas about how evil you are as it is. You'd probably feel guilty for the rest of your life. Have the baby; keep it if you want. It's all up to you. You're a pretty independent-minded woman. You'll manage."

3

My sister, Pat, was a graduate student at the university; she lived in a commune in a run-down neighborhood near the campus. When my plans were set enough to talk about, I telephoned the house for three days before I reached her. She couldn't possibly come to supper because it was her night to cook. Wouldn't I like to come there? No, I said, I had something private to tell her. I felt very ill at ease in her house anyway, I was so conservative and middle-class compared to its residents. She agreed, finally, to come over after dinner.

It was almost ten o'clock when she arrived, her long red hair damp and her face flushed from the effort of cooking and cleaning up for a dozen people. Apparently, she had sensed from the tone of my voice that this was a serious occasion, because she'd brought her gigantic, bony boyfriend with her. Even more that I, Pat shied away from emotional confrontations, and Herbie, a psychology student who smelled of Ivory soap, would insulate her from whatever I was going to say.

I resented Herbie's presence, so I let them sit nervously on the couch for a long time and wonder if the news they were to hear was good or bad. But as I made them a drink, I began to see that Herbie's insulation would help me too. I couldn't cry in front of a relative stranger. I would have to be cheerful and solicit their congratulations. I was still too queasy to drink, so I put iced tea in my glass, and then, squeezing in next to Herbie on the couch, I proposed a toast to the baby I was expecting.

"I know where you can have an abortion," Pat said immediately. "This girl at school just had one and only missed two days of classes. East Orange, New Jersey."

"I don't want to have an abortion, I want my baby."

"Baby? Christ. It's not a baby, now. It's just a little blood clot. This man in New Jersey only costs four hundred dollars, plus plane fare, of course. You've got to have an abortion," she said, as though it were a matter of fact.

"Mary, you've had quite a bit of therapy, haven't you? I'm sure you could get one legally on the grounds of emotional instability," Herbie said, scratching his balding head.

"'Emotional instability' won't quite do it, Herbie," I said: "You've got to be so sick that the pregnancy is going to push you over the brink of insanity. But, in any case, I don't want to have an abortion."

Pat was beginning to understand what I'd said.

"You can't have a baby without a husband. It will ruin your life. Please, be sensible." She was on the verge of tears, and she got up and walked around Herbie to try to hug me. "It'll be all right. I'll fly to New Jersey with you. The operation only takes about ten minutes. It's just a D and C."

At the sight of her pain, a great choking sound came out of me. It was a frightening, even terrible thing in our society to have a baby without a husband. You were turned out in the snow, alone to die, or practically so. I was pregnant, knocked up, and by a man who didn't give a damn in hell about what happened to me. I was in it completely alone. I couldn't stop crying. This was it—the worst that could ever happen to a woman.

"Does she have any tranquilizers in the house?" Herbie asked Pat.

"Oh, if only Daddy were alive, he'd take care of me, I know he would," I burst out.

"She identifies quite strongly with your father, doesn't she? You

29

can tell. The sign is that she doesn't talk like most women." Herbie was happy to be demonstrating his clinical skills.

"Jesus, you're an ass," Pat said to him.

Their exchange diverted my attention from my own situation for a second, and when I came back to it, I realized what maudlin self-pity I'd been sinking into. It was a luxury I could no longer afford. If I was going to be able to respond to a baby's needs I had to be strong. I went into the bathroom and washed my face. When the tears stopped catching in my throat every time I exhaled, I went back out to the living room.

"Pat, let's not talk about it any more. It's all settled. I am going to have a baby, and that's final. I'm sorry I cried. You know, I'm really quite happy about it."

Now Pat began to cry. "Poor Mary, you've always been so unhappy and alone, I just can't bear this. Where's the father? Why won't he marry you?"

When I told it was Ronald, she stopped crying. "That dirty fucker," she said. "I'm going to talk to him tonight. He'd better get divorced and marry you."

Herbie got up and took her hand. "Let's sleep on it, Patty. You need to sort out your own feelings before you say any more."

Pat began to cry again.

"I don't want Ronald to know," I said, following them out to the car. "No one knew we had an affair, and no one will know he's the father. I didn't mean to upset you, because I am really very happy. Really I am. It will be such fun for all of us. I know it will. Just think, you'll be an aunt."

"We'll be in touch," Herbie said, through the car window as they drove away.

The next day, Pat telephoned to say she was feeling more optimistic about it. A baby would be fun, and I was right to leave Ronald out of it. But I knew she really felt quite differently.

In the following weeks, I told the few friends I had, and they reacted pretty much as Pat had. Most of them were lonely young men who came by occasionally to eat a free meal while they watched the baseball game on television, or to discuss their love problems. Each of them told me how I could get an abortion. One offered to send me to Puerto Rico or Sweden. Another had a classmate in Boston, Massachusetts, who had just flunked out of a medical school in the spring and been cut off by his parents. He was desperate for money, and he'd probably do it gladly. One, an aging divinity student, told me very frankly that my attitude was morally reprehensible, I was flaunting the ways of society, and then, undoubtedly imagining me whooping it up in bed with some gloriously gorillalike creature, said "Disgusting" and walked out, never to appear again. Most of the others drifted out of my life quite rapidly.

I began to wonder how the newspaper would react. I decided to talk to one of the top executives and ask him for a leave of absence. That way there would be no long chain of gossip. My leave would be granted and I'd simply disappear for a while.

When I walked into his quiet, carpeted office, he was on the phone. When he had time for me, he acted rather distracted. Gee, they'd hate to lose me for that long. Four months, at the most, I'd said. Well, it could be arranged. Anything else he could do for me? I said no, thanked him and started to leave.

"Wait. I forgot to ask what you're going to do," he said pleasantly, tapping his desk top with a paper clip.

"Actually, I'm going to have a baby," I said, blushing.

"You're what?" He slapped the paper clip down.

I repeated it.

"This changes the picture somewhat. I'd assumed—well, never mind what I'd assumed. I'll have to check with some of the other officers."

He called me up that night at home and asked if I'd be willing to have an abortion. Otherwise, they'd have to let me go; yes, if I wanted to put it that way, "fire me." I offered to make up a fake husband, change my name and wear a ring. No, that wouldn't help; let's be realistic.

There was no newspaper guild at the paper to which I could appeal, so I went to a lawyer. The lawyer said it was their right to fire me if they wanted to, but he'd see what he could do. After a couple of weeks he reported that the paper would give me severance pay, about as much as I would have gotten from unemployment compensation, and would allow me to resign, so that a firing would not appear on my employment record.

I was crushed. Now I was really in trouble. I could survive for the next five months on the severance pay, but what would I do after that? How would I support the baby? Ronald, in his vaunted

31

capacity as head of my section, had told me I was no good, and this was pretty much proof. If the paper was willing to drop me, after six years and at the time when I most needed work, it was a good enough indication that Ronald's assessment of my talents had been accurate.

I had to find other work, quickly. I went to the state employment office and was told that I couldn't legally work after my seventh month. I was then almost five months pregnant. They recommended that I try to do temporary office work. Terrific—I type with two fingers and take a shorthand of my own invention. And the last thing I wanted to do was spend the rest of my life typing.

I panicked and began to exaggerate my troubles and my precarious position to myself. I feared hysterically that the baby would be born prematurely, at any minute, and die.

Dr. Browning told me such births were relatively rare, and suggested that I might really be hoping for an escape. I knew he was right, but I wouldn't admit it to anyone. He gave me some Thorazine to calm me down, and the first tablet I took made my mouth dry. I thought he was giving me a powerful dehydrant to dry the life out of my baby.

"Don't be ridiculous—we give it to pregnant women all the time. It's never hurt a single baby to my knowledge. If you want to worry about that sort of thing, there are a couple of other medicines you've had to take that I'd choose first," he said over the phone.

I was too frightened to ask which medicines. So—my baby had been poisoned. I grieved as I waited for the dead fetus to be born. Only, as I lay in bed, it fluttered inside me, moving for the first time. I had been given a second chance. This time I would do anything to see it born. I threw the Thorazine away, just to be safe, and called Ronald.

For a week I listened to his anger, his accusations, and then his fear that came out as threats: if I ever told anyone it was his child, he swore, he would come and take it away from me. Any court would give him custody; it would be a very simple matter. He'd merely have to show a judge his home, his family; no court would award a child to a sniveling, incompetent neurotic like me, he said. In my own panic and fear, I believed him, and I swore to him I'd never tell a soul; my sister knew but, I promised, she could be trusted.

Ronald then gave me a plane ticket to London. I'd enjoyed a trip

32

to England several years earlier, and he said I could live there very cheaply. It would be better for everyone if I went. He was probably right. At least in England no one would be around to take away the baby, or threaten me with abortion, or even speak to me. I could go my own way and get back some of the confidence I'd had in the beginning, before I was fired.

Pat was in the process of getting rid of Herbie and was down on Colton, where she said there was nothing for either of us. Of course I should go. She'd go in a minute, if she could find an excuse to leave graduate school.

Dr. Browning thought much less of the idea. He thought I should stay at home, where there were a few people to help me and give me some support if I needed it. Had I talked to my grandfather?

I would talk to my grandfather, but as far as support went, there was really only Dr. Browning, and he wouldn't be involved in the birth at all. In fact, he would be out of town for a month right around the time the baby was due.

I put my books in cartons, sold my furniture, and packed what few pieces of clothing would fit me before the baby was born. Then I got nervous about taking such a drastic step and called on my grandfather, who was, with Pat, the only family I had.

I'd expected him to be shocked and angry, but he listened calmly, merely nodding his wrinkled gray face. Finally he said I was handling a difficult situation well. He admired my courage. Of course, if I ran into trouble, he'd help. That was what families were for.

The next day, however, he'd changed his mind. He'd arranged for me to have a Caesarean abortion. When I shook my head, he gave me a few days to think it over, implying that if I did not accept his offer, I would no longer exist for him. But, as it turned out, he didn't really care one way or the other. When I called to give him my decision, he had already gone away for the winter, as usual. My existence had never been of much interest to him, but I had loved him in a casual, though none the less significant, way.

I arrived in London at dawn, the day after an international motor show opened. Hotel Booking, a tourist service, spent several hours trying to find me a hotel room. Just before noon, they located one on Belgrave Road, only twenty-five shillings a night. The room, it turned out, was on the fourth floor of the hotel, which had no elevator and no porter. The only working bath was on the ground floor.

I had not slept at all during the plane flight, and the pure white brilliance of the world at sunrise several miles above the Atlantic Ocean had split my head open with pain. The time change made me feel completely removed from the dirty red carpeting of the hotel stairs. I kept thinking I was still on the plane, and squinting my eyes. I was sure the effort of climbing to the room while carrying my suitcases would kill the baby.

I lay down on the pink chenille bedspread, intending only to get my breath before hanging my coat up. When I tried to move, however, I found that I was literally paralyzed with panic, which began thumping, then thundering, in my chest and throat. It was like the nightmare I had had so often: I opened my mouth to scream for help, but no sound came; I tried to move my arms and legs and failed, the effort leaving me drenched in sweat.

I watched the afternoon light flowing through the gray net curtains and across the cracked and chipped paint of the ceiling. It was quite simple. I was having a nervous breakdown. Hysterical paralysis. It would not kill me, and it would not hurt the baby. I kept telling myself that, but it did very little good. The maid would find me in the morning. I would be taken to a mental hospital in a strange country and there at least I would be safe— but would I?

In the morning, I could move and I could speak. But my feelings were paralyzed. I sat on the bed crying—I sounded like a dog whining—but inside, I felt nothing. I kept trying to stop. I got a towel from my suitcase and held it over my mouth while I walked down to the bathroom, and back up, but the sobs kept coming and coming. It was really quite grotesquely amusing; I knew what was upsetting me, but I couldn't feel it; I just wept.

The maid came in and, seeing that my bed had not been slept in, started to leave. Then she saw me standing at the sink in front of the window with a towel over my mouth.

"Are you sick, love?"

"No, just sad," I sobbed.

"Oh, now, it's no time to be sad, with a baby on the way."

She was the first stranger to look at me and acknowledge I was

34

pregnant. I put my hand down on my belly and it was nicely big, and hard.

"Your husband left you?"

I nodded.

"Never you mind about that," she said. "Come on downstairs and get yourself some breakfast."

After breakfast, I felt better. I called a friend who lived out in Hampstead. She came right in on the train and hugged me. It was wonderful news—a baby! I was so lucky. She'd been living alone herself for six or seven years, and she envied me. Why, she even knew a job I could get. An anthropology student in Earl's Court was looking for someone to take dictation from him and type up his notes at home. It would pay my rent. We went looking for a better room for me that afternoon and found one near Piccadilly. I called the anthropologist that night and went to work for him the next morning.

He looked like a thin, auburn-haired Lord Byron to me, but he was very cold and aloof at first. One day he dictated a letter with which he hoped to gain support for the liberation of a young Greek woman who was a political prisoner. In the letter he described how she had been pregnant at the time of her arrest but had just written to him to say that life in jail was easier now that she had the company of a darling boy born ten days earlier.

I began to cry and could not see the paper to write down his words any more.

"Very well, then, we'll finish this one tomorrow," he said. "That will be all for today." He left me alone in his study to compose myself.

I expected him to fire me the next day, but he proceeded with business as usual; only, when he was through, he asked if I'd like to have lunch with him. We sat in a little pub and drank half pints and ate dried-out shepherd's pie. He said I'd really shaken him by crying. I'd seemed so tough and self-contained that he'd been hesitant to talk to me.

After that he took me to lunch almost every day and drove me home in his arrow-shaped yellow sports car. I thought he was a very nice boy and began to dream about him. In one dream he was my baby, lying in the curve of my arm.

One morning I arrived at his house to find a silky-looking girl, naked underneath one of his sweaters, at the breakfast table with him. After he'd taken her home and returned, I raged at him for putting me in such a humiliating position.

He looked at me with shock.

"Oh, God," I said, "I have such a rich imagination. I'm sorry. I think I've been telling myself that you loved me, and were only waiting for me to have the baby."

"Yes, well, I was afraid of that," he said. "It's really a good thing, then, that you're going home."

I decided if the baby was a boy I would name it after him. James. It was a nice name, after all, and I'd never been involved with a James, so it was a safe choice.

I went back to America because I was worried about money. The nearer the baby's birth came, the more I realized what a responsibility I would have for preserving its life. The more money I had in the bank, the better off we'd be. I thought that in America I could live for free in a shelter for unmarried expectant mothers.

The shelter I approached when I got back to Colton said its costs were about a hundred dollars a week, plus several hundred dollars for the delivery. This was clearly out of the question for me, but I had several long talks with one of the social workers, who finally came right out and told me that I had to give my baby up for adoption. I agreed with her that in some ways it would be selfish to keep my baby and thereby deprive it of a nice, middle-class adoptive home—but I was selfish. Then she told me at great length just how severely I would handicap the child, how I would ruin its life. I could not possibly be a good mother. Look at me, running around the world irresponsibly in my eighth month. From the evidence I had very little to give a child. Most intelligent girls in my position found the courage to give their babies up. She knew of several dozen couples who were waiting to adopt.

On the surface, I dismissed her opinion, but inside, I was badly shaken. She was a professional social worker and a rather nice woman. She'd spent twenty years handling pregnant unmarried women. She was probably right in her evaluation of me. I would be a terrible mother.

"I'm concerned about the child, Mary," she said finally, "but

36

more about you at this point. You simply cannot bring up a child alone. You may try, but I think you'll live to regret it."

When she was convinced that I was beyond dissuading, she sent me to another agency which, she said, would help me get day care.

The social worker there took a more aggressive approach: What made me so special that I thought I could keep a baby? That was just plain irresponsible. We weren't talking about a puppy or a kitten. This was a human being. All right, she said, as I started to walk out, it was up to me. She'd help me find day care.

She spent more than an hour asking me questions about my family and Ronald's. When I couldn't tell her what color Ronald's mother's eyes had been, she thought she should talk to him. I said no, but it never occurred to me to ask why she needed such information to find me day care.

"It won't be easy to find a good sitter for you," she said, "but if there is one in this city, I'll find her."

I left her office feeling immensely relieved. She had been awful to begin with, but in the end, she'd become my first real ally. Everyone knew how hard it was to find good help, especially at the low wage I'd be able to pay. How lucky I was.

About a week before the baby was due, she called me up. How was I doing? She had some disappointing news. When she'd talked to me, she'd forgotten that her agency no longer found day care for people. They were philosophically opposed to it. And, as a matter of fact, it was illegal in the state for preschool-age children. Of course, if I could afford to pay $100 a week, she'd get a well-trained baby nurse who'd come into my house every day. She didn't want to leave me in the lurch, however, and she had a perfectly charming young couple who'd be thrilled to death to have my baby. My share of the agency fee would be only $125, whereas the adoptive parents would pay the agency several times that. Didn't I want to take this, the humane, course?

Before I hung up on her, she said she'd see me when I was in the hospital, just to make sure I hadn't reconsidered. She'd asked the hospital to notify her when I was admitted. The hospital social service staff was much more considerate—its members even offered to help find me baby clothes if I needed them—and they said that under no circumstances would they notify anyone of my baby's birth unless I requested it.

37

4

Several hours after James was born in the Colton City Hospital, a black nurse's aide came up to remove me from the whiteness of the recovery room. There were four mothers there, and I alone had produced a boy. I chuckled when one asked me if I too had had a girl, and so they turned and began talking among themselves.

As the aide pushed my bed through the dark corridors, I asked her where my baby had been put, and she stopped the bed by a nursery window and rapped her eyeglasses frame on it. For the second time that night a red raisin of a thing in a huge white undershirt was held up for me to admire, and for the second time I smiled not at the sight of a baby, but at the proof of my accomplishment. They said it was normal, they said it was male. After months of worry, after months of telling myself I really and truly wouldn't mind at all, not one bit, having a girl, that baby was quite a show.

"You seen enough?" the aide asked in an angry tone of voice. "All right with you if we move on now, MISS Hanes?" She had been looking through my chart as I watched the baby.

She took me to a closet of a room filled with asbestos-covered pipes—a nook, I later learned, that was usually reserved for dying ward patients. There was a four-bed room set aside for unmarried mothers, but that week it was full with girls from the maternity homes in town, and so the hospital gave me, a ward patient, a private room of sorts. It was kinder for all concerned, I suppose, to keep the unwed mothers segregated from those who have husbands.

In the room, the aide began poking around, unpacking a plastic satchel of sanitary napkins and baby products, a gift from the hospital and various manufacturers.

It was one o'clock in the morning, and I asked her if I would have to wait until breakfast time to eat.

"Looks that way, don't it?" she said. "Kitchen's closed."

I had had nothing to eat or drink since the previous morning. I asked her if she would get me some water, but she didn't answer.

"Mind if I take these home to my granddaughter?" she asked, holding up some baby powder and oil. "You won't be needing them, I guess."

"I need them," I said, wondering if I was expected to bribe her with all twenty-five cents' worth of them for a drink of water. "I don't have anything much for my baby."

"What you need now? You be giving him up for adoption, won't you? I seen in your record about you not being married, didn't I?"

"I'm not married, but I need that stuff. I'm keeping my baby."

"You don't say?" She smiled at me. "You going to keep that baby? Most white folks don't have enough love."

About a half hour later, she returned with a tray. There was hot tea, buttered toast, jam, milk, and a bowl of sugar—which I ate with a spoon, chewing every granule.

"Like as not, that'll cost me my job," she said casually, leaning on the white metal railing on the end of the bed to watch me stuff the toast into my mouth, "but you deserves a little something. Like I said, most white folks don't have enough love."

"You're right," I said, high in the euphoria of the moment. "It is just a question of love. I've got plenty of love, and isn't it a beautiful baby?"

"You can say that again, Lord love him, he's not half bad-looking for a white baby. Say that much." She left, slipping the baby oil into the pocket of her pink apron.

I was much too ecstatic to sleep, and I lay on my side all night

39

until the sky got pink over the gray gothic arches of the university medical school across the park. Out in the city, people were waking up and turning on electric razors and coffee percolators, and none of them had the faintest idea of the wonderful thing that had happened to the world during the night. My baby had been born.

A nurse brought me more food, eggs and salty bacon—an unbelievable luxury—and muffins. It was the most beautiful day I had ever seen, I decided as I licked the last smear of egg from the plate like some starving dog. I wrote on a scrap of paper to put later in my diary: "My baby was born last night, at 10:34. It is a seven-pound, two ounce boy. Everything will be different now. All the terrors of the past months are gone. I will never again have to claw my way through that icy gray railroad station of a world. Never again will my soul reel in that awful nausea of emptiness. And, perhaps most important of all, I will never again have heartburn. For the first time in nine months, I can swallow freely, nothing gnaws at my throat. I will throw away my milk of magnesia tablets."

By midmorning, however, my joy was gone. In my physical exhaustion, the brutality of the birth came back to me. I relived it, closing my eyes and shivering at its violence. The pain had been unlike anything I could have imagined. The baby hitting me like a train at thirty miles an hour, crashing its way out, ripping me open in great spurts of blood and dark juices all over the doctor's green shirt and the nurse's green dress. "Push!" they kept shouting, but in the holocaust of that pain there was nothing left to push with. And then in the overhead mirrors I had seen a tiny head rise in the bloodiness, and heard it bleat and then scream.

A nurse came in and gave me a measuring pitcher. She told me to walk down the hall and void in it. It was eleven o'clock. If I didn't, they would have to catheterize me and I knew what that was. I followed her down the hall and then collapsed on the wet, red toilet seat. I slipped the pitcher under me, saw how the antiseptic-painted insides of my thighs were the bright red of the toilet seat, and how my legs hung down from me like great sides of meat in a butcher shop. I was bleeding, and when I got into the shower to wash my legs, I noticed in horror that thick yellow droplets were oozing out of my nipples and my breasts were burning and hard.

40

I sat in my bed on an ice pack and sent back my lunch untouched. I rang my bell and told the student nurse that I had a headache. I needed to see Dr. Edwards, the doctor acting as my obstetrician.

"The resident on duty will be around to see all the patients after supper," she said, straightening my pillow. "It's almost visiting hour. You'll feel better when you see your husband."

Another nurse came in. She was a massive gray tank.

"Drink this. It will cure what ails you, all right." She handed me a pleated paper cup of mineral oil. "The headache's normal. Milk must be getting ready to come in. Wipe your nipples off good with these." She gave me a cup of gauze squares wet with antiseptic. "I'll be in with the baby in a minute. I bet you're anxious to see him, aren't you? Can't get him sucking too early, you know. You and another girl up the hall are my only breast mothers Can't understand it. God didn't make bottles to feed babies."

I left the gauze and antiseptic untouched and hobbled down the hall, with my johnny swinging open at the back, to a pay telephone.

"How you doing? Haven't heard from you in months. Thought you were in merry old England," Ronald said, with obviously affected cheer. "Where are you?"

"In the hospital. I had the baby last night. At ten thirty-four—the doctor said the time for the birth certificate—and I saw you suddenly, standing in a kitchen surrounded by dirty dishes, making a drink for a girl in a blue slip."

"Gee, how'd you know?" He giggled in nervous amazement. "What is it?" he asked, finally.

"The baby? The baby's a boy, a little boy," I said and began to cry. "I need help. Ronald, I'm frightened."

"Listen, take it easy, will you, for Christ's sake?" He lowered his voice. "You want me to lose my fucking job?" After a long silence, he said; "Well, good to hear from you. I'll be seeing you, get together for a drink, now that you're in town."

The Yellow Pages were chained to the wall, and I had to stand to look through them. My tears were puckering the paper in tiny circles. Diaper Services.

The first number I called was eager to deliver a hundred prefolds until I gave my name, "Miss . . . ."

"Actually, I'm just looking at the route map now and I see that's a bit out of our normal service route. Of course, if you'd care to make a two-month deposit in advance we might be able to work something out."

I had seen their trucks go past the house where I was living every day.

I called a second number and, making no effort to hide my tears, told them I was widowed.

"Oh! Today's the day our man normally makes deliveries in your neighborhood, so if someone will be home, we'll have them out there this afternoon, dearie," the woman said. "And congratulations. How much did he weigh?"

I told her, feeling a tinge of pride.

"God bless you both."

When I got back to my room, the nurse was there and, oh, yes, she had a clear-sided bassinette right there with her in my room. I could see the redness of the baby through the plastic, right there by my bed.

"All ready for your first meal?" she cooed to him. "Come on, Mummy, he's wide awake and waiting."

The coolness of the antiseptic felt good on my nipples, and I scrubbed away all the pus that was oozing out of them.

"That's the ticket," she said, and then, sensing my disgust, explained, "The yellow—that's colostrum. Means your milk is on its way."

She lifted the suddenly screaming, thrashing red lizard out of the box and toward me. "Let's give it a try now."

It clamped its jaws into my breast and I jumped with pain.

"Naughty, naughty," she said. "He's very greedy. Now you just take the nipples, little boy, and leave the rest where it belongs." She grunted and readied him for a second attack.

"No, no, no." She slapped his cheek as I bit my lip. "If he gets it in that way, just hit his cheek or work your finger in his mouth and break the suction. He'll crack your nipples if you don't." She started to leave. "Five minutes on each side and then you can play with him until I get back."

When she had gone and closed the door, I peeked down at the monster that was macerating my breast. My heart was thumping and I had to keep swallowing. It had no relation to that gentle hazy little creature, pastel pink or blue, that had cuddled in the curve of

42

my belly for so long and nudged me gently on the long winter nights. Whatever it was, with its slits of navy blue eyes, its scaly red cheeks, and its bony fists churning up and down, I didn't much want. Wolves, or was it rats? Some animal abandons its young or eats them, one of the two.

When the nurse returned for the baby, she woke us both up. My breasts felt light and feathery. The baby was coiled up like a snake in the crook of my arm.

"Beautiful, isn't he? What a love!"

I was too tired to argue.

In the next three days, I sent out more than three dozen birth announcements. Each had a personal note of some kind written on it.

To the social workers who had told me I could never have a baby alone, I wrote how excited I was about the prospect of starting our life together and thanked them for all they'd done.

To relatives who'd moaned about a child with no name I carefully wrote JAMES HANES all across the card, cramming it in as many times as I could.

To my grandfather, who had produced to his sorrow only a daughter who had produced only granddaughters, I wrote, "It may be a bastard, as you say, but at least it's a boy."

To the one or two people I still considered friends, I wrote a description of my heroic walk to the hospital, how my water had broken all over the caduceus inlaid in the tile floor of the hospital entrance, and how the admitting-room nurse had looked at my small belly and said unpleasantly, "You must be awfully early. Are you sure you're not just excited? We're very busy here, you know."

To others, including the publisher of the newspaper which had fired me, I wrote what a wonderful, adorable baby James was. But I didn't believe a word of it.

When a photographer came around with "Baby's First Picture" for sale, I bought the required minimum of a dozen and studied them for hours, hoping to see what the baby really looked like, who it was, and where it had come from.

I played the joyful-mother role well, and I spent an hour or so every day making myself look beautiful. While other mothers had visitors, I would be in the bathroom washing my hair, and then putting on make-up. I would smooth the sheets and lie back in

43

studied gracefulness, like Sleeping Beauty in her glass coffin, and wait for Dr. Edwards. I knew he would come back to see me, and when he did, the very sight of me was going to win his love forever.

As it was, he didn't show up until the fourth day.

As he walked up to my bed, he said, "Nothing here," and asked me to roll over so he could check the incision and stitches he'd left in my crotch.

"I've had a terrible headache ever since I last saw you, in the delivery room," I said, but he didn't answer.

"You can go home tomorrow," he said. "All you have to do is soak your ass four times a day for a week."

"I can't go home yet, Dr. Edwards," I said. "I'm not ready to cope."

"When will you be?" he asked crossly.

"Twenty-one years?"

"I'll give you twenty-one more hours, and then you'll be out, right where it hurts." And he left, without even looking me in the eye.

"Why didn't you tell us you had a spinal headache?" the head nurse asked several minutes later, when she came running in with a cup of pills. "Boy, Dr. Edwards just chewed the blazes out of me."

"I told everyone who came in here I had a headache," I said, smiling in secret pleasure. "I even asked to see him about it."

"Well, you're to lie flat and take these, now and every four hours, until you leave."

The pills made me high, very high, at first. I floated in the whiteness of the sheets. Dr. Edwards was just shy. He would be waiting for James and me outside the hospital when we left. He would just drive us home, that was all, but it was a good start.

I was sober that afternoon when Margo Novak, an old friend of my parents, arrived. She was a fat, often caustic, old-maid pediatrician whom I'd asked to come examine James. I was sure something was the matter with him, a congenital heart defect, or brain damage, and she would tell it to me straight.

"They put you where you belong, I see," she said, looking at the pipes. "This room suits you." She glared at me, and I knew that I had always been rather much in love with her.

"I examined your offspring," she said. "That's why I have on this gown and look—how many masks! I have a cold but I wouldn't be selfish; I will let you give him his first respiratory infection."

44

"What's wrong with him?" I asked.

"You. He has a mother who worries. He is perfect, a beautiful little boy. And we only need your signature and he'll be circumcised within the hour. If we wait and have to do it in five or six years, it will be a trauma."

"What can I say to him? How will I explain that the knife slipped?" I joked as I signed the paper. I was so glad to see someone I knew.

"Wonderful boy," she said, snatching the paper from me. "You don't deserve him. I will see you in my office in a month." She started out.

"Wait," I ran after her, grabbing onto the soft green of her operating-room dress. "Help me," I whispered. "I don't think he's wonderful at all. I don't even know what he is; he isn't the thing that was inside me. I don't want him."

She put her arm around my shoulder and her voice was almost tender.

"It is easy for others to think he is beautiful. To them there is none of the pain. You have been through a lot, you know. But you are a strong woman, and you will make a good home for that boy. You want him. You will love him. Give yourself time. Call me if you worry, keep up with the breast-feeding for six weeks at least; then you can stop."

"Do other mothers feel this way?"

"You are not other mothers, are you?" she asked, harsh again. "That, you had better get used to." As she turned to leave, her white-and-yellow hair scratched against my cheek.

5

It was a cold morning for April, and an almost wintry sort of drizzle was falling as on the sidewalk outside the hospital a student nurse handed me a frayed blanket containing my baby.

"Your husband coming around in the car?" she asked, pulling her yellow cardigan around her shoulders.

Dr. Edwards was nowhere to be seen.

"We'll take a cab."

"What a shame, going home all alone at such a happy time."

"Listen," I said, as I lowered myself onto the base of my spine in the back seat, "why don't you come along with me? I don't know anything about taking care of babies."

"You'll learn. Get Dr. Spock," she said, and waved as the taxi pulled away.

Dr. Spock. I'd read his book so I'd know what things to get for the baby—undershirts and safety pins. But he'd depressed me and made me feel so guilty that I'd hidden him in the back of a bureau drawer under some old stockings, as though his subject was much more lurid than child care. He attempted to draw his readers and their

46

husbands, always their husbands, into a happy and challenging communality of experience. I had no place there. I cringed with guilt as I read how mothers shouldn't go to work, unless it was very important to them, until their child was three. I was not doing things the nice way, the good way. And my child would suffer.

None of the books on pregnancy or childbirth had prepared me for exactly how tired I would be, and only one had mentioned the insane depths which a postpartum depression can reach.

With James under one arm and my purse under the other, I got out of the taxi and started up the five flights of stairs to my room at the very summit of a huge old house just outside of Colton. Halfway up the third flight, small black clouds came thundering into my eyes. From then on I took the stairs very slowly and on each landing counted to ten with my head lowered. I had to climb the stairs perhaps a dozen times a day, if I was to eat or drink, or wash my small amount of baby clothes, or earn my keep.

The house was owned by Katherine Peck, a willowy, black-haired divorcee who spoke in an operatic baritone of a voice which literally shook the window panes of my room when she called to me. She'd taken me in during the last weeks of my pregnancy and then had gone off to South America to visit her son, who was in the Peace Corps. She had expected my baby to be born and the two of us to be settled down by the time she returned. James was born three weeks late, and so she returned the night before we were to leave the hospital and found she would have to face the very situation she had hoped to avoid—a squalling newborn.

I'd been acquainted with Mrs. Peck for three or four years, during which we'd both been on the fringes of the civil rights movement. Her son had been a childhood friend of my sister's, but I hadn't gotten to know Mrs. Peck until we'd ridden to Selma together on a bus and I'd pressed my forehead against the cool glass of the window and let her talk on and on about her many artistic and talented friends. On the way back, I'd tried to sit with someone else, but she'd cornered me at the very back of the bus. She began a real aria about how moving an experience we'd just been through, but I was badly in need of sleep and so I groaned, "Mrs. Peck, the sun is setting and we went a long way to take a walk."

She mistook my discouragement for some sort of poetic metaphor about achievement in civil rights.

"How true, how true," she trolled. "You have the mind of a poet—that's almost a haiku!" She became a great admirer of mine and of the silly little newspaper articles I was writing at the time about the seasons changing in local parks, the futility of life as perceived at a sports event, or sad affairs remembered in a museum.

She invited me to several parties at her house, and I went and squirmed while awkward, beige-sweatered men tried to sing Schumann song cycles or retired science teachers read poems about spleenworts and hepaticas. Finally, I sent her a copy of *Swann's Way* and wrote in it, "You, of all people, must meet Mme. Verdurin." She took it as a great compliment. She would wave frantically at me across the church where I sometimes went and would whisper in the voice of an oboe, "My dear friend, God bless you," just as the choir started down the aisle.

She was not as distressed about my poor timing as I'd feared. Her maid, a black woman named Emma, fixed a special lunch for the two of us and carried it up to my room that day.

It was a nice meal. Was I properly honored? Of course. But I was too tired and frightened to eat. I put James in the laundry basket I'd fixed for him, and Mrs. Peck hovered over him briefly. In a crack of pure childhood terror, I saw her as the winged monster in one of my fairy tales, a shadow descending to grab my infant in its talons. I guess I had not forgotten how shocked and scandalized she'd been at my pregnancy, which she'd learned of when a social worker from one of the unwed-mother shelters had gossiped most unprofessionally at a cocktail party. Mrs. Peck had called Pat to find out if it were true. Several days later she arrived at Pat's apartment when I was there and offered me a spare room in her house. It was not up to her to judge me, she said, and if she could find it in her heart to understand and forgive me, perhaps others would also in the years to come.

Mrs. Peck sat down in the chair in my room and began to eat her lunch. She had an afternoon appointment to go skating with an old beau. I wouldn't mind if she went ahead.

I went into the bathroom and washed my face with cold water. Then I took some aspirin, and while I was swallowing it blood began to run down my legs. I thought I was hemorrhaging. What else could it be? What could I do? The hospital might help me, but what would happen to James? Katherine Peck might watch him for a few hours, but then what? If I left him with her, she'd hire a nurse, no doubt, and then present him, with the best intentions in the world, to her Christians Discuss group, a production I (a fallen woman) had avoided starring in a few weeks ago only very, very narrowly.

I sat on the edge of the tub and pondered the bleeding. Either it would stop or I would eventually lose consciousness on my way to death. If someone should find me in time, the police would be summoned and I would be rushed to the waiting arms of Dr. Edwards. With tears in his eyes, he would direct the stretcher to the morgue. James would go to one of those nice, normal, two-parent homes in the suburbs that were anxiously awaiting blond, blue-eyed babies just like him.

I took one of Mrs. Peck's monogrammed Turkish hand towels, folded it and put it inside my underpants. I would die more gracefully than I had lived, I thought, as I waddled into the bedroom.

Mrs. Peck was just finishing the last of her aspic.

"I think I'd like to take a nap now, if you don't mind. I'm feeling very tired."

"Emma, the tray!" Mrs. Peck said to Emma, who was pulling on one of James's fists.

The two women left, hurt or offended. I couldn't worry about it under the circumstances. If I lived, the worst that could happen would be that she'd kick me out of her house.

In the closet I found a plastic bag containing a spare pair of chintz curtains and bedspread. I took the bag and spread it over the bed. She would never be able to say that my bleeding had hurt her linen or mattress. Then I lay down. But I got back up again and pulled the laundry basket with James in it to the side of the bed. I left my hand dangling over into it. It would be so moving when they found me that way, frozen in a last gesture of maternal devotion.

It was getting dark when James's yowling woke me. The bleeding had slowed, but the towel and one of my two dresses were ruined. The plastic bag had not been in vain. I let James cry while I cleaned up the mess. I rolled the clothes and towel up in the garment bag and

49

stuffed it all under the mattress, much as I had hidden my first menstruation-stained underpants from my mother thirteen years earlier, lest she discover and make use of my sudden weakness.

James too was lying in a pool of liquid. Four flights down in the front hall, I'd seen a hamper of diapers. I climbed slowly down to get it, and then began the long, slow ascent back. The house was dark except for the kitchen, where Emma was fixing supper. Mrs. Peck was still out, and a good thing that was, for I could hear James through the entire house.

The diapers were not the neat triangles that the hospital had used. They were rectangular. I had to fetch Dr. Spock to learn how to fasten one on James.

I sat in the chair to nurse him and slowly eased his screaming face toward my nipple, but he caught it in a bite. I flicked his cheek with my finger and tried again. This time he took it correctly, and slowly I felt his body soften and grow still, except for the faint rhythmic fluttering in his throat.

I felt then a peculiar sort of admiration for the ugly little lizard. He was savage, an animal, the origin of a human being, instinctively taking what it had to have to survive, taking it from me because I was there. And because he was my baby. He was my baby. I had really had a baby.

I sat there, letting him suck and rocking from side to side in the darkness. I loved him; I had become a mother after all. When he fell asleep, I turned the light back on and looked at him very carefully. He was so quiet and round and pale now, like the moon. I uncurled his fists, and lifted up his undershirt to look at his little stump of an umbilical cord. It was like a scab now, but I remembered how that cord had glistened gold in the light of the delivery room as Dr. Edwards had pulled it up for me to see.

James was back in his basket and I was buttoning my shirt and thinking how I would put on the radio and hear some music to celebrate my happiness when I heard Mrs. Peck screaming. I found her bent over her beloved *chinoiserie* cabinet in the downstairs hall. Tears were streaming down her face and she kept wailing, "God help us, God help us."

Emma had on her hat and coat and was walking out the front door.

50

"Oh my God, Mary, Mary, help me," Mrs. Peck cried. "Martin Luther King has been killed—can you bear it, can you bear it? Oh, my God, the irony of it all."

And so the world sort of collapsed into riot and grief around the warm little circle James and I had found our first night home.

I got Mrs. Peck upstairs and into bed and summoned her doctor, who came with tranquilizers. Then I called my sister, who came late that night to weep with Mrs. Peck so that I could sleep. Mrs. Peck reciprocated my sister's kindness by inviting her to stay the weekend, which she did.

Sunday morning they sat at the breakfast table and shook their heads as they read the newspaper. Entire city blocks were being destroyed, people killed, stores looted. The nonviolent civil rights movement was dead. No one had thought the revolution would come so soon. Mrs. Peck was making plans to go to Geneva, because the Swiss were so peaceful. My sister said this was a very sound idea and winked at me.

But her wink and almost everything that was happening outside the circle of my arms was beyond me. I tried very hard to read the newspaper but I fell asleep. I couldn't understand why Emma failed to show up for work, and I brooded about this, for it meant I had to take care of the kitchen and the meals.

I was trying to get Dr. Novak on the telephone when Mrs. Peck's voice pierced my ears. She absolutely demanded, she said, that I come right down to see one of the pinnacles of human history—a mule train, would you believe it—bearing Dr. King's body to the grave.

She couldn't understand my indifference, and Dr. Novak couldn't understand my concern.

"Babies cry, in case you didn't know it," Dr. Novak said. "You want me to come out and hold him for you?"

"He stopped crying about five hours the night before last, and about four hours last night. Listen to him!"

"Give him some sugar water," she said and hung up.

I was trying to dry him after his bath in the sink, and he began crying so vigorously that he flipped himself right over and onto the floor as I reached for a diaper. He kept right on crying, so I wasn't worried. If he was an idiot because of it, I wouldn't have to save to send him to college.

51

Mrs. Peck suggested that the problem might be that my breasts were so small that they weren't giving any milk; she was just suggesting that, but whatever the problem was, she did hope it got straightened out soon.

Finally Dr. Novak called back to ask if he was still crying. Was he wetting his diapers between each feeding? He was probably getting enough milk then. She came out to see him.

"Some babies are like this," she said. "Call it colic, if you want. It will be over by the time he's four months old. Nobody said the first few months were fun, but you have to endure them. Now, young man, what seems to be the matter?"

She gave me some drops which I fed him every four hours, before each feeding. They worked for a day or so.

"You are very tense," she said to me over the phone. "How can you expect to have a peaceful baby? It is to be expected that he will cry. The sooner you are on your own, the better. I could not stand it where you are myself."

I found that by taking James in bed with me and lying with him across my stomach we could both get some sleep. Dr. Spock said you should never take a baby in your bed, but I figured he was writing that for married people like himself who probably thought of a bed first as a place for sex, not sleeping. Yes, I might some day, possibly, use a bed again for sex, and if I did, a sure way to make James anxious to get into it then was to act as though it were sacred ground reserved for adults only. If I welcomed him into my bed now, he would probably fail to develop much interest in it later on.

So we began sleeping together, but he still cried all day, buckling back and forth in his basket.

"About your lack of milk," Franny Sprague, Mrs. Peck's daughter, said, "you know there's nothing to be ashamed about." She had come to inspect me, her mother's foundling.

I got a set of scales from the diaper service at Dr. Novak's suggestion. In the week he had been home, James had gained half a pound.

Franny sat with her mother in the sunlight drinking Dubonnet, and at three, Emma put the chicken salad back in the refrigerator.

"They'll start fighting any minute now," she said to me. "I'm going down to the cellar to do the laundry. If I was you, I'd go upstairs and take me a long nap, with my door good and locked."

I took her suggestion, only the door wouldn't lock. I heard the shouting start at three twenty. At three thirty, Mrs. Peck burst into my room, in tears.

"My mother ruined my first child's breast-feeding. She dried up my milk just like that. Don't listen to my daughter. She's been telling me how you're starving James. I told her to go to hell and I'm going down and tell her again. Look at me" —she ripped open her blouse—"I have no breast, now, not an ounce, and I went on to breast-feed two children, each one until it was nine months old. Have confidence in yourself. If you don't, you'll never make it."

Confidence. Yes.

Franny Sprague sent her husband over that night with a pot of geraniums and a bottle of Duff Gordon cream sherry for me. He handed me the sherry in a paper bag. "She says a shot of this before each feeding does wonders. She ought to know. Of course, I know nothing about such things; I'm merely a surgeon."

The sherry helped, especially at the midnight and dawn feedings. With a little of that stuff in me I didn't care whether I had milk or not. I continued to nurse him into June, but nursing was not the big issue to me that it was to Mrs. Peck and her daughter.

When James was two weeks old, I forgot to worry about his crying or anything else, because postpartum depression hit like a tornado. I'd be washing the dishes for Emma or going upstairs with an armful of towels, and suddenly I'd be crying uncontrollably.

At night, alone with James at the top of the house, I heard strange sounds. I would awake in terror, expecting the door to break open and wolves to come upon us. I pushed a chair against the door and sheltered him on one side with my body and with a pillow on the other.

In lucid moments, I knew something was wrong and that I had to get help or protection. I was drowning in my own feelings, many of which had to do with my inability to respond to Mrs. Peck's needs as well as James's.

There was a popular song being played every hour or so on the radio then. It asked, "Do you know the way to San Jose?" where lots of friends and peace of mind awaited everyone. There was a line about putting a little money down and buying a car.

One leaf-dappled though still cool morning, after I'd cleaned up the breakfast things, I wrapped James in a blanket with a dozen diapers and a clean shirt, took my checkbook, which showed a balance of just over $200, and left Mrs. Peck's house forever to buy a car and go to San Jose.

6

There was a car dealer on the main highway about a mile from the Peck house, and I walked down there, stopping to rest on several of the softer-looking lawns we passed.

Underneath the red-white-and-blue plastic banners, half a dozen dusty old Volkswagens were parked, and I began to check them over. The only thing I really cared about was whether or not it had a radio, preferably FM, because I knew I was in for a long, boring trip, and James would probably cry most of the way, although the morning air had temporarily anesthetized him.

"Can I help you?" the used-car salesman asked in an Are-you-going-to-make-me-call-the-police tone of voice. He looked me up and down twice, rather scornfully taking in my baggy blue jeans, sneakers, old raincoat, sweater and milk-splotched man's shirt, which I realized I had forgotten to button after James's breakfast.

"I want to buy a car," I murmured, withdrawing from his little brown BB eyes.

"Going to buy a car, eh? Where's your husband?"

"San Jose—that's in California."

"How much you thinking of investing?"

"As little as possible. Fifty dollars?"

"Whoooo-Whoooo!" he said, waking James who of course opened his eyes with a yowl. "In a fifty-dollar car you'll never get to San Jose, if that's what you had in mind."

I took James into the car showroom and left him on the royal-blue carpeting that surrounded a new Ghia.

"No." I told the salesman, as we walked back out to the used cars, "if I go to San Jose, I'll fly. But I certainly want a car that will hold up for at least five or six thousand miles. Otherwise it's not worth the time to write the check, is it?"

"I could let you have this model for a hundred dollars," he said, kicking in the direction of an old blue Adolf Hitler-vintage model. "But with the baby, well, it's your life and your decision. I wouldn't let my wife near it, myself. What's your husband doing in San Jose? Hmmm?"

"He's just been discharged from the Army and he's visiting his mother. She lives there." I said, nervously, beginning to volunteer too much information. "He's been in Vietnam, you know."

"He didn't come home to see his baby first?"

"Well, he's very close to his mother."

"Still, you think he'd want to see his own baby. How old is the kid?"

"Two weeks."

"First one, I bet."

"Yes."

"And he didn't even come to see it?"

If he knows I am lying, he'll never sell me the car, I thought. "We haven't been getting along too well, actually," I said, looking at my sneakers. One of them was untied. "We are thinking about getting a divorce. I mean, he wasn't ready for a family. He didn't want any children."

"How old is he?" the salesman asked, leaning closer and closer to me in his cloud of Sen-Sens. I was leaning farther and farther back until my behind touched the warm metal side of the car.

"How old is he? Forty-eight," I said without thinking. It was a nice number.

"Oooh, boy!" the salesman whooped, and I, certain that he was expressing his triumph at having finally caught me in my lie—who serves in the army in Vietnam at forty-eight?—burst into tears.

But his hand came down on my shoulder.

"You poor kid," he said. "Any guy that's not ready for a family at forty-eight is never going to be ready. He's a real loser, that one. You're better off without him." He pulled out a maroon-plaid-bordered handkerchief from his pocket and handed it to me. "I could tell you'd been through the mill when you walked in here—I got you might call extrasensory perception about people. It's part of being in sales. Now, dry your tears. I'm going to give you a real good deal."

But I couldn't stop crying, even though I was laughing at myself and the entire situation. I kept choking out great sobs.

"When was the last time you ate?"

"About an hour ago."

"Sure. I bet you haven't had a decent meal in months."

"Eggs, sausage."

He nodded and pulled me over to the shadow of the building. "I'll let you have that car we were just looking at and a full tank of gas too, for a hundred and twenty-five dollars. How's that sound to you? But you better keep it just between the two of us."

"That sounds a little high," I said, my tears slowing down.

"High? Listen, this morning already, honest to Pete, I've had two calls about that very car. I quoted them a price of a hundred and seventy-five dollars, and both parties are coming by to see it. One's on his way in now from Camden Center, so if I was you, I'd act fast, providing of course you're really in the market for a good car."

"OK," I said. Camden Center wasn't that far away. "But I'll have to call my husband and clear it with him. It's his money, really, you know."

"I like you," the salesman said, "And I want you to have that car. Now, if you go all the way home and call your husband, you may miss out on it. I'll let you have it for a hundred."

"Fine," I said, "I'll just go inside and call him on your phone, collect of course."

The salesman looked at his watch. "Up to you. Phone's on the desk. Only thing is, it's ten o'clock here, what is it there, in San Jose? Eight or nine? If it was me, I wouldn't want to be woke up. I'd be liable to say no."

57

"It should be around eight in San Jose, and they get up really early—they're farmers." I was laughing now, because I was imagining Ronald, who had never in his life gotten up before nine o'clock, sitting at a San Jose breakfast table and holding his throbbing head while his 200-pound wife made him yet another helping of her famous pecan and sour cream waffles. She liked to see a man eat a good breakfast, she always said, "Chocolate or maple syrup, honey?"

James was still yowling in the salesroom, and I used a phone on the desk closest to him to dial the recorded weather forecast number.

"Mrs. Hanes?" I said, "Is Ronald up yet? Good. Put him on." The ruse was probably unnecessary because no one could hear my voice over James's screams, but I was having fun.

"A Volkswagen, yes, a hundred dollars and a tank of gas. No, I need a car today. All right. Good-by."

I told the salesman: "He says seventy-five dollars, or a hundred with two new tires."

The salesman cursed and took the latter option. Two new tires were put on, but I discovered several weeks later, when I had had to replace both of them, that they were new retreads.

After I'd signed all the papers for registering the car and making a first installment on the minimum amount of compulsory insurance, the salesman looked at me and grinned.

"First time I ever sold a car to a person who hadn't even driven it," he said.

I had to wait for several hours in the showroom while the license plates and insurance sticker were obtained and my bank was contacted to make sure my check was good. I threw James's wet diaper away in the ladies' room, and then I sat on the showroom floor and read the picture pamphlets about new cars while I gave him his lunch.

"You know, I seen a German lady do that once in public when I was in the service over there," the salesman said, trying to hide his embarrassment. "They don't see anything wrong with it over there, any more than they do in some of your savage countries."

"You must be putting me on!" I said merrily. "Listen, will you do me a favor? Get me a Coke from that machine over there. I don't have any change and I don't want to move right now. You have to replace the fluids the baby takes."

58

"Sure," he said, helplessly, and he bought me a packet of stale cookies as well.

It was late afternoon before James and I were seated in our preowned car, ready to hit the road to San Jose.

We were well into the city of Colton, where I planned to pick up the turnpike and head west, a logical start, when I realized that I was quite insane. I had always acted out my depression in freaky, manic ways, but this had to be one of the worst. I was coming down badly. I had about twelve dollars in my purse—how far would that get me in tolls, gas or food? Furthermore, I didn't know anything about San Jose except the cheerful, bouncing promise of Dionne Warwick's voice. In fact, I'd never been farther west than Denver, and that trip had been a mistake.

I was almost out of diapers, and my rear end was so sore that I was driving barefoot, because I could survive the discomfort only by sitting with one sneaker under each buttock to lift the pressure somewhat, off my scar. And also something was the matter with the car. It trembled violently every time I shifted gears.

I would not go back to Mrs. Peck. Even if I wanted to go back there, I was sure she wouldn't take me in. I'd missed lunch—she'd been having three friends in to see some blankets and stuffed llamas she'd bought on her trip—and Emma would have needed help. Also, Mrs. Peck was funny about money. She'd taken me in because I was destitute, or at least too poor to finance a stay in an unwed-mother shelter and still have enough money left to live on until I returned to work. She must know that I was low on funds after paying my hospital bill. To spend my last dollars on a car would, in her mind, put me in the same category as what she called those ignorant welfare mothers.

I drove around the parkway trying to decide what to do. James seemed to be adjusting to the irregular trembling of the car very well. It had apparently eased his colic and he would wake up to cry only when we hit stop lights. The rest of the time he slept peacefully on the seat beside me.

I parked on North Street by the park and gave him his supper. My need to be milked was becoming as regularly urgent as his need to be fed.

It was just after five o'clock, and cold was coming back with the orange fading of the light. Pigeons were rising and falling on the paths as people rushed home to their own little worlds, to cook their own little suppers and laugh over the tedium of the day before watching the same old tedious television shows. Security. A string of young women, round and lush-looking, curled past, roommates no doubt; secretaries going back to their apartment to make tuna-fish casseroles and chocolate cakes for their accounting-student boyfriends. Their faces were fresh and creamy.

A wave of self-pity came over me. Here I was wizened and sore and prickly and bleeding, a lot of twenty-six-year-old bones aching inside worn-out blue jeans, sitting in a wreck of a car while the night got cold, with no place in the world to go and no one in the world who cared about me. I'd never be lush or free. I'd never rush home, my feet slightly tired in nice shiny high heels, to take a bath and powder my body in strange places where the scent would be a nice surprise.

I had James and what did he care for me? I was a nipple. A bottle and a pillow would have served him as well, actually more comfortably.

I couldn't cope. I left James in the car, locked the doors, and went across the street into the Perry Hotel, where nine months earlier I would not have ventured in flat shoes, let alone bare feet and blue jeans.

I had just one dime and I used it to call Dr. Edwards because I understood his cold indifference: it was a defense. He really loved me and would understand and come to take us home with him.

"I'm sorry, Dr. Edwards is no longer at the hospital," the operator said. "He left at the end of March."

"I know he was leaving," I said, "but he was in the hospital during April. He came back to see me there. Would he be in some research department in the medical school? I need to find him."

"Honey, right here in front of me is a note saying he left the hospital at the end of March. Could one of the other doctors help you?"

"No," I said. "I have to find him. Give me his home phone number. He's not listed in the phone book."

"Honey, I couldn't give you his home number if I had it, which I don't. I'll give you a number at the medical school. You could try that after nine tomorrow, and they might know where he is. Are you

60

sure one of the other doctors can't help you? You don't sound too good."

I hung up. There was one other thing I could do. I would go to the lake and find Stanton. The last I'd heard, he was going to be there until May.

When I got back to the car, two old ladies, one with an apricot poodle, and a pimply boy with a slide rule on top of his notebooks, were standing beside it.

"Is this your car?" the boy asked anxiously.

"Yes."

"There's a baby inside and something's the matter with it. It's crying real loud."

"I can hear, I can hear," I said, unlocking the door.

"Imagine leaving a little baby alone in a locked car," one of the old bags said, pursing her maraschino-cherry lips at me.

The other old lady's dog lifted its woolly leg and tried very hard to squirt out a drop against my tire.

I sighed in deep agreement with them all.

"She's not fit to be a mother," I said, shaking my head. "She does this all the time, leaves him in my car, sometimes with a note, 'Give me a good home'; she thinks it's a great joke. Just wait until I get my hands on her."

I cuddled James to me. "There, there," I said. "Aunt Mary won't let anyone hurt you. I'll take him home now—his father is very understanding," I said to reassure them.

Then I started the car and began to make my way north through the rush-hour traffic to the lake and Stanton.

7

We used to spend the summer and some weekends at the lake near Stanton's family, on a point of land with thin yellow beaches and tall black trees. The Montgomerys' place was a graceful sort of field-stone château complete with carved boxwood trees and a fake drawbridge over the ditch that drained the stinky little swamp behind our cottage.

We began to go there when I was ten and my father had found himself, as my mother put it, by accepting a job as vice president of a company whose main product was preserves. She was jubilant, and he, at first, was dangerously bitter. He referred to himself as a jam salesman, and once when they were going out to dinner, he'd harangued her about how he was going to take a case of jam with him and sell jars to the guests. She ran upstairs with a headache, and he went to the party alone, leaving the case of jam in the middle of the front hall.

In any case, he grew to like his job and became very successful. We moved out of the old maids' apartment building and into a house, and we could go away during the summer like other decent people, my mother said.

Although I was properly impressed by the Montgomerys' world, it was their shy, ugly failure of an only son who consumed my long daydreaming hours.

For two years I watched him sailing off alone at dawn in his boat, or walking along the beach with a frightening-looking German shepherd.

I was twelve before we ever dared speak, and then it was only to say hello, but it was enough to build another few years of dreams upon.

I was in my bathing suit, and I remember walking from the damp cool of the rug onto the hot wooden boards of our porch and seeing him standing there with a little soldier's hat in his hands. He was talking to my father, who was slouched in the bottom of a butterfly chair.

Stanton's head had been shaved by the Army, and his uniform looked as though it would crack if you touched it. In fact, that was the way Stanton had always looked, stiff and rigid as though he were holding himself against some excruciating inner pain.

He was telling my father that our dog, a scruffy, drooling half Airedale, half buffalo, had gotten into the pen with his mother's Pekingese, who was in season. His face flushed purple with embarrassment when he saw me.

"I hate to ask, sir," he said to my father, "but would you keep him tied up for a few days? I mean, he might not have—well, he might not have been successful, if you know what I mean."

"Christ, that's terrible," my father said. "I didn't think old Rover was that old. Might have missed, you say?"

Stanton failed to catch the humor, such as it was. "I've got to be going, sir," he said. "I've got to be back at the base tonight."

"Sure. Oh, this is my daughter, Mary. We let her out on weekends, under sedation of course."

It had been a long day of tonic and mostly gin.

Stanton blushed again and practically limped forward to shake my hand. "Nice to meet you," he gasped. "I've seen you for two years now, of course, but, well, we'd never been introduced."

"Well," my father said, "you tell your mother to let me know if old Rover made it. I'll take care of the puppies for her—drown them—be the best thing, I guess. Like to drown my own some-times," he said, getting up. "Children, that is."

"I don't think that will be necessary," Stanton said. "Mother will call the vet if there's any problem."

I watched him walk down the driveway to where his mother's chauffeur had parked not quite as far behind the trees as I think Stanton would have liked.

"Damn good thing the war ended," my father said, fishing the little minnows of ice from the water in the ice bucket and dripping them off his fingers into several more inches of gin. "Damn good thing. Can you see him on Pork Chop Hill? Twenty-five years old and scared of his shadow. What an ass. That's A double S." He bounced the lime rind off my behind.

I walked down to the beach and sat on the cool sand at the edge of the lapping water. Stanton. His eyes were the color of the lake on a cloudy day. I too was glad the war was over; he would not be killed. He was the only human being I'd ever seen who looked as out of place in the world and as unhappy and scared as I felt. He was a grown man, of course, thirteen years older than I. And it was a strange thing he'd started in me, that small branch of electrical feeling, fine and faint as the foreign black hairs that were sprouting there.

I didn't see him again for five years, until he came home when his mother died, several months after my father's death. He came up to the lake from town after the funeral. I was out in the middle of the cove, treading water. My fingers were puckered and my nose was running from the cold of the lake, but I wanted to stay in as long as possible. There were not many hiding places on the island, and my mother, at home alone, had been drinking a good part of the day.

I saw Stanton in what seemed to be a white suit, standing on the shore watching me—or the water. I swam and waded in and climbed up beside him. His suit was grey-and-white striped seersucker and his necktie was black. His teeth were clenched in nervousness.

"I wondered who you were," he said, hands tight behind his back, looking me in the eye and then up and down. "I thought you were a trespasser and I was going to have to call the police."

"That's right," I said. "I heard the serfs were organizing." His hair was longer now on the sides. On top, it was beginning to disappear.

64

"Mary, you've gotten pretty smart," he said. "I heard you'd gone east to college. Briarcliff, was it? Bennett?" He looked down at the pool of water that was dripping down around my feet.

"Bennington. How was the funeral?"

"Most enjoyable. You should have been there. One of mother's great-aunts—she's in her late nineties—had an attack. Everything had to stop. An ambulance arrived and removed her on a stretcher. The minister couldn't remember where he'd been in the service. He read the lesson twice."

I laughed. "At my father's funeral, when we had to say the Lord's Prayer, my sister and I got the giggles and went completely out of control at 'Our father, who art in heaven.'"

He looked at me, teeth clenched for a minute, and then a small smile started at one corner of his mouth and suddenly tripped right out in a burst of laughter.

"But it's so sad," he managed to say finally. "Poor Aunt Emily is probably dead herself by now, and I'm fairly certain none of us bothered to check with the hospital. In fact, I'm not sure which hospital they took her to. I went on to the cemetery and then came straight down here."

"Well, let's go call. Come to my house because I'm cold," I said.

"No, you go get dressed, and I'll go back home. If everything is all right and Father doesn't mind, I'll take you to dinner some place. Would you like that?"

But Father Montgomery did mind, although Aunt Emily was merely suffering from food poisoning, it turned out. A fishcake she'd had for breakfast had already been identified as the culprit and the cook warned to throw out the leftovers.

"It is my last night here, you know," Stanton said on the phone, "so I think Father has grounds for wanting me home. I'm going to New York tomorrow and then back to Africa." Much to everyone's horror, especially his investment-counselor father's, he was attempting to develop a resort hotel and recreational area on the Ivory Coast.

Late that night, he woke me up by throwing stones at my window. It was very hot, and his suit was soaked in sweat. Still, at seventeen I thought it was very romantic to be called upon in such fashion.

We sat on the porch and slapped at mosquitoes for a few minutes, and then he said, "Would you mind?" and dropped his head in my lap, where it stayed rigidly, mumbling sometimes about Africa, sometimes about his father and how God had not created Stanton equal or some such thing, but mostly snoring, until the clamminess of morning and the laughter of a flock of crows as they rose up from their nests around the swamp woke him up.

"I'll write," he said as he backed off the porch. His face was white, and little beads of sweat had immediately popped onto his forehead, despite the chill. "It's been a wonderful time for me, Mary. I'll write."

But I knew he wouldn't. I understood that pale sweaty fear of his: he had showed too much of himself to me.

When Stanton came back into my life eight years and almost twice as many men later, I was four months pregnant. And if I had not been stinging with rejections, I might have laughed at this thirty-eight-year-old's adolescent shyness, and the clumsy stiffness of every gesture he made, at his knowing so little about women that he thought nothing of my bulging breasts and stomach or my dizzy spells.

I'm not sure whether I loved remembering that summer of another era and the tender feelings that had no place in my life any more or whether I simply needed someone to hug for a few moments of reassurance. Much to my later shame, however, I let him court me—that was his phrase—every night for two weeks before I ruined everything by telling him that I was pregnant.

He thought for a few moments and then offered to marry me right away. We'd leave for Africa, and no one would have to know the details and dates of anything. When the baby was born, people would naturally assume it was his child.

"Oh, God, yes," I said, my spirit suddenly soaring up from under all the hate and fear, "yes." But then I shook my head. "I'd be using you, probably. I don't know you, in so many ways. We've never even kissed properly, the way men and women usually kiss. How can I marry you? I have to work this thing out for myself, have the baby."

We were in the Montgomery house; he was standing in a window looking out over the tennis courts, which were lighted even on this October weekend for his father's young partners. "You'll give the baby up for adoption?"

"No. If I could do that, I'd have an abortion. I guess it's the closest

I've come to feeling religion. But I feel that life has asked something of me and I have to follow through, no matter what the consequences."

He came and sat beside me on the couch and put his hand firmly over mine. "If you go ahead and have the baby alone, then everyone will know you're—will know you've had an illegitimate child. I never could marry a woman like that, with that kind of baby. My father would die," he said, and then he dropped his head into my lap again, but this time he was crying.

It was two weeks later that I left for London. This time Stanton did write, at first from Africa, and his letters sustained me. They were stiff and controlled and utterly impersonal, but they were the only mail I got. I'd sit in front of the electric fire in my room in Piccadilly and read how the hotel laundry claimed it had lost his evening shift but two days later he'd seen it on the bellboy, and spin a fantasy around it. Then for a month there was no word from him, but in late January he wrote from the Mayo Clinic, where he was recovering from a tropical disease he had contracted. He'd almost died, he said, but now he was sitting up and eating with a fork and spoon. When they released him he was going to the lake to rest for a few months—until May, anyway, he said, when his father would begin coming out on weekends and disrupting—inevitably—his son's peace of mind.

"Out of order," he wrote at the end of the letter, and I smiled at what I am sure was his unintentional irony. Stanton's body might be run down, but never would his behavior or his thoughts be outside of the established order of his world.

8

I left the car and James at the end of Stanton's driveway and walked across the drawbridge and onto the wet lawn around in back to see if the house was completely dark.

There was a glow in some of the upstairs rooms—from the hallway, I assumed—and one light downstairs, in Mr. Montgomery's study. The old man must be there lecturing Stanton, I thought, and I crept up outside the slant of light the study windows cast and peeked around into the room.

First one, and then another, and then a third golf ball rolled across the red-and-blue Oriental rug and tapped the dark wooden wall before bouncing to a stop. The old man must be in there alone, practicing his golf. I had to step into the light to see the rest of the study, and when I did I saw Stanton, pale and skinny, standing there alone in a maroon velvet smoking jacket, with a golf club in his hand.

I watched while he hit several more balls, aiming them toward an overturned wastebasket, and missing it each time. Then I backed away and ran around to the drawbridge and down to my car again.

Golf. It enraged me, for some reason. Didn't he have anything better to do? If he'd been reading, or watching television or playing solitaire, I could have knocked on the window. But golf! I hadn't even known he'd played the game.

It was just as well; I was exhausted and dirty, and James was due for another meal. I would call Stanton and see him in the morning.

I had to break a window in the cellar door to get into our cottage. It was not really ours any more, anyway. When my mother died, it had gone, with the rest of her estate, not to her ungrateful children but to her father. For some reason he had not gotten around to selling it, and it had been there eating up his money, he said, waiting to be used by some of his employees or young friends for a weekend house party.

I turned up the heat and started the hot water so we could bathe in the morning. There was very little food, a couple of cans and a bottle of whisky. I made myself a drink and warmed up some dry-looking ravioli, and then called Stanton.

He said he was just getting into bed. Where was I? Was I all right? Should I be there all alone? He'd be over in the morning.

The bed was so cold it felt wet, and it smelled faintly of mildew. I lay there, hazy from the whisky, feeding James and looking out over the swamp at the lake, just beginning to glitter in the moonlight. Maybe we would stay there, James and I. We could manage to live, somehow. I could fish and my grandfather would never find out. We wouldn't stay for long, just until things were worked out with Stanton, just until I got my strength back.

In the morning the sunlight filled the room, and the bed was soaking wet and warm from James. I hung the bedding out to dry on the porch and we took a bath together, James lying on the floor until I washed and then coming to rest on my thighs while I cleaned him.

In a closet I found an old Mexican dress of my sister's. I put it on, I diapered James in a linen hand towel, and wrapped him in a black turtleneck jersey that had been mine. I felt very cheerful. Our own house, no one to yell for us, no needs to fill but our own. And Stanton on the way.

I had a can of peaches for breakfast, and then I put on my old raincoat and sat on the porch with James lying across my knees, and looked across the lake. I was sort of dozing when the idea came to me that I should spare James from the agonies of the world, a world

69

where families dissolved over a new life, where black and white could not live together and where blacks destroyed their own neighborhoods and each other in retaliation for the death of their leader.

I would put him in a little boat and cast him out to sea, as Mary Hamilton had done in the folk song, that he might sink or he might swim, but he'd never come back to me. I was wanting to get rid of him, the poor little seven pounds of him which were—as I waited for Stanton, my salvation—suddenly weighing very heavily on me.

Poor James, poor mouse, my baby. I took him inside and put him in the middle of the living-room floor to sleep, but of course he yowled. I went upstairs to get another hand towel to diaper him, and when I came down, Stanton was standing on the porch, peering in under the shadow of his hand at James.

I ran out to hug him, but he looked at me with such a strange mixture of feelings that I stopped with my arms up, as though to shield my breasts. He opened his mouth and then closed it without saying anything. In the brightness of the sun, he looked as green and feeble as I felt.

"It's good to see you," I said, and he shook his head; then finally managed a thin smile. "Let's take a walk," I said. "The baby will be all right for a while."

"I didn't know you had him with you," Stanton said, but his back was turned to me as he started off down the driveway toward the water.

"Where could I leave him?"

He didn't answer. "I was surprised that you were in the cottage," he said. I was almost running to keep up with him. "Your grandfather told me he sold it before Christmas."

"Sold it! But all our stuff still's there."

"Sold it furnished, I guess," Stanton said. "People . . . bought it, elderly couple . . . here . . . weekends."

"Great, I've been there illegally," I said, now running. "Please, could you slow down? I'm still a little sore."

But it was windy then as we came out onto the shore, and I don't think he heard me. He picked up a stick and flung it into the water, and then a stone, and all the while he was walking ahead of me, just out of hearing range. He was saying something, but I couldn't get it.

I kept jogging along, shouting at the navy blue of his parka, "What's that? I can't hear you. Walk slower, I can't run."

Finally, I just sat down on the ground and let him walk off into the distance, and he got almost around the point before he turned and found I wasn't following him.

He walked back, slowly now, still throwing stones, but looking scared and defenseless.

"You should be in bed somewhere," he said, sitting down beside me, "You look terrible. I didn't realize, I didn't think, I mean you said to walk."

"I just need to catch my breath."

He began talking again, about Martin Luther King's death and how the answer was black capitalism. White imperialism had made Africa what it was today, and white dollars in the hands of black businessmen would rebuild the American ghettos. New businesses must be started and blacks trained to run them, and eventually to own them.

I couldn't understand why he was talking to me about all this, now of all times; it was like his golf-playing at night.

"Businesses," I shouted at him in anger. "What in the hell are you talking about, black businesses and capitalism? You want to castrate them and make them like a lot of—of yous." That really knifed into him. Quickly I tried to cover it. "Blacks have to decide for blacks what's best, and it may not be what's best for you."

"You bleeding-assed liberals think the world has to change to fit each and every one of you. Well, it won't." He got up and stood kicking the earth beside me.

I covered my eyes. Then I stood up and took hold of his arm. "If we're going to fight, let's fight about what's really making us angry," I said calmly.

He put his hands on my shoulders. "I don't want to fight with you at all. Look at you—there's nothing left of you—you've wasted away. You're running around in the middle of the night looking for help. I just hoped you'd let me take care of you. I want to love you; I know I can."

"That's what I wanted—that's why I came," I said, leaning against him, putting my arms around his strength, "I'm just so tired, Stanton. I have to have some help."

71

"I'll help you, I'll do anything I can, but—"

"But the baby?"

"It's not too late, is it? I mean, there can be other babies, our babies. But not this one, not now; I can't have the world knowing this one isn't mine. Even if I adopt him, he's still a bastard, and everyone will know it. Why, my father . . . you can understand it, can't you? What does this baby have to do with you and me anyway?"

I could see the darkness of the water over his shoulder. That blueness, I thought, and his strength were all I wanted. What did I want with that red lizard sucking the skin off my nipples? Where could I go if I didn't hold onto Stanton?

"Stanton, that's my baby," I said, not knowing quite why, not really wanting to say it, "and we come in a package now. Just as much today as we did when you think you fell in love with me. You take us or you leave us." And I turned and left him there by the lake.

I took my time about packing up to leave. I carefully folded all the yellow-stained bedding and put it on top of the washing machine in the cellar. The remaining hand towels and the dress and jersey were mine, or at least they should have been, so I stole them. I put my old jeans in a paper bag in the back of the car and fussed about, arranging James on the front seat in his blankets. Still no sign of Stanton. I knew he would be along any minute, but I wasn't just going to sit there waiting for him. A little chase would do him good.

Quite near where I turned onto the main highway from the road to the point, there was a gas station. I stopped and went into the outside telephone booth and pretended to make half a dozen calls, while I watched the turn for another car to nose out onto the highway. None did.

He would now be a minimum of twenty minutes behind us, but if I drove very slowly, he would be able to catch us.

After about an hour of very slow driving in the breakdown lane, I finally saw his black Mercedes in the rearview mirror. I pulled out into the middle lane and resumed normal speed. He was driving so fast, it was a wonder he hadn't been stopped.

I was watching the car in my rearview mirror. I didn't want him to know I saw him, and when he pulled out from behind to come alongside of me, I kept my eyes straight ahead as long as I dared.

Then, prepared to break into a grin of incredulous joy, I very casually looked over into his car.

But it was not Stanton. A priest with a red, gaunt face, his thin spike of a neck curving out of a giant porcelain collar, was slowing down, cigarette in his mouth, to reach for the lighter. Not Stanton but a priest, complete with a statue of the Blessed Mother on his dashboard.

Some time later I saw him again as he pulled out of a roadhouse parking lot, where no doubt he'd had a quick snort. He cut in front of me so sharply that I had to slam on the brakes, and James bounced off the seat onto the floor, where my dirty dungarees and the stolen towels cushioned his fall. I pulled off the road and picked him up, rocking him back and forth until he stopped crying. His head was so small that I could almost have crushed it with one hand, and in front, where the bones had yet to close beneath his bald scalp, his still-empty mind seemed to undulate back and forth as his crying slowed.

"You're not too bright, but you're awfully handsome," I said to his ugly little gnome's face.

There was nothing to do but go back to Mrs. Peck's, and to hell with what she thought.

There were a billion women he could have chosen to bear him. Why had this strange, demanding soul, my son, picked me?

9

The Peck house was blazing with a fiftieth-birthday party for Henry, Mrs. Peck's brother, a would-be concert pianist. Ever since Martin Luther King had been safely in the ground, Mrs. Peck had thought of nothing but this party, and she had been very hurt when I'd failed to get excited about it.

I sat in the car for a few minutes wondering if I could keep awake for three or four more hours to drive around the city, or whether I should wait in the cold darkness of the garden until the party was over. I just couldn't face it; I had to lie down and sleep.

I decided that I could tiptoe up to my room without being heard. The house was big. James was awake, so to make sure he would not cry and give our presence away, I opened my dress and fastened him onto my breast. If I went in through the back, Emma would see me, so I turned the front doorknob very gently and gave the door the softest possible one-handed push.

A great chiming fanfare of bells pealed forth like Christmas morning. I had forgotten that when Mrs. Peck entertained, the inside of her front door was festooned with bells to welcome the arriving guests.

"Why, Mary! At last! Just in time for dessert!" she trilled, coming up from the dining room to see who had arrived so late. "A very, very special cake!" Then she said under her breath, "Get rid of the baby and change your clothes, immediately. I won't ask you where on earth you've been or tell you how sick with worry your poor sister and I have been." Her eyes riveted into me and she raised her voice again. "Quick, quick now!" She walked back to the dining room.

I slipped in and sat just outside the candlelight in a chair I arranged in a shadow, where I hoped I'd be invisible, and took the glass of champagne and plate of birthday cake Emma gave me.

The wine went down easily, but the cake, with its heavy cream roses, stuck on my tongue. I couldn't swallow it; my throat and my stomach were too full with the heavy fatigue and desolation of the day. I tried to scrape the frosting off my tongue by moving it under my upper teeth. The sweetness then clotted on my teeth and lip. I had no napkin, so I bent down and wiped the mess onto the hem of my dress, and when I looked up I saw that Mrs. Peck was watching me through a crack in the crowd about her table.

I knew that it would be only a matter of seconds before I lost the champagne. I stood up, put my plate on the chair, and started for the door.

"Mary, where are you going? My dear, you must, I insist, you must tell Henry that marvelous story about the time you interviewed the father of American music himself. You know who I mean," she said, and then, lowering her voice as though I were beginning to speak, she whispered to the table, "She used to be a newspaper reporter, you know. Remember her?"

"I can't, I'm sorry—I just can't talk," I said, inching backward.

"What do you mean, my dear? You're talking perfectly well; I can hear you distinctly," she said, drawing herself up like the queen she loved to play. "The story, for our birthday boy."

"I mean, I'm sorry," I said and ran from the room, managing to be sick just outside the door—I hoped out of hearing—on the tile of the hall floor.

After that, relations between Mrs. Peck and me were sort of strained.

75

The next morning I heard her calling the police about "a frightful old car, abandoned right in my driveway!" I had to rush down and claim it.

"Yours?" she asked coldly. "Never mind, officer, I have the culprit." The car, she said, returning to her breakfast tray, was to be kept off her property, down the hill on the street, please, out of sight.

I moved the car and limped back up the driveway. I was more tired than I had ever been in my life, and there were a dozen or more cassettes waiting to be typed. During the last weeks of my pregnancy, Mrs. Peck's minister, hearing of my poverty, had sent word that I could have a job typing for a friend of his who was dictating a manuscript. I took it gladly, but since James's birth I had gotten far behind in my work.

I put the tape-recorder earphones on and began to type, but James's crying was so loud that my ears were literally numb. I could not possibly work with him in the same room. I put him on the bathroom rug and shut the door on him and began to try to catch up.

Of course, I felt some maternal stirrings for James, but it was not easy. He was so uncomfortable and so noisy, and there was nothing I could do to quiet him. When I was called downstairs on some small chore, I'd feel relieved to be away from him, and then immediately guilty.

When he'd finally fall asleep around ten in the evening, I'd sit by the open window and watch the stars and shiver as the frustration and anger at my poor, miserable baby slowly passed out of me. But there were other feelings, deeper and more complex. A despair, a hopelessness and a grief for all the pleasures I had lost. In the past, I'd always been able to act out such feelings, but now I was trapped in one room with a baby that hated me—or so I felt—a baby I was trying very hard to love. I couldn't run off into the night to make love with some glorious stranger, or sleep alone in the woods. I was a mother, and there was nothing I could do but sit, while my baby slept, and crash back and forth with the doubts and regrets.

One morning in June when James woke up screaming as usual at three, I heard voices instead of music on the radio as I lay dozing and feeding him. I woke up sharply. Robert Kennedy had been shot in the head in California.

Mrs. Peck was a Republican, and when I told her hours later, she shook her head sadly and then went about her business—a tennis match at the country club. The smell of the wisteria outside my window began to sicken me as I typed.

By afternoon one of my breasts was swollen hard and bright red and I had a fever. I lay down on the bed, but James's screaming kept shaking me away from the sleep I so wanted. When the pain began to break out into my arm, I crept downstairs and tried, for the last time, to call Dr. Edwards. To him alone would I dare say; "You were right. I should have given my baby away."

An intern with a very rushed voice came on the line. He told me to squeeze the milk out of the inflamed breast every four hours, not to give it to James, and to put ice packs where it hurt. I should take aspirin, and if I was not better in the morning, he would see me at the clinic. He'd see me now, but the women were lined up six deep. It might just be milk fever, anyway, and if so, it would pass.

I pulled down on my sore nipple, and the milk shot out in tiny blue needles that dribbled down the side of the glass. When the glass was half full, I looked down at it and suddenly threw up all over James and the bed. As I stood up, the glass slipped from my hand and crashed on the floor, spattering my poison milk all over James and the rug.

I picked James up and held him on my healthy side and cried for a long time. I wasn't quite sure why, but it had something to do with the violence of the world I'd brought him into, the cruelty and the poisons where we least expected them.

When James's screaming woke me up, it was dark. Mrs. Peck and her supper guests were on the terrace way below my window, and I could hear them laughing over their after-dinner drinks. My fever had broken and I felt better, just shaky. I got up and slammed the window shut. I couldn't believe they could sit there and laugh as though nothing had happened, as though no one in the world was waiting to die. And somewhere I knew Ronald was sitting back in the warm night and chuckling softly with the girl beside him.

I fed James with my good breast and then cleaned up the mess before bathing myself and him. Then I put on the radio again. The announcer said that the senator's brain was swelling from the wound, and the next few hours would be critical. The doctors were waiting. I lay there waiting for sleep and planning how in the

77

morning I would take James and walk down to my car and drive us fast into the first concrete wall I came to.

But in the morning, Robert Kennedy was dead and my breast was normal. Milk fever had passed. I called Dr. Novak and told her I wanted to wean James.

"Good," she said. "What inspired you to take this giant, independent step?"

I didn't dare tell her that I'd poisoned him long enough. So I made up a lie: "I've decided I don't want to be involved any more. I don't want to care. I don't want to feel." Of course, it was not a lie at all.

"A few more weeks," she said, "and I promise you, it will all be over. He will stop crying."

There was a small apartment over Mrs. Peck's garage that had been vacant since Christmas, when, Emma said, Mrs. Peck had discovered its occupant, a medical student, entertaining a female overnight. In May, the gardener-handyman began to clean it out on rainy days. I'd see him coming out of it with a vacuum cleaner or floor waxer, and I began to suspect that I was going to be moved from the house to the garage.

One morning in the middle of June, a moving van arrived and an old man in a deerstalker cap hopped out and directed the movers as they carried cartons and then charred pieces of furniture into the garage. Perhaps I had not fallen so badly from grace after all. Maybe I was to remain in the house.

But after the movers left, when the old man was eating lunch with Mrs. Peck, Emma told me I was to move in, that afternoon in fact, if I wanted. It was even furnished, because the old man's summer place had been ravaged by fire. Mrs. Peck had agreed to let him store what little he had salvaged in the garage, provided I could use it. Mrs. Peck said he wanted to talk to me about some of the things that were there and had asked Emma to tell me to stop in after I'd helped with lunch.

The old man, a retired professor at the university, was reciting Latin to Mrs. Peck when I knocked on the living-room door.

"My dear young lady," he told me, "I just wanted you to know that the furnishings belonged to my wife. I'm confident she would have wanted you to use them. I ask only that you not disturb the boxes, as they contain a few pieces of china and glassware which I have left, in my will, to the state historical society."

I knew he wanted to be thanked, and I tried to oblige him for Mrs. Peck's sake.

One of the first things I did, of course, when I had moved into the apartment and locked the door behind me, was to open a carton. It contained five or six dusty glass Ball Mason jars, a stone Dundee marmalade jar and three tinny-looking forks.

The furniture was a help, although I had little use for eight end tables, or the five ladder-backed wooden chairs whose straw seats had pretty much rotted away. There was a dining-room table, however, and a bed with a sagging mattress that rested on rope webbing. The couch had actually been on fire; its back was burned away and its cushions still damp. I covered it with newspapers, hoping somehow to cut down the smell.

The burnt smell faded as the summer wore on, and by the time I left, I noticed it only when I came home at night, or blew my hay-fever-clogged nose sharply in the morning.

Right after I moved into the garage, Mrs. Peck closed her house for the summer and left for Geneva, taking Emma with her as a treat. She sent me by Emma a check for $500 with a note explaining that she was sure I needed a little reserve after I'd spent my money on that automobile. The night before she left, she invited me into the house for supper alone with her at her long dining-room table. James was alone in the garage, yowling, and I kept worrying about him, so I only half heard the small talk she made.

She was much too proud to tell me what was in her heart: She'd believed in me, given to me, sheltered me when my own family had turned its back on me, welcomed me into her house, even to parties; all she'd wanted in return was that I like her and respond to her small needs. I had failed her badly, but she was turning the other cheek.

"In Geneva, we'll rent a car and drive to Germany for a week. Emma must see the vineyards of the Rhine."

"Fantastic, she'll love it. How wonderful of you," I kept saying, shaking my head until my neck was stiff, not so much from the motion but from the tension. I was too proud to say I was grateful. I knew how lonely she was and how much she needed just a little love, a little applause, but I was too tired to listen and clap, too wrapped up in my own needs, and if I opened my mouth to speak, I knew only fear and sadness would come out. I would die, I vowed, before I let Mrs. Peck or anyone else in the world know how I felt.

We finished a bottle of wine with our coffee and shook hands and said good night and good-bye.

"Have a wonderful trip," I called gaily, as I walked out to the garage.

"You have a good summer too, dear Mary," she answered, "Feel free to sunbathe on the lawn."

I didn't have much time for sunbathing, however, because on the first Monday in July, I went to work in the office of the man who had been mailing me the cassettes. His name was Bill Mitchell, and he was a popular, quasi-religious writer and lecturer. His regular secretary had gone away for the summer with her family, and he needed someone in the office to answer the telephone and the standard kind of letter he received and to arrange his fall and winter calendars as speaking engagements were made.

He was traveling around the country to visit friends and speak at various summer schools. When he had a few minutes in the airport between planes, or in a taxi en route to a campus, he'd dictate a chapter of the book he was writing. I transcribed it from the cassettes onto paper and eliminated any inadvertent repetitions he made working in this piecemeal fashion.

He was a nice man, his voice slow and gentle in my ear, and it had been his idea that I bring the baby with me to the office. James sometimes dozed happily on the desk top in the sunlight, but usually he screamed with colic.

It was an office building on the skids. Next door was a two-man advertising agency with no secretary and apparently only one account, a Japanese tuna-fish canner. Down the hall there was a nest of lawyers, an irascible father and three sons. I'd see them standing in the doorway to the office building sometimes when I went to lunch, and I thought they looked like salesmen at one of those eternally going-out-of-business-sale shops, lurking outside to buttonhole gullible-looking pedestrians. Maybe once a week their secretary would come in and tell me they had an important client, so could I pick the baby up or something—anything—as long as I kept

80

him quiet for an hour? Well, maybe only forty-five minutes; she'd come and tell me when it was all clear.

Then James and I would go walk in the park across the street. The fresh air always quieted him. If it was raining, we'd go in a Unitarian church which, having harbored draft dodgers and AWOL soldiers all spring, thought nothing of one screaming baby boy. If there was a funeral or some other service in progress, we would run three blocks down to the public library, where I found that by walking very fast I could keep one room ahead of the security guards for almost a half hour. I'd go down to the record section and grab any album that was on display and play it at top volume. The noise usually intimidated James somewhat. If worst came to worst and the record-listening booths were filled, we would ride a bus, out to the end of the line and back. But this was only in times of extreme emergency. It cost seventy cents round trip.

But Dr. Novak turned out to be right. James's colic was over before too long, and he screamed only when it was time for his bottle. Our life settled down into a routine. The days were not difficult, although sometimes we ran into friends of my family or people I had worked with on the paper. This usually made my face burn, and theirs too, almost always. Most of them tried just as hard to avoid seeing me and James and I tried to avoid seeing them.

In the evenings, we would go to market, a daily process, as the apartment had no refrigerator, and at least every other night we had to do the wash at a laundromat. My sister was very busy falling in love and getting engaged, but once or twice a week, we would have supper with her and George, her thin, serious fiancé, an archaeologist.

Night was the difficult time, when I was too tired to do anything but undress and lie under the hot, slanting roof while James sucked loudly and energetically at his bottle. The telephone company was on strike, so no phone could be installed. This increased my feeling of isolation, though there was no one I had to call. I had no key to the Peck house, and the nearest neighbor in the summer-deserted suburb was a quarter of a mile down the road.

Often I would be awakened by a scratching at the garage door below or what I thought was the growling of wild animals underneath the window. I paid no attention until one night when I got up to go to the bathroom and looked into the driveway to see a car parked in front of the house. In the house, a dim light moved slowly past the kitchen windows and upstairs to the living room.

I grabbed James and my purse and in my nightgown and bare feet ran through the darkness down the driveway to the street, where I'd timidly continued to park in deference to Mrs. Peck's memory. Unfortunately the car keys were not in my purse. So I ran on down to the main road and stood in the orange light of the street lamps waiting for a car to come along.

The first car passed; the second stopped. A woman in a white dress was driving it.

"Is your baby sick?" she asked, rolling down the window.

"No, but there are robbers in the house—could you take me to a phone or to the police?"

She took me down to the village and the police station.

"Lucky I came along," she said, "I don't normally drive here at this time, but I'm on private duty and I lost the patient, so I'm through early. Normally, I work eleven to seven," she said, looking over to see if I was interested.

"Did it upset you, the patient dying?" I asked, clutching James to me.

"Sure, always does. This was a real baddy, too. Young girl, my age exactly, twenty-three. Cancer all through her. She had a four-year-old daughter. Look," she pointed to the back seat and a wicker basket of gladiolas. "Her husband made me take those. I don't want them— I'm superstitious—but I can't just throw them out, can I?"

"I would. I wouldn't keep them for one minute," I said. "Her husband will never know."

"Yeah, you're right," she said, as we pulled up in front of the police station. "Here, I'll wait until you get inside, make sure everything's O.K."

The sergeant at the desk radioed to a cruise car and then looked at my old flannel nightgown—in the middle of summer—with its front ripped open low enough to permit the feeding of James, and James naked except for a very wet diaper.

"I'm sorry," I said, "but I don't have a phone. I live over the garage and I could see someone in the house."

82

"One of the boys will take you back. Are you a neighbor? We'll need you to make the report."

"No, I'm just living over the garage. I'm a friend. You can contact her daughter; she was there the other day." I gave them Franny Sprague's address up at the lake.

A fat young patrolman waddled into the room and pointed at me. "This the lady you want me to take home?"

"No, Charlie, that's my wife."

The nurse was sitting in her car outside. "Everything OK?" she called. "Look, I took your advice." She pointed at the metal-net trash basket on the corner, where the flowers sat in the bottom.

"What she want to throw flowers out for?" Charlie asked as we drove up the hill. "Perfectly good flowers; I could've used them."

"Go back and get them then," I said, crossly.

"I will, but we'll be all night here," he grumbled.

But the police were brief. The trespassers had disappeared by the time the cruiser arrived, but the back door was open and the burglar alarm had been disconnected. It looked like a pro job, they said. They'd send men up for prints in the morning.

I walked through the house with them, and I couldn't see that anything was gone. The robbers had missed the big Renoir in the living room and the Henry Moore. There might be some jewelry gone, I said; Franny Sprague could tell them.

Charlie followed me up the stairs to the apartment.

"Not bad. How much she charge you?" he asked.

"Free. She can't rent it, something to do with fire-department regulations."

"Not bad! I guess they didn't come up here," he said, poking around. "No refrigerator?"

"No."

"Well, I better get back and get those flowers," he said.

I put James in his crib and walked out to the police car with Charlie.

"Take care now," he called as he drove off.

When I was alone on the dark driveway, I decided to take one more look through the house, and I wandered through it until the black silence began to frighten me. I took with me a clock which I needed and some drink to put me back to sleep.

Franny came down the next morning and spent most of the day going through the house.

"You know what they took?" she laughed to me on the phone at Bill Mitchell's. "You won't believe it! Only two things—a little dime-store clock Mother had by her bed, a two-dollar General Electric model that's gone, and a decanter of Grand Marnier which Mother always kept on her bookcase. They must have been after narcotics or something; you know the house is still listed under Pop's name in the phone book." Katherine Peck's ex-husband was a psychiatrist who had moved to the West Coast after their divorce.

"I'll call Mother just in case she can think of something else, but I'll bet that's it! A clock and a liqueur! Any messages for Mother?"

"Give her my love," I said.

"I'm sure she'll be grateful to you! What heroics!"

Late that night I took Mrs. Peck's little crystal decanter and poured the rest of the Grand Marnier down the drain. I put it with the clock in a paper bag and drove downtown, where I left them on top of a trash can in an alley behind an all-night diner.

In the weeks to come, I wondered if Franny Sprague had gone into the apartment and seen them there—it was incredible to me that anyone could be so observant as to notice two such trivial items missing from a large house. If Mrs. Peck confronted me, as I was almost certain she wouldn't even if Franny told her, I was prepared to die denying the theft.

It was one of the things I liked to think about ("What? She saw what in my apartment? Nonsense!") That, Bill Mitchell's book and my Dr. Edwards fantasy were about all I dared think of. Everything else was packed away behind great walls, containing people I had loved and things I had done, and I walked around those walls very carefully in my mind, lest I weaken them in any way and drown in the grief they held.

The Dr. Edwards fantasy had something to do with the walls. The insanely elaborate details I gave to it, day and night, obsessively refining and embellishing it, kept me going, I think, through the summer.

10

John Edwards was the angry and antisocial little doctor in charge of the prenatal clinic when I went to the Colton City Hospital.

Most women were lucky enough never to see him and were examined by a different intern or resident each week, according to one of the student nurses; but, she said, laughing, "You lost."

The intern who examined me first thought there might be some problem because I had taken steroids for asthma during the early months of my pregnancy.

He was a blond and rosy-cheeked, corn-fed young man, and it surprised me when he grumbled, "You get to be one of Edwards's girls. He catches anyone who might possibly be interesting."

So I lay back on the paper-covered examining table, my legs still in the stirrups, and waited for almost two hours until Dr. Edwards got through in his laboratory.

When he arrived, he sort of scuffled into the small examining room, almost tripping on the tails of his long white coat. He was probably just over five feet tall, and he looked much too young to have ever shaved, but he was mean, or at least he looked very irritated, as he picked up the history the intern had taken of me.

As he read it, he'd shout out questions, checking what the intern had written without even bothering to look up at me: "Mumps in 1952? Father died, cancer; mother, heart—heart what? Thrombosis? Occlusion? O.K. mother died, coronary occlusion."

When he was through, he slapped the record down on my belly.

"Don't get your hopes up," he said, his eyes almost shining. "A lot of women who've taken the medicine you have run into bad problems. There was a paper published on it last month, and we delivered one here ten days ago: no central nervous system."

"I'm certainly glad I lay here with my legs up in the air for two hours to hear that," I said. I pulled my legs down and began to get up.

"Nobody told you to get up," he said and pushed me back down. "And I don't like your attitude. I tell you you've got a high-risk baby and you answer me with sarcasm."

"Would you rather I wept and begged you to help me?" I asked. "Look in the record again. Look where I was treated before. The doctor who wrote the damned article you're talking about was on the staff there, for Christ's sake. I saw him and he felt my dose had been small enough not to cause any problem." I grinned.

"Well, then, you're wasting my time, if that's the case. Why don't you deliver your own damn baby? What's your name anyway?" He flipped back to the front of the record. "Yes, I remember you! You used to write for one of the papers around here. Why in the hell did you get pregnant? Look! You're not even married! You've ruined your life!"

"I know—a lot of people have told me that. Now, tell me I should have had an abortion or I should give the baby up for adoption!"

"Appearances can be deceiving," he said, "but my impression is that you're much too whimsical to be a mother. It's a serious job, you know. And look at this"—he almost leaped for joy—"just look at this! You've gained sixteen pounds already. The baby isn't even due for a month. Any woman who's that irresponsible, who'd let herself go that way—"

"You're sick," I said. "You're really a maniac. I can't believe a big hospital like this would have you on its staff." I stood up and started over to the corner to get my clothes off the little stool. "You wouldn't say that to me if I were married, and besides, I know that's not an unusual weight gain. I'm going to write a letter to the hospital administration about you, I really am."

I had one foot awkwardly into my pantyhose when he shouted, "I don't give a God damn what happens to you or what you do—just get my name right: Edwards, John N."

When the door slammed, I sat down on the stool and started to cry.

"Boy, he's really in good shape today," the student nurse said, patting me on the back. "He's terrible, he always is. All he cares about is his research. His wife left him a couple of years ago; you can see why. I don't think he has any friends."

I was dressed and combing my hair when he returned with a hypodermic syringe in his hand.

"All I'm here for," he said quietly, staring at the floor, "is to get that poor little bastard out of you alive. That's all I care about."

"That's all I care about," I said. "What in God's name do you think matters to me?" I began crying again. Everyone cared about my baby—how it'd be doing in five, ten, twenty years, warped by only one parent and sniveling its way up in the world as a bastard. To me such worries were really expressions of concern about the family name, or the shortage of Anglo-Saxon Protestant babies on the adoption market. This psychotic little doctor was the first person who cared about the first step—that the baby was born alive, a fair beginning in this world.

"If you're sincere," he said, "pull down your pants."

The student nurse gasped.

"So I can give her the injection, for heaven's sake," he snapped, "I'm not going to trust it to you—you're much too kindhearted. You'd probably throw it out."

He jabbed the needle into my behind. "Don't go more than six feet away from a toilet in the next few hours," he said.

"What did you give me?" I was still sniffling.

"Something to get rid of the fluid. I think you're getting toxemia, I do. You look like it to me. When I see you next week, I want you to have lost at least five pounds. Then we can begin to work together."

The next week I had lost seven pounds, but I think very little of it had been fluids. Lacking a proper diet to follow, I merely eliminated two meals a day, and ate only meat and vegetables for supper.

87

"That's a start. Now go get some rings, so I'll be able to tell when your hands start to swell. Besides," he said, flicking my abdomen with his index finger, "I'm embarrassed to be seen in the same room with you and that and no rings."

"Come on," I said. "This is the one place I'm not embarrassed. Half the women out there aren't married."

"But I don't look at any of them," he said, and then quickly attacked again. "It's a little late for you to be embarrassed; you should have been embarrassed on those balmy spring nights. Keep up the diet."

Five weeks later, when the baby was a week overdue and I had lost thirty-one pounds, he told me I could resume a normal diet in moderation, but still no salt.

I sometimes wonder why he thought I had to lose so much weight. I wasn't exactly skinny, but at the same time, I hadn't needed such a desperate crash diet. Dr. Browning looked at me and shook his head, "No more dieting," he said.

But Dr. Edwards was furious when in the sixth week of the diet I lost only one pound. Perhaps he was a nut, or perhaps he was trying to lift me out of my depression by giving me an absorbing physical task at which I could succeed through some self-discipline. Anyway, I was proud of my physical accomplishment, I'd done something well. The fact that when the baby had been delivered I would at five feet seven inches probably weigh just over a hundred pounds didn't seem important at the time. But the whole following year I was sick with one chest infection after another, and I caught and passed on to James every kind of bug that came within a mile of me. Dr. Browning had been aware, as Dr. Edwards apparently had not, that asthma weakened my resistance to respiratory infections. It seemed plain that what little resistance I'd had was gone with my thirty-two pounds.

When the baby was three weeks late, Dr. Edwards told me at my weekly appointment that he was leaving the hospital at noon that day.

"You have four hours to produce, if you want me to deliver your baby," he said. "After lunch, there'll be no more babies for me ever. I'm going home to Portland for the weekend to celebrate."

"It will never come in time," I said, bleakly. "Don't make me be with some stranger. I'm afraid."

"Afraid! You're the woman who said there was no problem. And I tend to agree with you, now. The baby's going to be fine, I'll bet you. I should have turned you over to the interns long ago—I just enjoyed fighting with you."

"I'm not that scared about the baby," I said. "I don't want to have it all alone. I'm afraid it will hurt."

"Well, we'll change your orders. Knock you out when you walk in the door, you want that?"

"No. I want you with me."

"Well, I can't induce you; there's just no medical indication for it. Go for a walk, a nice fast walk. Maybe that will work." And he left.

I had my coat on and was on my way out of the hospital when he caught up with me. "Don't be afraid, Mary," he said, walking out to the street with me. "You know, you're really a beautiful woman in your own way. I know you'll get married some day and everything will work out for you."

"I know," I said, crying because of his tenderness. "I'm not worried about that. It's just been a long road, having this baby, and I wanted you with me at the end. I'm so lonely, I'm so sick of strangers."

He looked around nervously, as though he were afraid someone would see him talking to a patient on the street. "Maybe things will come sooner than you think," he said. "Look, my plane for Portland doesn't leave until two. You've got some time—get walking."

At three o'clock I was still walking. I climbed the driveway to Mrs. Peck's empty house and spent the rest of the afternoon typing Bill Mitchell's cassettes. At six, my stomach was hurting. I hadn't had anything to eat since my breakfast boiled egg. I started downstairs to fix myself some supper, but I realized it wasn't hunger. I sat on the steps and timed the contractions—one every three minutes.

I called a taxi. There would be an hour's wait, the voice told me. It was only a mile and a half to the hospital. I walked it very slowly, thinking what a nice spring evening it was, how the crocuses had been up that day for the first time, and how it was a good night to be born, even though Dr. Edwards was gone.

In the labor room, the nurse who was wiping my forehead and listening to the fetal heartbeat finally called to one of the interns who were rushing up and down the corridor outside.

"Well, somebody's got to look at her," she said. "I think she'll deliver without you boys ever even checking her."

"It's not going to be me," he said, in the doorway. "She's down as Dr. Edwards's patient. I won't touch her."

When I came out of the next contraction, Dr. Edwards, in a little green suit, was standing beside the bed holding my hands in his. I remember thinking how big and muscular his arms looked in the short-sleeved suit, and how tall and strong he had suddenly become in my eyes.

"I'm the one who should be crying," he said, wiping the tears from my cheeks with the nurse's washcloth, "Do you realize that my mother made a yellow cake with chocolate frosting just for me, and right now it's getting stale in Portland? I've given up a whole weekend for you! Come on! If you cry, you can't help me."

One night at my sister's apartment, a beaded sort of young man who wore a deerskin jacket despite the 90-degree heat sprawled across the table and asked us to witness something. That was his way of putting it.

The janitor in his apartment building, a really square guy, like with two kids and a wife and all, had come home one day with "this old, beat-up Wise Potato Chip truck, you know, the blue job with the wise old owl on the side winking at you? He gets out all his tools and starts working on it, and the next thing we know, he's converted it to a camper. Fine, it's June and time for a camping trip with kiddies. But no, one day, he just takes off alone—splits—and he hasn't been heard of in a month now. His wife's out there emptying the garbage every morning, kids screaming below. I ask her where's he gone? And she says, like he always wanted to find himself, you know what I mean?"

My dream of Dr. Edwards was born in that tale. As I spun it out over the next two months, I would sometimes tell myself it was going to become a short story, and I'd write down notes—which were always pretty much the same—in my diary, but I had no real desire to communicate it. I protected it and fed it, and it grew to occupy almost every waking moment that was not grabbed by Bill Mitchell's telephone or James.

The dream usually began with the truck coming into the driveway outside Mrs. Peck's garage. It was a rainy Sunday morning, and I watched through the window, waiting for driver to realize his error, turn around and leave. Finally, there would be a loud honking, and Dr. Edwards would get out and look up at the windows of the house.

I would grab James and run down to greet him and the Wise truck.

(The "Wise" bothered me. I knew it was too much, if I ever wrote the story. I liked it, though, and I kept it in the fantasy after considering some names of alternative local potato-chip companies. And it had to be a potato-chip truck, although I was not sure why—perhaps it was something to do with the fragile nature of the food, so greasy, vulgar, and devoid of any genuine nourishment. Ultimately, what could be any less significant than a potato chip?)

"I've been looking for you," he'd say, without a smile or any evidence of emotion. "Not the baby, you. I wanted to say good-bye. I'm leaving town, you know."

The rain would begin to drip off my nose and James's, not to mention his.

"Won't you come inside?" I'd say, formally.

"No, no more houses. Get in the back of the truck if you're scared of the rain," he'd say, wrestling with the door handles, which were just a bit above his reach.

"You see, I'm sick of bringing life into this world. What for? Sure, I could go back to my lab and try to find new ways of preventing life—that's what I liked, birth control—but what the hell. I've always wanted to spend all my time taking pictures. I'm quite a good photographer. But you didn't know that, did you?"

The inside of his truck was dark brown and stuffy. On one side, there was a clumsily made plywood table on which he'd placed darkroom equipment, and on the other side was a cot-sized mattress covered only by a rather shrunken green army blanket. I put James on the bed, such as it was, and Dr. Edwards and I sat on the edge of the truck, with our legs dangling out into the rain and our backs against a couple of cardboard cartons.

"There should be a market for my pictures," he said earnestly. "At least enough of a one to buy film and developing chemicals, gas and a little food for me."

In reality, in the delivery room, as he had sewed me up after extracting James, he had begun to talk rather compulsively in the

91

almost postcoital sadness that comes after a job is done. Most of the time, these days, he'd told me, he felt there was no point to life except that small purpose you found in your work. When that failed him, he would blow out his brains as Ernest Hemingway had. He was through with people and relationships. He had a dog now, who was always glad to meet him when he came home, a dog who loved him no matter what, a great Dane, Jack the Giant Killer. I'd lifted my head up as high as I could to watch his eyes above the surgical mask. "Jack kills the giants of loneliness?" I'd asked, and he'd nodded.

In the dream, he told me all that had changed, although he still had no need for people. But he no longer missed them. Jack the Giant Killer had gone to live on a farm in Iowa. Now, he had found himself, he had gotten over all the misery of losing his wife, and he could go freely because he had nothing to run away from.

"If I'd run before," he said, "There would have been people and things to haunt me, to catch up with me. Not so now." He slapped my knee. "Well, I'd better be on my way, hither and yon, wherever my camera takes me."

James in the dream was beginning to yowl, and Dr. Edwards was obviously annoyed by the sound; he looked like a cat with its ears back, tail switching.

"What's going to happen to me?" I asked him, pressing my face down into his shoulder in a sudden burst of panic. "What will I do with all the sadness and grief and hate inside me?"

He pulled my head away by my hair. "That's up to you, isn't it?" he snapped. "It's certainly not my problem! Now get the little bastard out of here—I've got to get going."

As James and I were climbing down from the truck, he'd say, "Wait a minute. One of the reasons I came by was to show you my family album." He'd pull a dusty old red velvet book out of one of the cartons. "Ever since I was a child, I've been taking pictures of people who matter to me, people who have touched me in some way. When I get a picture of someone that I can really love, that satisfies me, I put it in here. Take a look at it." He'd try to hand it to me, but my arms would be filled with James.

"Oh, all right," he'd snarl, "I'll hold the damn baby."

Leaning into the truck to shelter the album from the rain, I'd open the cover to see a rather grotesque collection of photographs:

92

"Mother—1951" showed a woman in a sleazy rayon nightgown standing in the kitchen, her face contorted with hysteria, and a carving knife poised to enter her breast.

"Uncle Hugh—1953" was a man with very shiny shoes and neat pants cuffs lying in the street. He was clutching his chest, and his face was twisted in the agony of a heart attack.

"Grandmother Carson—1957" was a heap of old bones and elbows, crumpled on a stretcherlike bed, bound by heavy cotton restraints, tubes running into her nose and mouth and arms and legs, tubes draining the contents of her bladder and stomach into glass flasks on the floor below;

"Christmas—1962" showed an ornate tree, with tinsel and an angel, but behind it was a casket banked with light and dark carnations, and in it lay a young man, waxed into a mannequin, with a floral crucifix held serenely in his hands.

"Thanksgiving—1964" showed a family, perhaps a dozen people at a circular table, yelling at one another in fury.

The last photograph in the book showed a woman like Botticelli's *Birth of Venus*, with fine and delicate breasts, her hair rippled out across a pillow and her face calm and exquisite as a huge, hairy, naked, barrel-backed male body descended between her parted knees. It was labeled "Jane Edwards—1966."

"This last one, this is your wife."

"Former wife. Rather lovely, don't you think?"

I'd nod in agreement.

"Well, now you know," he'd say, smiling for the first time, taking back his album and handing me the thrashing James. "I'm off."

"But what will I do, where will I go? You're my only hope," I'd cry.

"That's right." He'd climb into the driver's seat and turn on the engine.

As the truck started to pull away, I'd scream: "I can't bear it, I can't bear it. I want to die! Let me die!"

The truck would back up a few feet, and the window on the passenger's side would roll down just enough to emit a camera lens. Click! Then he was gone.

11

One heavy August morning I dressed James in a fancy white lawn suit my sister had given him and took him down to Family Court to file a nonsupport claim against Ronald. This was the first step, my lawyer said, to getting a paternity settlement.

In the beginning of my pregnancy, I'd had no intention of ever asking Ronald to help support his child. After all, he'd wanted me to have an abortion, and I'd refused. To have the child born and to keep it was my decision, one in which he had no voice. It seemed unfair, initially, to make him pay. But when he sent me off to England and promised to write but never did, and when he refused to offer the casual reassurance I sought when I was in the hospital, I became angry and changed my mind. He had practically forced himself on me; I had taken precautions, he had not; mine had failed, and the child was a responsibility which we shared. The ten to twenty dollars a week for which my sister and my lawyer said I should ask was a rather small sum compared to what I would have to pay out over a twenty-one-year period.

My lawyer, John Philips, was a young law-school graduate whom I'd known casually before I got pregnant. I liked him because he was so terribly shy and timid that I became quite confident and bold in his presence. I knew he did not have the makings of a great trial lawyer—with his shy black eyes and occasional stutter—but he was the one who had gotten the newspaper to give me severance pay when I was fired, and more significantly, I could trust myself in front of him. I could talk about my affair with Ronald without crying. In the presence of a more dynamic, assertive man, I knew I would melt and flow away in tears.

John was standing on the courthouse steps when I arrived with James and several diapers in my arms. He was wiping his forehead and pushing back his fine black hair, which was as damp as his forehead from nervousness. We went into the clerk's office, and John began whispering to him.

"You'll have to speak up, son," the tough old clerk shouted, but John could not bring himself to state the delicate nature of our business in an audible tone. He tried to get the clerk to step outside with him and was pushed aside.

Encouraged by John's timidity, I stepped up and yelled the facts over the sound of James's crying. I answered a few routine questions; the father's name and address, how long had I known him, had I ever lived with him and how old was the baby. Within ten minutes a summons had been issued for Ronald.

I was high all day, lifted partly by the strong and competent image of myself which John had evoked, mostly by the fact that Ronald would now have a police record. I was going to get even with him, I thought, as I typed Bill Mitchell's cassette.

"At this very moment, rrrright now, the sheriff is knock, knock, knocking at your father's door!" I sang in operatic style to James. James always bubbled over with giggles when I sang to him, and he stuck his toe down out of his little chairlike box and kicked the box of paper clips off Bill Mitchell's desk. All five hundred of them clicked splendidly to the floor.

Two weeks later we returned to court for a hearing. John waited in the courtroom for our case to come up while I stood outside in the hall, trying to quiet James and reading the notices on the bulletin board. I screamed when someone pinched my behind and almost dropped James in my fright.

I turned around to see Ronald for the first time in ten months, walking away with a man who must be his lawyer.

Several minutes later Ronald stood up in the courtroom and said to the judge in a loud voice, "Not guilty."

I ran outside and sat in John's car. I thought about leaving James there on the seat and going home to cut my wrists. But that would make it too easy for Ronald.

"We'll get that son of a gun," John said when he found me. "Did you see what he had on? A madras jacket! No client of mine would ever show that kind of disrespect for the court. He's a real loser, Mary; you're lucky to be rid of him."

"You didn't see him pinch me when he came into the courthouse."

John was too angry to answer. He just skidded the car out of the parking lot and into the traffic, and for the first time, I thought he might actually become my advocate. I changed my mind the next day when he phoned to confirm that I hadn't had intercourse with any of the following men, whose names had been put forth by Ronald's lawyer. John felt, I thought, that if I had done it once with Ronald, I was a loose woman and must have done it with every other man I had found. Eventually he seemed to accept my story, but I wasn't sure he was happy with it.

I told him how Ronald had been hired to head the entertainment section, the part of the paper I was then working on. He was a rather unattractive man, I thought; from the moment he arrived he smirked at me like a jack-o'lantern across the city room, and several times he'd asked me to go out for drinks with him. I'd always refused not only because he was unattractive, but because I knew he was married.

His invitations became more and more frequent, and he intimated that he was about to divorce his wife. In any case, I came to see quite clearly that I would have to become involved with him or look for another job. I asked to be transferred within the paper, and my request was turned down. I was just what Ronald needed, an editor said, to really liven up the section.

I knew I could never get another job. I was a "lousy, superficial little writer," Ronald told me frequently, and damned lucky that the newspaper had hired me. His judgment was more convincing to me than those offered by such people as the editor.

96

One night in a rainstorm he offered to drive me to the bus station. I had a bad cold and a fever, and thought, why not, for heaven's sake? A ride was nothing. I was not a helpless little girl, and he was not a dark stranger asking me into his car for a candy bar.

Of course, he took me all the way home, and I ended up grotesquely twisted underneath him, with most of my clothes on, screaming for him to get out now that he'd had what he came for.

After he left, I filled the tub with hot water and Mr. Clean, and scrubbed myself in a desperate effort to wash away what I honestly felt had been a sin, adultery. My guilt was compounded in my mind by the fact that I had not fought him off successfully. I had struggled, I had said "No" repeatedly, but I had not screamed for help; I had not kicked him. I had been too afraid, and I knew as I let the Mr. Clean burn into my skin that my fear had been symptomatic of my lack of self-esteem and my weakness of will. I was ashamed.

I had a friend at the paper, a middle-aged man who was very fatherly to me. I stayed after work one night, steered our conversation toward Ronald and hinted at my problem.

"You'd better not let him touch you," he said, and I interpreted the disgust in his voice as being directed toward me.

"I won't," I said, knowing that I really had no choice.

A year later, after many, many miserable fights and scenes with Ronald, I finally took myself to a psychiatrist.

"Forced? You might have been forced once or twice, but not for this long," the psychiatrist said. "You must enjoy it."

"Perhaps I did, but I can't remember any pleasure now," I said.

After a couple of months of therapy, I was able to get rid of Ronald. And, just as the psychiatrist had said, I was not fired. I had given Ronald whatever power he had over me as part of my "quite monumental" effort to avoid taking responsibility for my own life. With the psychiatrist's help, I began to try to take some of that responsibility, and I was proud of myself for the way I handled Ronald at work and avoided him at home—until that one night when I was too rushed to fight with him.

John Philips and Ronald's lawyer made a settlement two days before we were due in court for a paternity trial. I accepted $2,000 a year for two years as a complete settlement of all Ronald's obligations.

John gave me a typed agreement to sign.

"It's the standard form for this sort of thing," he told me. "It's designed to protect him from any further claim from you."

I read it and was amazed to see how it favored Ronald. He was made to sound like the innocent victim of a promiscuous woman's whim.

"I won't sign this unless you put in the phrase, 'He admits that he is the father,'" I said.

John said that would be difficult, but I laughed at him. "What do you mean, difficult?" I demanded. "You want instinctively to protect the man in a case like this. You're supposed to be my advocate. I want Ronald to publicly recognize his son."

The agreement was retyped with my phrase in it, and Ronald signed it without much delay.

"Congratulations," John said, handing me my copy.

I smiled, but it was a very thin salve to my deeply wounded pride.

I felt myself practically destroyed by Ronald's "Not guilty." I began to bathe twice a day and carried Dial soap to Bill Mitchell's office to scrub my hands and face several times during my working hours. And I sank even deeper into my lethargic depression.

Right before Labor Day, I received two pieces of news that jolted me to action.

The first, a letter from Bill Mitchell's secretary, said she was coming back to town and would like to have her job back the day after Labor Day. She understood my position; if I couldn't find something else, she'd let me stay on for another week or so, but she did need the money too—a husband's salary didn't go very far these days.

About an hour later, I was reading the help-wanted advertisements in the back of the paper when Franny Sprague telephoned. She was in town, and could I have lunch with her? Oh, the baby! That was right. She'd come up to the office with some sandwiches.

She arrived at one twenty, saying she'd been unable to find a sandwich shop. Was I starving? Yes, well, she wouldn't stay that long; they were still at the lake and she was just down for the day, to see her gynecologist. A terrible fright—she and Bill thought she was pregnant again, could I imagine that? Well, thank God, something had just gone wrong with her hormones.

98

She looked well, her skin tanned and hair bleached by the sun. She took off her linen jacket—did I mind?—and sat there in her slip and skirt. It was hot in the city. How ever did I stand it? Her feet were killing her too. Would I mind? Honestly, she hadn't had on a pair of shoes all summer, just slippers when they went out to cocktails or the club. She couldn't remember when the sailing had been better.

Well, she'd get right to the point. She and Bill—well, really, it was mostly Bill—I knew how men were—anyway, they were worried about Mother all alone in that big house with just Emma. Mother was a sitting duck, up on top of the hill there. And after the goings-on this summer, they were even more concerned.

Now, as I probably knew, Mother had always had a man living in the garage, and that way, she had some built-in protection. I could see the wisdom in that. Well, it just so happened that one of the policemen who'd been involved that awful night, a bachelor one, Charles Brians, had gotten in touch with her. He'd taken it completely upon himself, she guessed, to get her name and address from the sergeant, and he'd driven up one Sunday to talk to her about the apartment.

I could see how, from their point of view, he was the ideal tenant for Mother, couldn't I?

"Of course," I said. "What a lucky break."

The only hitch was that he had a lease where he was now and it ran out on—she raised her eyebrows gingerly—August 31. So, he'd like very much, if it wouldn't put me out awfully, to move in that Labor Day weekend. Now if I was stuck, they'd all put their heads together and work out something. After all, we wouldn't want this young man here sleeping in the street, would we? She reached down and pulled James's toe.

James was lying on a towel on the floor and jogging in place. His arms and legs would move rapidly up and down for a minute or so, and then he'd freeze like a bird dog, focusing on the squares of sunlight cast on the gray walls. Then, having absorbed that, he'd be off again.

"Don't worry," I told poor, embarrassed Franny. "Heavens, I have a whole week, don't I? Surely I can find something in that time."

"Well, you just let me know if there are any problems. Mother would never forgive me if we didn't see you happily ensconced somewhere. If you get stuck, Bill may be able to help. There are always nurses at the hospital looking for roommates."

After she left, James and I went downstairs to the cafeteria for lunch, and I read the apartment ads. It had been a year since I'd paid any rent, and the apartment I'd had then had apparently been an incredible bargain. Now, for $150 a month I could get an unfurnished efficiency out by the airport runways.

I went back to the office without finishing my lunch. Christ, everything had fallen in at once. Thanks to Ronald, Mrs. Peck and Bill Mitchell, I had about $3,000, enough money to survive in a hotel if worst came to worst for a few months, until I found some sort of work, but where was I ever going to find a baby-sitter? I called the state department of child welfare to see if there was any day care and was again told that day care was illegal for preschool children. I was advised by a social worker in the state welfare department to whom I was referred that the best solution was to come right down and apply for the Aid to Families with Dependent Children welfare grant.

I called up a family service agency and said I needed help. I scooped up James and ran across the park. At the top of an old brownstone house, an ancient, chain-smoking social worker told me how her doctor thought she had some sort of pulmonary lesion and wanted her to go right into the hospital for X rays, but her mother, who was eighty-seven, had just had another stroke and she couldn't think of herself at a time like this.

James, just five months old, babbled merrily on the floor, grinning at me.

"You know, if I'm going to counsel you," the social worker said, "You'll have to leave the baby some place else. Could you get a sitter? We can't talk while he's making all that noise, now can we?"

"A sitter's my problem," I said, and my story spurted out—no job, no shelter, no sitter.

"Well, have you thought of adoption?" she said, coughing purple as she rummaged around in her desk for another pack of cigarettes. "We've got a lot of good homes waiting, and I'm fairly sure one of them wouldn't mind such an old baby. A boy, though, I don't know. Sometimes they want a girl, you know, because the family name won't be passed on through her."

"You mean they'd rather just lend their name to someone who's not their flesh and blood?"

"Well, it's perfectly natural. We always tell our parents that there can be no guarantees about what they're getting. We do our best, we're very thorough, but there are circumstances beyond anyone's control." Before I left, I asked her if she counseled any mothers who had kept their babies. Of course, a few. Would she get a group together? Others must face the problems I faced, or must have solved them.

I called back a week later. She was just going off to the hospital now; it looked as though Mother was out of the woods for a while, so she was going to get herself in shape while she had the chance. No, she'd checked my group idea with her supervisor and it would not be possible.

In the paper I found very few jobs offered that had any possibilities. There were plenty of secretarial positions, some paying quite well, but I couldn't do it. Bill Mitchell had been fine, but I wasn't going to leave James to type for a sausage maker or address fliers for an automotive supply house.

I did leave James with my sister one afternoon and drive out to a suburban textbook publisher. A very sweet old woman told me how I'd be writing descriptions of the texts for salesmen to take to the professors at various colleges. She would be my supervisor, and if I worked very hard, well, she was due to retire in three years. She showed me the desk where I'd sit next to Adrianne, who was out sick, and told me they were pretty liberal—you could take a coffee break in the morning, and most of the girls brought their lunch and ate in the lounge; you had a half hour. I couldn't stand it.

I thanked her and told her I'd call her if my interest waxed. She seemed very surprised and shook her head sadly.

There was a second paper in town, not a bad one, and I had a friend there. At least he had been a friend. I hadn't talked to him in a year. I called him up.

"Sam Callahan? he's managing editor now," the man at the city desk told me. "I'll switch you to his secretary."

"Hey, Sam, how about giving me a job?" I asked when I finally got him on the phone.

"How the hell are you? How's the baby? News travels fast," he said, avoiding my question. "Look, I'm taking the afternoon off—

101

why not?—it's a Wednesday. Doctors do it. Aggie, the girls and I, we're going to the lake. Come along."

Sam had married a dental assistant during his senior year at college. She was a dainty little girl, with frosted hair and silvered fingernails. She sat in the front of their station wagon and smiled back at me.

"Sit down, girls," she said to her two small daughters, six and four, in pink-checked sundresses with sunflower appliqués, just like hers.

I had on my old dungarees and a shirt. I didn't own a bathing suit any more, and James was looking like a convict, his bristly big head popping out of a dark striped shirt, and his arms punching up at me in left and right hooks. After each jab, he'd yell "Aye-aye" boisterously.

"So you had a boy," Callahan said, as he started the car. "I wish to hell you'd tell us your secret. We're trying a third time—you don't mind me breaking the news, do you, honey? What do you bet it'll be another girl?"

"I sort of wanted a girl," I lied to Aggie. "I figured a girl was more fun. There are more things you can do with girls. What can you do with a boy?"

"Hell, anything you can do with a girl and more," Sam said. "Girls, you want a brother—don't you?"

The little girls nodded primly.

"Well, I don't want a boy," Aggie said, fiddling with the little rhinestone cross around her neck. "You have to worry about making them masculine, and especially in your case, it must be a worry, isn't it, Mary?"

"That's what I've been told," I said. "If it's a boy, it'll be a queer—that's what everyone says. One social worker called me up the day we got home from the hospital just to make that point one final time; 'Boys, particularly, need fathers.' I had James on my shoulder and the phone under my chin, and before I could answer, he vomited all over the mouthpiece. What could I do? I just hung up."

"Funny, neither of the girls ever threw up, unless of course, something was wrong with them."

"Aw, hell, honey, what are you talking about?" Callahan said. "They puked all over the place. All babies do."

102

"All right, Sam, have it your way."

We drove in silence for a while, and then Aggie turned back to me.

"It's none of my business, of course," she said, smoothing the silk of her elder daughter's hair, "but, Mary, I do think you should wear a ring. People talk enough as it is. You could get one in the dime store. I think you owe it to your family and to your baby."

"Aggie, I had two rings, a wedding ring and a fake engagement ring, and I took them off when I left the hospital. I guess I thought they made me look married and out of bounds to any men I might meet."

"Well, men try to pick me up rings and all sometimes, don't they, Sam?" she asked kittenishly. "Don't you think Mary should wear a ring?"

"Aggie, what's gotten into you? For the love of Mike, lay off. I suspect Mary has other things to worry about."

"She's probably right, Sam," I said. "I'll get a ring."

"Let me tell you what we're trying to do with the paper," he said, looking at me in the rearview mirror. He began to describe how he was attempting to give the paper a new tone, so it could compete for its share of the circulation; and the emphasis was to be on youth. Even the sports section was being revamped. They were going to do a lot of hiring, maybe a couple of dozen people, before they were through.

"Of course, there's no one I'd rather have than you," he said, as we waited at a red light. He turned around and smiled at me. "But I don't think I can swing it. I checked with the higher-ups and they said no, too."

"Why?" I asked, not really surprised or disappointed.

"What do you mean, why? Because you have James."

"I guess that makes sense," I said. I was embarrassed for having put Sam in an awkward position.

I picked James up by his arms and began bouncing him around on my knee, playing the Irresponsible Mother game. The game involved my pretending to be a series of important and responsible people demanding to hold the baby because his mother couldn't be trusted with him.

"Give me that baby," I said becoming a social worker. "His mother's too neurotic to—whooooops!" and I almost dropped him,

103

spreading my knees to let him fall and then jerking him back up just as he was about to hit the floor. He'd roar with delight.

"I'll take that infant; suffer the little children to come unto me," says the bishop. "Whooooops!"

"Send that woman to jail and give the baby to me," says the judge. "Whooooops!"

In the end, the mother says, "What's this old mouse doing here in my house? I'll just have to take him and drop him—whoops! right in a big hug."

"I've got to get something quickly," I said to Sam, when I realized Aggie was watching our game with her mouth gaping open. "Friday's my last day of work."

"Wow, I didn't realize it was that urgent," Sam said. "Jeez! Why did you leave everything to the last minute?"

"It sort of fell on me, and I hadn't planned—I don't know why."

"Why don't you go on welfare?" Aggie said. "Of course, they'd deduct something from your payments because you don't pay any rent at Mrs. Peck's, do you?"

"No. But I've got to be out of there this weekend too."

"Well, no problem then," she said, enthusiastically, "Maybe you could get in one of the projects."

"Look, the first thing to do is find a decent place to live," Sam said, glaring at Aggie. "When you're all settled and have found someone to take care of James, that's the time to start serious job-hunting. Have you read the help-wanted ads?"

"Yes. But how can I rent a place when I don't know how much money I'll be making? And if I can't get a job here, I'll have to look somewhere else, so I don't want to be tied to an apartment."

Sam parked at one of the state-owned beaches, and we walked down across the hot sand. I stuck the old black umbrella I'd swiped from Bill Mitchell's office in the sand to shelter James.

"It's a shame," Sam said, pulling off his T-shirt. "I wish I could put you on, but baby, in something like this, friendship just can't enter into it. We're in a tough competitive situation. We can't send you out representing us."

"I know," I said, "I'm sorry I asked."

He leaned down and gave me a wet smack on the cheek. "Why don't you move in with Aggie and me for a couple of weeks, until you get a job? Aggie's not doing a damn thing, are you, honey? She can even watch James while you go looking; then you won't have that worry."

Aggie was smoothing Bain de Soleil on the back of her elder daughter. "Sam, why don't we talk about that later? It's such a nice day—let's just enjoy it."

It was a nice day, golden August, and the sky was deep blue. The beach had just a few people on a weekday afternoon, a couple of boys nearby tossing a multicolored beach ball, while their black cocker spaniel ran yelping between them, and nearby, the littler Callahan girl, her head a helmet of smooth gold hair, shoveling sand into her fish-painted bucket. There were a few round marshmallow puffs of clouds, and beneath them, far out on the lake, was a trio of sailboats.

"It's a perfect day," I said, feeling suddenly cold in my intestines. "It looks like one of those pictures in a child's coloring book: 'Color this and tell us how many mistakes you can find.' You know the kind I mean, the kind where, when you started to crayon, you'd see that the dog only had three legs, or the sails were on backwards or the man was missing an ear?"

I took off my dungarees quickly and pulled my shirt up over my head. Without even looking at Aggie, I walked down to the water in my grayed nylon underpants and old, yellow-stained nursing bra and waded right in. For a few seconds, I thought the cold was going to kill me, my head pounded and my feet were gone, but gradually I began to tingle with life. I flapped around and spouted like a whale.

When I came out, Sam was lying on the sand with his arm over his eyes. James slept peacefully beside him.

"What happened to Aggie and the girls?" I asked, trying to keep the smile out of my voice.

"Oh, Aggie gets upset about things," he said, without looking up. "She'll be back eventually."

I started to get dressed.

"Listen, I had an idea," Sam said into his arm. "Way out on the west side, there's this think-tank deal, a bunch of oddball professors and businessmen, futurists. It's called Faraday, Brinks and Crummel. It was just a little outfit until three weeks ago, when it had several million dollars' worth of Federal poverty-program funds dropped in its lap. Now, it's tripling overnight and hiring like crazy. We're running a feature on it. It's looking for writers and editors.

Give them a call when you get home. Use me as a reference. I'll snow them for you."

"Thanks," I said. "I guess I'll have to call them."

"But listen, Hanes, do me a favor, will you?" he asked, still keeping his arm over his eyes. "On the application blank, write that you're divorced, and get rid of that bra, will you, for the love of Mike? It looks like it came over on the *Mayflower*."

Faraday, Brinks and Crummel was much too busy growing, I soon discovered, to pay attention to practicalities such as employment application forms, and I made no mention of my marital status during my interview because I felt such a conventional bit of information would have soured the company on me.

12

Faraday, Brinks and Crummel, known as the Company to its employees, was a maze of immaculate, starkly white rooms. In the center sat Andy Crummel, like a fat little spider. Although he was white, he was wearing a dashiki and he had a string of sunflower seeds around his neck. He said to be perfectly frank from the start—that he was one of three senior partners in the Company, and roughly two thirds of its guiding force.

He spent twenty or thirty minutes telling me how ghetto dwellers were demanding that meaningful change happen in their lifetimes, and his soft voice seemed to wander up and down the walls, slipping into pockets of brief inaudibility.

I sensed that he was extremely interested in whether or not I was listening to him, so I leaned forward and wrinkled my brow to simulate concentration, which I actually found quite impossible to attain. He was wearing sunglasses with mirror lenses, and when his curly dark hair was not floating down across them, all I could see was my own image, pale, ugly, and very distorted.

His desk, a slip of white marble on chrome legs, was banked with jade trees, and a canary, in a many-tiered Japanese cage painted red, was chirping periodically in the corner behind him.

Glass-framed photographs of four little blond girls hung on the wall, and I decided that despite his deeply lined face, Andy was only in his mid-thirties.

"Well, now you know something of my philosophy, of what the Company is about," he said, beginning to caress an unsharpened yellow pencil,"you'll have to meet Johnston Faraday, or course, to fully understand what we are."

He looked perplexed. "I've wondered where you were, Mary. I saw that your articles were no longer appearing in the paper and it concerned me. It concerned me—how shall I say it? It concerned me because you were one of the few people writing in Colton who really knew where it was at. You understood what it means to be poor and black, and now you're here. It's really wonderful. What can I say—a miracle! We need you."

I wasn't about to argue with him or to suggest that he must have me confused with someone else. After all, I thought, I had written one or two articles that had a connection of some sort with poor blacks—I must have—and it was possible that I'd touched upon something only he was sensitive enough to see.

"I only have one question about you, Mary, and that is, quite frankly, if you'll be able to relate to the people. I know you'll feel them, but will you make music with them?"

"I don't think I relate very well to anyone," I said. "And music, right now, I'm not interested in that, except as much as you have to make to get by."

"That's what I was afraid of, that's what I was afraid of," he said, shaking his head. It had slipped through my fingers.

"One thing, though, I've never had any trouble at all talking to people, getting people to open up and talk to me. It's the second and third stages where I fall off," I said.

"Well, fine, fine. Because all you'll need to do is stay on that first stage. We have field representatives to form meaningful relationships, some of which will probably last a lifetime. Will you let us have you? Will you come tomorrow?"

He got up and I took his cool, waxy hand.

"I have to finish the week where I am," I said, hesitantly. "But I'll be here Tuesday, after the holiday?"

108

"Ah, yes, Labor Day, the great American holiday. If you must, you must. Finish where you are, but hurry to us."

"What time do you begin work around here?" I asked, aware somehow that I was asking the wrong sort of question.

"Mary, we never stop work, but you'll see all that for yourself."

I started to leave, but turned on the doorstep. I'd forgotten to ask about money.

"Money? Oh, dear. Name your price."

"I was getting ten thousand . . ."

"Sold, sold. That's what it is."

He closed his door and left me to stumble about through the corridors and find my way out.

I had a hard time of it, and I felt incredibly clumsy and stupid when I finally confronted the receptionist. She was a long, lithe, suntanned girl with a crew cut. She had on a white knit dress that didn't quite cover her orange-and-blue-diamonded underpants.

"What?" she asked angrily, looking up from her crossword puzzle.

"What time do people get started here in the morning?"

"They don't," she giggled. "They get started at night, in bed, usually!"

"Work. Nine?"

"That sounds great to me. Say, you don't know anyone who's looking for an apartment, do you?"

It seemed she'd been at a party the night before and seen this really fantastic place—it just blew her mind and she had to have it. She'd signed a lease for it, right then and there at the party; she must have been out of her mind—she already had an apartment with ten months to go on the lease. She was stuck with the old one.

I had left James at my sister's, and she was going to dinner at seven. I told the receptionist—her name was Kathy—that I'd take her old apartment; two rooms and a kitchen—"if you like to cook"—for only $160, if we could get it all settled right then, by six thirty.

"What's the rush? You got tomorrow before the weekend; I mean you could see the landlord then, couldn't you?" she said, dialing his number.

No, I had to work tomorrow, and tonight I had a date at seven.

"You have a date?" she asked, incredulously. "Hmmm."

The landlord would see us in an hour at the apartment. She called the answering service to cover the phones and shouted back to Andy Crummel that she was leaving.

"This place is amazing," she said as we left. "They expect me to hang around until five o'clock tomorrow, when everyone else left yesterday for the weekend. I'm telling you, it's unreal, the whole place. No one believes it. You'll see."

The apartment was on the top of a three-decker, its paint peeling, beside the parking lot of a shopping center.

The landlord lurking in the dark wet hallway looked like an aging tadpole. He was green and almost froglike from too many basements.

"Look, Kathy," he said, "You're a nice girl; I want to help you out, and if this lady's a friend of yours, fine. But before we go up there I got to tell you, there's going to be no subletting. I'll let you off and write her a new lease—that way, I'm in control. Get what I mean?

"The hallways will be completely renovated starting next month, with new stairs and lights put in. Got the men lined up," he said as we puffed up to the third floor. "And we'll be putting locks on all the doors. Kathy has a dog, but that's just 'cause she's my girl. No pets."

Kathy's door was open. It had no lock, although I noticed a hook on the inside. A big brown mystery of a dog started wagging its tail and dribbling urine all over the Finnish rug as we walked in.

It wasn't a bad place, I thought, glancing around. It was light and had high ceilings. There were some scrubby weed trees edging the parking lot beneath the bedroom window. That was nice. Kathy had obviously put a lot into it. The walls were covered with Finnish textile prints, and she had a lot of expensive Scandinavian furniture.

We went back to the landlord's office and stared at his oil-green carpet while his secretary typed a new lease.

"You'll just fill out an application," he said to me, "Although Kathy's word's all I need."

There was a print of the Sacred Heart, all bloody and crowned, behind his desk.

I wrote down, "Divorced," and under "Children" put "1."

"Kathy's put a lot of improvements, so the rent goes up to a hundred and seventy-five a month, not including your gas and electric, and we'll need a month's rent as a security deposit."

He took my application and I got out my checkbook.

110

"Wait, hold everything. No kids. Sorry," he said.

"It's a five-month-old baby, and it will be gone all day while I work," I said, forgetting that James would no longer be coming to work with me. "If there's any problem, you can just tell me and I'll move, but I'm sure there won't be."

He let out a puff of cigar smoke. "Make that rent a hundred and eighty-five," he said and handed the lease back to his secretary. "No carriages in the hall, now."

"I don't have a carriage."

"O.K, give me a check for three seventy and it's yours."

I gave Kathy a ride back to the Company.

"Watch out for him," she said. "He's a real creep, the landlord. He told me the same thing about the halls when I moved in three years ago. I can't wait to get my stuff out of there. I should get some guys to help me tomorrow night; then you could move in Saturday. Would that be all right?"

The next morning I called the university and asked if there were any student wives who did baby-sitting. It seemed to me my best chance of getting a young, intelligent baby-sitter inexpensively lay in finding someone pretty much in my position, with a young child or two and in need of money. As it turned out, the university published a list of such women, and James and I went out and got a copy of it on Bill Mitchell's time.

I sat in the car and read through the list. There must have been fifty names. I narrowed it down to two—because they lived fairly near Kathy's apartment—and then to one, because the name sounded Jewish. Poor James, with his canned baby food and helter-skelter, unsanitary life with careless, preoccupied Mary, needed a little Jewish Mothering.

As it turned out, Trina Friedburg was not Jewish and she was more haphazard and casual than I. But she had a daughter six months older than James, and there were a lot of books around the house. She was young and healthy, with pixielike brown hair and big brown eyes. Her husband was a law student.

I sat at the kitchen table while they finished supper, and I liked them despite their supper—canned meatballs, sauerkraut and creme-filled donuts. James, on the floor, looked up at Trina and grinned—with love, I thought.

Sure, she'd take little Jim in every day, for forty a week plus overtime, and diapers and food. That was O.K. "Huh, Jim?" she said, giving him a nickname I disliked.

James laughed and waved half an Oreo he'd found on the floor.

On the way back to Mrs. Peck's, I looked at James sucking his shirt, on the seat beside me. He was losing his mother. Was I going to pay out forty a week plus to warp my child's psyche? Oh, God, it was probably already warped, or it would be by the time we turned into the Peck driveway. He'd smiled at Trina just about the way he smiled at me, or at the meter maid at the corner outside Bill Mitchell's office, for that matter.

If anyone was going to suffer from the daily separation, I decided, it would be the mother. While I might not miss his screams and spills, I had become accustomed to him. In just the few hours I'd spent at the Company, I'd felt like something of an amputee. His constant needs did speak of my relevance. And, as much as I hated to admit, I was sort of fond of him. Just a little bit.

So, I'd make a big effort and get used to missing him all day, and then I'd recover. But I knew, although such prescience did little good, that I'd never recover from the guilt, the doubt, and the pleasure of leaving him.

Late that night, Mrs. Peck arrived home from Europe. About twenty minutes after her cab left, she came running up the steps to the garage apartment.

"This is terrible, terrible," she said, throwing her arms around me. "I never meant for this to happen. I only moved you out here because I knew how much you wanted to be on your own. But this is too much. I told you, you must not work until James is at least three. I told you, I was prepared to help you out. If you want to do some work for Bill Mitchell, that's fine, but not a full-time job away from home. You must have these precious years with your son. It's a small thing for me to give them to you, to try to make things as they would have been if your parents were alive."

"If my parents had been alive!" I laughed. "No, you've given and given and I have nothing to give in return. I have to get back in the world."

"Well, I just wanted to make it clear to you, you always have a home here."

"I feel that way, I really do," I said, surprised at the sincerity behind my words.

112

"Well, with that out of the way," she said, "I must make myself a highball, put my feet up."

She was halfway down the stairs, when she stopped and called back to me: "What is your job, anyway? Franny neglected to fill me in on that one."

To my surprise, I couldn't answer her. Andy Crummel had neglected to fill me in on that one, I realized only then.

13

I was outside the Company at 8:15 the first morning, but its thick glass doors were locked, no one came to answer the bell and the telephones, on Kathy's desk just inside, rang continually.

At 10:05, Kathy hopped out of a white Porsche and swung across the sidewalk. She dangled the keys in my face and asked, with an elfin smile, "Looking for these?"

She dropped her pocketbook on the floor and began to fiddle with a fingernail, as the telephones rang on and on. "I told you we were very casual about time here, didn't I? Well, I thought Andy would." She thought it was terribly funny that I'd been just standing there for two hours.

"I came early, Kathy, to talk to you about the apartment. I knew it looked nice because of all your stuff, but I've never seen such dirt. I can't use the kitchen or the bathroom, really. Are you going to clean it up?"

She picked up the phone. "Good morning, Faraday, Brinks and Crummel. May I help you? No. I'm sorry, he seems to have stepped away from his desk. May I have him call you? Fine. No, no. The telephones have been out of order. The repairman just left," she winked at me. "Oh, I can imagine! How annoying. I'll have Mr. Crummel call you as soon as he has a minute."

She pressed another button: "Good morning, Faraday, Brinks and Crummel. . . . "

I could see she wasn't interested in my problems with her former apartment.

When James and I had arrived at the top of the three-decker with our single suitcase of worldly goods, the apartment we'd leased had been missing. In its place was one of the worst hovels I'd ever seen. Entire walls had rotted away to reveal old fuzz and splintery ladders. No wonder Kathy had invested so heavily in hangings. Where her carpets had been, old linoleum, in half a dozen layers of various hues and designs, was peeling up. The windows stayed open only with the help of a book or milk bottle; several panes were cracked and two were actually missing and replaced with what appeared to be wax paper.

But the filth which she had left behind was the most upsetting part. Dust, old magazines, shoe boxes and wire clothes hangers were to be expected. So were filmy jelly glasses, sprouted potatoes and an inch of burnt fat in the broiler.

But there were other things—examples of absolute piggery —which I simply could not face. One of the lesser annoyances was the very vivid evidence that her dog had relieved himself for several weeks, I calculated, in the two closets. After inspecting the bathroom, which had been tactfully closed during my initial visit, I was tempted to follow his example.

"I don't think I can live there. What can I do?" I asked her when she finally ran out of phone calls momentarily.

"Oh, scrubadubadub!" she said. "Get out the old elbow grease."

I nodded and went to find my office.

That night, Mrs. Peck came calling with a basket of delicacies, including smoked salmon and wine, and recoiled in horror at the house she'd intended to help warm.

Two days later, a professional janitorial service arrived, and three men spent a day and a half throwing out garbage and cleaning the place. And she then sent a painter, but he shook his head and left after painting only two walls.

After two weekends of solid work, I was ready to buy a few

necessities at the Salvation Army, like a bed (we'd been sleeping on the floor on a blanket) and a table and chairs, but it was months before I could bring myself to unpack the suitcase.

My office at the Company seemed like one of the choicer ones in the building. It was on the outside, and it had a window overlooking a dingy back street.

At 5:30 on my first day of work, when no one had showed up to tell me what my job was, I left my empty desk and went home to fix supper for James.

The second day things were busier. Half a dozen secretaries were in the offices, making telephone calls about hairdressers' appointments or their poodles' infected ears. One argued for two and a half hours with her husband, who was presumably also at work, about what they would get her mother for her twenty-fifth wedding anniversary.

At 4:45, a fat little man with three briefcases got out of an old white and rusted Nash Rambler, which he'd parked in front of the fire hydrant outside my window. He waved an elbow at me through the glass, so I walked out to the front door to see who he was.

He juggled the briefcases around, somehow managing to get all three of them tucked into the left side of his body, opened the door, and came in and shook my hand.

"You're Mary? Glad to have you. I'm Johnston Faraday. Come on back to my office with me."

Johnston's office was like mine—one mahogany-finished door on iron legs and a folding chair. He had a telephone, however, and he picked it up to talk to Kathy.

"Tell Andy to come on in, if he wants to talk to Mary with me. Otherwise, I'll see him in ten minutes. Where is he? Will you find out!"

Kathy came in a few minutes later.

"Andy says to tell you he's hung up at home, but he should be in next week."

"God damn it," Johnston said, "What's his number? I came all the way from St. Louis to talk to that son-of-a-bitch at five o'clock."

When he had Andy on the phone, he was surprisingly mild. "Andy? You got problems?" He listened for a long time and said finally, "Well, you know the deadline's next Friday? You think so? O.K., I'll let you talk to her."

116

He shook his head and, putting his hand over the telephone receiver before giving it to me, said, "To know Andy is to love him."

Andy apologized to me profusely. Then he got down to business. He was in a bit of a mess and needed me to bail him out. On his desk was an alligator notebook. Inside that should be two folders of notes for a report on his neighborhood project that had to be in Washington, in the Feds' hands, by a week from Friday. If I could write the report from his notes, I'd be just saving his life. It didn't have to be fancy or very long. Maybe a hundred pages, with enough detail to convince them we'd been busy. If I'd write it and get it typed up, he'd be in Thursday to sign the cover letter.

Johnston Faraday had lit his pipe and was reading through some papers from one of his briefcases when I hung up. He was sweating into his peach-colored shirt, despite the chill of the air conditioning.

He told me he'd hired Andy because the Company needed his "particular expertise."

"No one can talk to the Feds like Andy—he used to be in insurance, you know. He can charm the flies off of honey."

"Apparently," I said, and then told him that in my desperate need for work I'd been seduced into coming to a job which I knew nothing about. "What's the neighborhood project?" I asked. "The thing I'm supposed to write the report on?"

"It's one of our centers of activity," Johnston said, and then described how the Company had many centers of activity in many fields of expertise, but at the moment, I only need concern myself with Andy.

Andy had landed several million dollars' worth of contracts from a Federal agency to organize neighborhoods. He was creating corporations in major U. S. ghettos. Once organized, the poor would use these corporations in some cases as a vehicle for the decentralization of political power and governmental services, and in other cases as a way of at least making their voices heard in assuring meaningful delivery of services to their constituency.

I didn't have the foggiest idea what he was talking about. I smiled, nervously.

"What's funny?" he asked anxiously.

"Nothing—it sounds interesting. A smile of pleasure, I guess."

"It will be up to you to cover for Andy—what you've seen today is, I'm afraid, fairly typical behavior—and to write a series of

117

booklets for use by our field representatives and for publication by Feds on the various areas of citizen input. Basically, these booklets will tell the folks out there how they can gain the power and the ability to control their own lives. Kathy should be able to round up a copy of Andy's proposal. It's all there.

"If you feel you need any help, there's also a list out with Kathy of all our fringe members in the Company. Just call one of them up and tell him you need some input from him."

I got the list of fringe members, and once, in writing the first manual—on how to start a neighborhood organization—I tried to get the fringe member whose listed expertise was group dynamics. The university told me they had no such professor there, and a check of their records showed a student with that name who had dropped out the previous year.

From my second week at the Company, when I saw my "Preliminary Remarks and Intermediate Report on the Establishment of Neighborhood Organizations" go out over Andy's signature, I was terrified.

Andy arrived in the office at 11:30 P.M. in a kimono, just in time to sign the report and get it into the mail to be postmarked on the due date; he did not read it.

"Do you feel you understood my notes and came to terms with the material?" he asked me as I drove him home, all the way to Northshire. He was too upset to drive himself that night, and his wife had been too tired to wait to take him home.

"Andy, does your caged bird sing?" I asked.

In truth, I'd found his notes totally illegible, all four pages of them, and even his secretary had been unable to make out the names of the cities he'd been writing about. From the proposal, I'd gotten an idea of what we should have done, and I'd basically rewritten this with a few words of color about local events which I'd dug up from newspapers in the public library.

"Beautiful, beautiful," he said. "I knew you were the girl for us. You must come in and have some brandy with me right now."

And then, because I was certain I'd be fired anyway as soon as the report hit Washington and a congressional investigation was launched, I told him about James.

"I can't come in," I said. "My baby-sitter's put in a very long day."

118

"Don't tell me," he said, covering his eyes. "You have six, I see six, you have a six-year-old girl."

"Six months and a boy."

"Well, you'll have to come in some other night, then, and bring him. My wife, Flora, is a genius with babies. And she loves them."

When I went to the Crummels' several months later, I immediately liked Flora. She was a fat, red-faced woman in a greasy quilted bathrobe. She had about a yard of yellow hair which couldn't have been washed in weeks. She was rushing around putting wine glasses on the table and getting cheese and soggy crackers into Andy and his sixteen Pakistani student guests, who'd been sent by a group for international friendship of which he was a member. Her girls were bribed with streamers of lollipops to stay in front of the television and keep James with them.

By the time I left, when dinner was over at ten thirty, she still hadn't found time to put on her dress.

"What the hell," she whispered to me, as we carried the couscous in to the table, "if they are new to this country for real, they'll think this is standard hostess attire. A lot of these visitors are fakes, you know. Students and their families having trouble making ends meet. They call up every month and give a different name and say they're just here to visit an electronics plant or a hospital. They get enough free feeds to last until the check arrives from the old country."

As I was helping her dry the dishes, she asked how I was liking my first few months as a mother.

"Oh, wonderful, wonderful," I lied.

"God, I hate babies," she said. "I'd just as soon come in and coo to them once a day and leave the rest to the state. They're a terrible bore, as far as I'm concerned, until they get to be around eighteen months—maybe not until two or three. Depends on the child."

"They are boring," I said, "and time-consuming, but you feel a terrific bond to them, don't you?"

"Sure, but you'd have that for a dog or anything you put an equivalent amount of time and energy into. Not to mention money."

"Maybe you're right," I said, wondering if she could be a spy sent from the child welfare people to gather proof that I was an unfit mother. "They certainly do wear you out."

"Especially you," she said. "Having to work on top of it all! I know, I was in grad school with my first two, and Andy, honestly.

he's more work than help. He's three times the work all the kids are together. Their tantrums are nothing—but nothing—compared to his. Poor man, he's under terrific pressure, but what can anybody do? Keep up appearances, keep the books balanced and then pray there aren't any more riots. I wish he'd get out, though. Insurance was a bore, but at least he wasn't home clutching his stomach and crying for weeks on end.

"How do you like working for him? That's not fair—don't answer. He's a child. I don't see how anyone can stand him. I couldn't if I didn't like fucking him, which you don't do, do you?"

I shook my head.

"I wouldn't care," she said. "Not too much." She didn't look quite as tough as she sounded, her small eyes looking at me shyly from under her sweaty red brow. "I didn't think you were fucking him, just because he likes very fat women, usually. Mother problems. He needs a mother. Maybe I should leave him? What do you think?"

"God, how can I tell?"

She laughed. "How can you tell? Listen, I like you. Will you go to a Women's Liberation meeting with me? Not right now; Andy's in need of all the support I can give him, and it would kill him if he knew I was interested in feminism. Maybe in a few months; I'll call you."

120

14

When the first sooty leaf below the bedroom window turned yellow, I caught cold, and from then on all winter, there was not more than a day or two at a time when either James or I was not sick.

Trina rapidly came to depend on my forty—or more often sixty—dollars a week, and she took James into her house in sickness and in health. She and her plump little daughter, Pammie, bounced through the winter without as much as a sniffle.

We spent Thanksgiving in bed with colds and fevers, but by Sunday night both of us seemed better. We walked out in the steely gray dusk to buy canned soup for our supper. In emergencies, James ate the noodles and pieces of meat mashed up and I drank the liquid with toast.

When we were coming back to the apartment, Franny Sprague and her husband were getting out of their station wagon in front. They had some baby furniture, she said, which they could no longer use. A crib and an elaborate split-level affair in which you were supposed to bathe a baby. I never used the latter; James and I always showered together, quickly, standing gingerly on a rubber mat that almost hid the stains in the bathtub.

Both pieces of furniture were still in their factory cartons, and it was quite obvious that they had never been intended for a Sprague child, the youngest of which was still crib age in any case. But the crib was a welcome present. The Company paid only for the hours you actually worked. When you were sick you were out of money, and I was beginning to go into debt.

Franny sat on my bed and watched James crawling back and forth across the room, over feet, rugs, outstretched legs, and laundry bag—anything she put in his way he merely assessed and then scaled.

Dr. Sprague was in the corner trying to assemble the crib. He'd grunt and curse, and metal rods would crash onto the floor. Every once in a while he'd shout "Pliers" or "Phillips screwdriver" or "Hammer," and I'd rush to knock on a neighbor's door.

"Well, I'm glad you weaned him," Franny said, after she'd observed James in motion for a few minutes. "But you know, you did it awfully soon—when was it, three, four months? You could have kept right on nursing him until he was ready for a cup, next year."

"He already uses a cup," I said, proud of Trina's accomplishment, born, I think, out of a desire to economize on the amount of milk consumed. From a bottle, James would take eight ounces at a suck, but in a cup, his interest failed after a few sips.

"Oh, that's very good," she said, with some doubt in her voice. "But does he get enough sucking?"

"Well, I give him a bottle at night in bed, and he does have his thumb, all day."

"That's my point, that's my point," she said triumphantly.

"Franny, shut up, will you?" Bill said. "How about a small, regular screwdriver?"

"He is right," she said, when I came back with a pocket screwdriver. "You should never listen to what anyone tells you about your children, especially clumsy surgeons." Bill sent the hammer skidding across the floor to hit her boots. "It's all speculation, pure and simple. . . . but one thing I think's important. Don't get too attached. I mean, you shouldn't. It's different for me—I do have Bill around. Margo Novak told me you and James were still sleeping in the same bed. That's bad."

"That wasn't out of perverted desire," I said, "I didn't have a crib.

122

I don't like waking up in a pool of cold pee and being chased from one side of the bed to the other all night. But why shouldn't I be attached to him just as much as you are to your children?"

"Well, it's just not nice, somehow. I don't know, maybe I'm being purely subjective."

"Oh, God, no, never," Bill said. "Will you please come hold this for me, Franny, and stop talking."

"William, haven't you got that thing together yet?" she said, rushing over to hold the side. "You know we were supposed to be in town ten minutes ago. You're so stupid with your hands." She held the side up while he tried to get a screw into a small hole. "Honestly, let me do it," she said. "You hold this."

Bill Sprague held the crib side and stared placidly up at the cracks in the ceiling.

"There," said Franny. "All right, William, you can let go now. It's done."

As they walked out, Bill, whom I'd seen only once before in my life, gave me a big kiss on the cheek. "Open your hand," he whispered. "I think it'll hold him anyway. If not, call my secretary. She'll have a carpenter out."

And, like a clown in an old-time comedy, he dropped five big screws, two springs and a nut of some kind into my palm and winked.

The Spragues had also brought a carton of sheets and baby clothes, some slightly worn but clean and welcome.

I made up James's new crib and put him in a blue pair of pajamas that had a cottontail and a hood with rabbit ears. He looked like a little prince in such luxury, a crib and pajamas.

As I was getting undressed to go to bed myself, I noticed that he looked flushed. I changed his diaper carefully without waking him and he felt warm. I figured it was the unaccustomed covering of pajamas after eight months of sleeping naked.

An hour or so later, I was awakened by a thumping and a sharp whistling sound. I turned on the light and saw through the bars of his crib that he was kicking about and struggling for breath.

God, I thought, I've really maimed his psyche. His first night in his own bed, away from mama's bosom, and he has an asthma attack. I rushed him into the bathroom and put the shower on as hot as it would go. I left him on the floor in the steam and then hopped

123

up and down, trying to decide if I dared call Margo Novak at midnight. She'd really bite my head off.

I went back into the bathroom and took his temperature—106 degrees. O.K., I said, rehearsing how I would answer her enraged, "You call me at this hour over a thing like that?" Dr. Novak, my son's life is more important than five minutes of your sleep.

"I'm terribly embarrassed to bother you at this hour," I said to her groggy hello, "but James is having an asthma attack and he has a temperature of a hundred and six."

"An asthma attack—so now you're a doctor," she said. "Let me hear him."

"I don't think you can. He's in the bathroom. I thought steam would help."

"Yes, I'm sure it will help. You have some brains after all. But really, Mary, you are an idiot. Pick the boy up, bring him to the phone so I can hear this 'asthma attack.'"

"Will you hold on while I get him?"

"Maybe I'll go out for a walk?"

As I picked James up, I swore I'd get another doctor first thing in the morning. It really didn't help anything for her to make me feel so stupid. She was the world's best mother, all right, only she'd never had any children of her own.

"Enough! Enough! I've heard enough!" I heard her shouting out of the receiver I was holding next to James's mouth.

"Take him back to the bathroom. I don't suppose you thought to close the door so the steam would stay in?"

"Ha, ha. I did," I said and deliberately cracked the receiver hard against the floor.

"I think he must go right away to the hospital," she said when I came back. "Can you drive him quickly or do you want me to get an ambulance?"

I knew she was joking. "I'll just have him slip into his superbaby suit and he can take himself," I said.

"I think he must be in a hospital," she repeated. "It sounds to me as though he could need a tracheotomy at any moment. He should be where it can be done under sterile conditions."

"I am not going to take him to any hospital," I shrieked. She was not joking at all. "He'll die there. I won't abandon my baby! you can't make me take him to the hospital. I won't."

124

"I'll send the ambulance for you—to go to the state hospital where you belong."

"O.K., but James isn't going anywhere."

"All right, there's no time for me to argue with you. I should be there in twenty minutes. If he stops breathing, or if he seems to be getting worse, or looking blue in the lips, throw him in your car and go. If you can't do that, call the police."

When she arrived she had a cardboard box with a vaporizer in one hand and her black bag in the other.

"I have a vaporizer," I said. "I just thought the shower was quicker."

"Yes, but your vaporizer is hot, right? A great help to a fever."

I started her vaporizer by his crib while she examined him in the bathroom.

"So, he has a bed of his own. How did you come to part with him?" she said, coming into the room with him in her arms.

"You always jump to conclusions about what a bad mother I am. I never take him in my bed."

"Of course not, and the rubber sheet is for you?" she nodded her head toward my bed, where the pad I had used to protect my sheets and mattress from him still lay. I had been too sleepy to think to remove it.

"Well, I gave him an injection and I think he's on the mend. Aren't you, James, my boy? Now, we'll give him another which won't be very pleasant, a little penicillin to start."

I sat on the edge of my bed and watched her. She'd taken off his rabbit suit and it was hanging out of her coat pocket. Beneath her coat, she had on some sort of crimson velvet pants. Most unusual.

"Let me take your coat," I said, going over to the side of the crib.

"Wait until I finish giving him this, if you don't mind," she said, and, as he started to scream, "There, there. I don't blame you one bit."

I hung her coat over the chair. It wasn't red velvet pants, but some sort of lounging-pajama affair, with tiny diamond buttons, and she smelled very fruity and exotic. How pathetic, I thought, getting all hundred and fifty pounds of herself sexed up to lie at home reading medical journals. She certainly didn't do anything else, with her disposition and at her age.

"Now, I still would like him to go to the hospital," she said,

125

coming to sit beside me on the bed. "Just as a precaution. I don't want to stay here all night, and he should be watched."

"I'll watch him. He's not going to any hospital."

"This kind of attitude we usually see in stupid, uneducated women. I cannot understand it."

"Well, you think I'm stupid."

"That is beside the point."

"No hospital. I won't. I know it's stupid, but I just can't do it."

"You afraid to be here without him? Well, my dear, you are the one in charge, in case you didn't know it. You are supposed to take care of him. He is a little baby."

I began to cry. "It just makes me feel so frightened and lonely, the thought of it."

"Well, now you have him out of your bed, you get rid of the rubber sheet. Maybe someone older than he will come along to protect you."

"Oh, God, that's not what I need. Besides, I'm too old—no one would want to sleep with me. It makes me feel lonely thinking of him lying alone in the hospital, listening to me walk away."

"I assure you, he's much too sick to do any such thing, at least tonight."

"I don't care."

"O.K., I'll wait here an hour or so. You get some alcohol and rub him to bring his fever down. I'll let you get the dried-out hands, as long as you're too old for it to matter." She picked up a magazine from the floor and began to thumb through it.

As I began scrubbing James's arms and legs with the alcohol and cold water, I talked to James. I wasn't talking to him, of course, but to Dr. Novak, but I didn't dare tell her directly what I wanted her to know.

"Once upon a time," I said, smoothing the burning alcohol into a fat little leg, "there was a little girl who lived on a farm in the middle of nowhere. She was three and a half, and she'd never seen another child in her life, but she had a mother and a father, and a nurse whom she loved. The nurse slept in the room right next to hers, and as the little girl lay in bed at night, she could see the nurse sitting in a rocking chair and drinking Pepsi-Cola and listening to the radio.

"One day, the little girl's mother went away for quite a long time,

126

and when she came back, she brought with her a basket with something little and pink inside it.

"'That is your new baby sister,' the little girl's nurse said. 'Don't touch!'

"That night the little girl didn't go to sleep in her room; the baby had to be there by the nurse, her mother said. The little girl went up to the third floor to the attic to sleep. It had been made into a bedroom for her, with her bed and toys, but it was still the attic, and there were no lights. She cried when her mother said good night.

"'Help,' she screamed, seeing the wolves coming in a pack in the shadows across the rough floor boards. 'Help!'

"'Shut up' screamed her father, but the little girl couldn't stop crying.

"Then she heard water running downstairs. A bath? But rough hands grabbed her and dragged her downstairs and threw her, pajamas and all, into the tub filled with icy cold water.

"'That will teach you to be hysterical. There will be no tantrums here.' Then the hands pulled her, still screaming, upstairs and left her wet and cold on the bed.

"Every night this happened, and the little girl tried not to cry for help, but the wolves would get so close that she could feel their hot breath on her face.

"Then one day, the little girl's parents put her in their car and drove for hours. She lay with her head in her mother's lap because her face was burning. They took her into a building which smelled funny and had glaring lights, echoing halls and white, white beds. Women with white hats were running around. One put her cold hands on the little girl and took her clothes off and put her into bed.

"'Bye,' said the little girl's father. 'You'll be well and away in no time.'

"Then her father and her mother walked away. 'Don't leave, don't leave,' she screamed, 'Mummy.' The cold hands held her down. A man in a white coat came and gave her a shot. She could hear her parents' voices getting smaller and smaller in the distance, and then they disappeared only to be suddenly loud and clear again. She thought they were coming back, but no, they were only on the sidewalk outside the window.

"'Stop, stop,' she screamed, but they kept right on fading again, laughing and talking as though nothing had happened, as they left.

"And it was a month before she saw them again, when they came to bring her home. There was a war going on, gas was rationed, and there was not enough to get to town to market and to the hospital to visit a little girl. And her mother had had a cold.

"Her father tried to carry her out to the car, but she wouldn't let him near her. Her mother had brought her a new coat, a red-riding-hood coat, and she wouldn't put it on. The nurses took her to the car and she lay alone in the back seat and hid her face and kicked the arm rest.

"'Just ignore her,' her father said. 'They obviously spoiled her, catered to her.'

"At home in the kitchen, her old nurse was holding the baby and feeding it through a bottle. She didn't even look up when the little girl came in. The little girl snatched the bottle away and threw it at her mother. It hit her in the face, painfully, and then spilled white milk all over the dark fur of her coat.

"'Get her out of here. I don't know her. She's a monster,' her mother screamed—prophetically, for she was, ever after.

"Never again was anything she did quite right, and usually it was wrong, and never again would she let anyone near her, especially anyone she might care for. But for years to come, even twenty-five, she'd wake at night hearing the sound of her parents' voices as they left her helpless and abandoned in a strange and terrible place, and she'd quake with fear, and her intestines would run cold."

James seemed cooler. I slipped the thermometer into him and his fever had broken. It was 103 degrees, practically normal for a baby.

I looked over cautiously to see if Dr. Novak had been listening. Apparently not; she was reading the same old magazine.

"His temperature's down," I called, not daring to look at her.

"Really?" She closed the magazine and came over to look at him. "No doubt through the chill of your sad tale. We'll give him some aspirin now, and I think he'll survive. I'll call you in the morning, and if there's any change for the worse before then, call me. His fever may go up again in three or four hours. You don't need to call for that. Give him some more aspirin. I left you a very mild sleeping pill on your dresser. Take it. You'll be able to hear him if he needs you."

She put her coat on, and got her bag. As she walked to the door she said, "You can return my vaporizer in a day or two, as soon as you get one of your own. About your story, that's very sad, and of course it explains just everything, but it excuses nothing. Everybody had an Aunt Agatha who kicked her downstairs. Only fools and weaklings use this as an excuse for their own failures."

"Wait a minute," I said, "I'm not—"

"You can wallow in it all you want, but when it comes to your child's health and safety, not to mention the convenience of others, you must get out of it and march."

I started to cry. "Get out," I said. "I try so hard with you, and all you do is laugh at me and make me feel stupid. I'm so sick of it all. Take James and get out. I don't want either of you. I don't want anyone. Leave me alone."

She came back in and began rummaging around in the black bag. "No one says it's easy. You've had an upsetting night. I do pick on you; you're right. I was like you, I think, when I was younger." She patted my shoulder and left.

"Good night," she called from the door.

When the door was closed I began to cry again. I loved her; why had I been so nasty? I hated and feared her, but this was balanced by an overwhelmingly strong adolescent admiration and love.

I went over to the window and watched her walk through the pale blue cone of light to her car. Just before she got in, she turned and looked up at my window and waved at me. I cringed with embarrassment. She'd seen me watching after her, in a moment of remorse and affection. It was almost three. I took her sleeping pill and then, feeling confused and jittery, began to vacuum-clean the living room.

One thing was clear. Whether I loved her or not, there were plenty of pediatricians in the world, and it was ridiculous to have one who so unsettled me. I needed an ally in bringing up my child, not someone to set off my inner ambivalence. When I thought she'd had ample time to get home, I dialed her telephone number. I would tell her quite simply that I appreciated her help to date, but I felt it best for all three of us if I got another doctor for James.

Almost immediately a sleepy male voice answered.

"Is this Dr. Novak's?"

"I'm sorry, she's on a house call. Let me hit the light. What seems to be the problem? Can it wait? She should be back fairly soon."

"Are you the answering service?" I asked, not wanting to leap to any conclusions—not much.

"No. Shall I have her call you?"

"No, never mind. It's Mary Hanes. She just left here a while ago and—"

"Oh, good, then, Mary. Everything worked out all right, did it?"

"Yes, I guess so. But—I forgot to thank her."

"Oh, how nice of you. I'll tell her."

"She won't think it's nice," I said in a burst of self-pity to a kind masculine ear. I'd split them up! Then I thought, what's the use? Why harangue him in the middle of the night? He was not my father. She was not my mother.

"Sorry to have waked you," I said.

"Quite all right."

I got into bed and slowly began to drift toward sleep on the bosom of Margo's pill. So it was for that nice voice that she wore the crimson pajamas. At her age. While she'd been with me, he'd been waiting at home worrying. She was a good doctor. So they said. I'd give her another try. Why rush it? She'd been like me. Maybe there was hope.

130

15

On icy cold mornings, the mile and a half to Trina's on the tiny back streets of Colton, in the old Volkswagen with its bald tires, seemed as long, arduous and perilous as the conquest of Mt Everest.

The preparations for it were often an almost insurmountable obstacle. I feared the cold terribly, and once I had steeled myself for that, I'd begin carrying things down to the car. First a day's diapers and food; then, most mornings, the laundry, which I left to be fluff-dried at a laundromat; then there would be my papers and books, my pocketbook, and both James's and my medicines. And finally, James, all bubbly and gay despite his running nose, fever, infected ear and sty. Each load meant three flights down and three flights back up again. Often, the car would be parked at the opposite end of the block. We'd be ready to leave when I'd remember I'd forgotten something.

I'd gnash my teeth in fury at the world that made it so easy for some people—mostly women, spoiled with solicitous husbands who'd meet them in the driveway to carry in a shopping bag of two TV dinners and a six-pack of beer. Most women had no idea what it was to have it rough. One of the nicer women at work had two daughters, aged one and three. Her husband was a successful businessman, and she'd returned to work because she was bored, a commendable step. However, she did nothing but complain to me about how stupid her housekeeper was (she couldn't make out the menus by herself) and how tired she was when she got home at night, really too tired to listen to the maid's dilemma about what vegetable to serve. The greatest trial of all was when one morning she had menstrual cramps and her husband coldheartedly left the house claiming he had a breakfast meeting, which meant she had to take their three-year-old to nursery school herself on her way to work. It was almost six blocks closer to his plant than it was to the Company.

I'd listen to her trials and nod in sympathy, feeling very superior inside. Some day, somehow, she'd find out what others, in other words Mary, had to contend with, and she'd be embarrassed for having complained—to me, of all people.

One morning the car wouldn't start. Apparently this was an experience it found enjoyable, for it began to repeat it at least three times a week.

One day the garage owner, a stumpy man with a German accent and the body of a tractor, was late getting over to start it. He found me huddled in the car with James.

"Baby? You have baby? Where's your husband?"

"Left me."

"No good, no good to leave a woman alone with a baby, and you have to work?"

I burst into tears.

"Move over," he said when the engine was going, "I drive you where you going. Taking baby to baby-sitter. Very good."

He chatted along, very much at home, it seemed, with streaming women. As he drove me back to his truck, I asked him if he was married.

"Bless us, yes," he said. "A fine woman she was and she gave me three sons and died giving me my little girl, an angel."

"You want to get married again?" I asked, at that moment feeling he was the man for me.

"What for now? I had my children."

132

After that, he charged me only three dollars instead of the usual four to start the car, and I thought he was getting up his courage to ask me to go out with him.

However, one morning during a blizzard, I stopped in to have chains put on and went across the street for a newspaper. When I came back, I stood in the office waiting for someone to show up.

"This old bug's had it," I heard a voice say. "Belong to a student?" I looked in the pit area and the voice came from beside my car.

"No, poor lady," my future husband said, looking up from an engine. "Her husband left her with a baby. Can't say's I blame him. She's ugliest thing I ever laid eyes on. Gray hair and the tits on her, you couldn't find them with the lights on."

When he came out, he smiled at me, I guess never thinking I might have been sitting there for more than a minute.

"That'll be five dollars."

I handed him the money. "I won't be back," I said politely.

"Sorry to hear that—well, take care."

"You too, and keep the lights on—you might miss something."

I walked out through the snow to the car, too sick to stew about it.

I had gained back very little weight since Dr. Edwards's crash diet, and about every other week my low-grade chest infection flared up to full-scale bronchitis with high fever and disabled me, so that all winter I was either dramatically sick or dragged down—so tired, continually, that I was rarely able to stay awake after eight or nine o'clock at night. I used to fall asleep with a book in my hand and all my clothes on, only to wake up at midnight or so to get undressed, bathed and into bed.

My ill health and increased depression were such that I began to find it impossible to talk with anyone except on some matter of business at hand. Not that my door was being knocked down with people wanting my friendship, but the chatter of the people at the Company began to weigh on me. I'd slam the door loudly when I heard people in the hall. I'm afraid what really annoyed me was the fact that they never did try to talk to me. I was older than most of them, twenty-six, and more unhappy, cross, and forbidding. Once or twice a fat, big-breasted Carnegie Tech graduate named Carol came in to talk to me, or rather to find out what was with me.

"Why do you wear such old clothes?" she said. "You always have on the same gray skirt and either that black shirt or a gray striped one. Don't you like pretty things?"

"Yes, I like pretty things," I said, trying to be compassionate. After all, she was years younger than I, and obviously good at asking the wrong kind of questions.

"Are you embarrassed because you're so thin?"

"No. Thinness isn't anything to be ashamed of."

"Not always," she said, looking at my flat chest.

"If you mean am I embarrassed to be flat-chested, look in *Vogue* some day. Besides, I find the mature man is apt to be less interested in the breast than he is in legs and what lies atop them, not to mention the head," I said, sounding superior, I knew.

"Why don't you go buy yourself some nice clothes, then?" she asked, now leaning across the papers on my desk, with her long black hair within my sore nose's inhaling distance.

"No money."

"Oh." After a few seconds, she said, giggling, "Poor Mary, we'll have to take up a collection for her."

I kept my door closed after that.

Andy called me into his office. I wasn't happy, was I? Whatever made him think such a thing? He heard I was not getting along well with my colleagues. Did I want to talk about it?

No. How could I say that I already hated myself when I came to the Company, and the work he had me doing was not helping me to like myself any better?

I was moved to the other side of the building into a dim, windowless cubicle where I sat and wrote:

"This country was founded by men and women who sought freedom to live the kind of life they wanted, the kind of life that had been denied them in their homelands, where a religion or form of government different from what they believed in prevailed," I wrote to start a brochure on how to organize your neighborhood.

"America was to be a land of freedom and opportunity for all, but somewhere along the way, its founders' dream has been obscured. Today, there are millions of Americans who are denied their share of the basic necessities of life because of their race or national origin.

"These people must organize and gain political power to control their own lives. The first step in this is to form a neighborhood corporation."

It was all a bitter, cruel joke. Thousands of taxpayers' dollars, poor people's among them, paying me to write such drivel. What did I know about gaining power to run your own life? What did I know about dealing with slum landlords and getting repairs made in run-down buildings; what did I know about joining the mainstream of American society?

I scarcely made it up the stairs on that last trip of the night with the dirty diapers to collapse in bed. Life was running over me. My apartment at a luxury rent was a slum with a trickle of heat and rats that danced in the kitchen at night, leaving their greasy footprints on the sink. The tin cans in which I stored even paper napkins all bore their teethmarks, little wobbly cuts in the metal surface, going down from the top about an inch. I kept a flotilla of rattraps in the doorway to my room at night, and it was just a matter of time before James lost a hand or I a toe in one of them The landlord laughed and pointed out that Section Bladeebla of the lease said vermin control was the lessee's responsibility.

If anyone was removed from the mainstream of the good American life, surely it was I.

When I was healthy enough to walk down the street with my fellow Americans, I felt dangerously conspicuous and out of place. I wanted to be alone inside the shell of my apartment, where I was safe. The only people I ever spoke to, really, were Dr. Browning and Pat. I looked forward to my visits with them passionately, planning for hours beforehand what I would talk to them about, what questions I would ask them, and sometimes I even made lists so I would not forget to share something with them. Of course, I knew they were only pretending to like me, that they, in fact, dreaded seeing me and would, if the slightest excuse presented itself, skip out on me.

I saw Dr. Browning once a month, and in between times when I got really sick, which was so often. Pat I saw on weekends when I was relatively healthy.

I liked to try to see Pat on Saturdays, in the afternoon or evening if she and George weren't going out. That way, I divided the long lonely stretch of Friday night to Monday morning. Of course there was James, but I couldn't talk to him.

135

He and I would spend Saturday morning cleaning and getting laundry together. He'd lie on the floor or sit in a little chair and watch me. Then we'd go out to market and the laundry, and late in the afternoon we'd walk down to Pat's apartment. She had a floor-length mirror which kept James busy discovering himself while we'd talk or sew or cook supper for George.

We used to play a lot of Monopoly with George, and whereas in the past it had always seemed like the most boring of games, I came to love it: it took forever to end, and that meant James and I could stall and stall about going home. James would fall asleep on Pat's orange-and-blue bedspread, and I'd take forever to decide whether to put a hotel on Park Place or just a house. Pat and George would be exchanging glances. I knew they wanted to go the movies or to a party or to get into the bed which James had taken over. I'd get him up and go about carrying his things down to the car. Lots of times I'd forget something on purpose so I could go back again.

When I was laid up with bronchitis and fever, Pat would come by to get the dirty baby clothes and sheets and take them to the laundry on her way to work. In the evening, she'd bring groceries. And she'd play with James before going home to George. I loved James when he and I were alone and I enjoyed his company, but he was not really fun until he was shared. Pat could make him laugh more than I had the heart to do, and she had long hair which he loved to pull down over his face. They would sit in the corner of the bedroom when I was sick and play together, and snuggle. After she left, I always cried with loneliness until James would laugh at my wrinkled-up face, and I'd take him to bed with me.

We would sit behind our wall of rattraps and listen to the radio. He'd pull himself up, holding onto my knees, and wave back and forth in time to the brighter songs. Then he'd throw things off the bed for an hour while I tried to sleep. We'd make caves with the covers and be fierce bears growling at each other. At night we would watch the lights of the shopping center and, leaning my face into the sour-milk smell of his softness, I'd make up stories for him about Santa Claus and the rich people who went into the stores to buy their Christmas presents.

"You need a rest," Dr. Browning told me. "You're completely debilitated. Take a week or two off. Maybe you should put James in a foster home for a while until you get back on your feet."

136

But I didn't have the money to take even a day off unless I was actually immobilized.

If I did not miss any days of work through illness, my take-home pay was about $153 a week, or $612 a month. Rent was $185, utilities and telephone averaged $25, and baby-sitting took between $160 and $200 a month, depending on how much overtime I had to pay Trina for. Medical expenses for James and me were very high. It was not unusual for our medicines alone to cost $40 a week. With $10 a month for gasoline and $60 for automobile, life and health insurance. I was already out of money before I began to add the cost of food, laundry and miscellaneous things like a spool of thread or a newspaper. Ronald's money and my savings were disappearing very quickly.

I started economizing by leaving the lights off at night. I could see to warm baby food and soup by the light of the gas stove, which had to be on anyway, and read by candlelight. But then I was afraid of fire around James.

When Christmas came I held out the utilities money. It was very little for presents, but I bought a small tree and a string of colored lights, and an arty sort of stuffed hedgehog for James. I felt my own loneliness very acutely as the holidays approached, and I transferred my needs and desires onto James. James must have a memorable first Christmas; I would make up to him at least on that day what he lacked in the way of family.

He was fascinated by the colored lights, and he crawled around beneath the tree and sat up to pull off the paper-doll chains I'd made to decorate it. I think he ate several pine needles before I thought to put the tree up on the table, out of his reach.

Christmas night we ate our supper of turkey noodle soup and applesauce by candlelight with Bach's Christmas Oratorio playing loudly at 32 rpm on my old, defective phonograph. It was cold outside, and snowing, and by seven o'clock I realized there was no heat coming out of the radiators. The furnace had gone off again.

We put on sweaters and our coats and got into bed to keep warm. I held James in the cubbyhole of my arm and told him the Christmas story, about Mary and Joseph and the baby Jesus, and I cried a little, because it seemed suddenly so relevant to me; the mother and her little baby lying in swaddling clothes in the manger because there was no room for them at the inn.

137

First James and then I fell asleep, and when I awoke it was just about eleven o'clock the same night. I left James in the tangled sheets and went into the kitchen to put the kettle on for tea. It was so cold in the apartment then that I could see my breath, even in the warmth of the stove.

It had been a good Christmas, I thought, certainly good compared to the previous year when I'd been all alone in London, laughing bitterly at how wrong my Dickensian image of British Christmas had been. There had been no rosy-cheeked children singing carols or scooting across the snowy streets with fat geese in their arms for Christmas dinner. It had been almost hot—in the upper fifties—and a yellowish rain had fallen.

In the late afternoon, I'd walked over to Green Park and then back to Leicester Square, in the hope that I would find a movie theater open or a cafeteria where I could get tea. But everything was closed, and the streets were deserted except for a few hearselike black cabs. In the doorway of a dark and empty Wimpy's, I saw two other human beings, an East Indian couple holding hands and staring solemnly at the dismal afternoon that made it impossible for them to use the cameras that were hanging around their necks. I smiled at them, and the man had nodded rather listlessly back at me

When my tea was ready, I held the cup against the heavily frosted windowpane and let it melt a small hole in the ice. I looked out at the parking lot and watched the snow shining down in the glow of the floodlights, which burned all night to frighten off illegal parkers. I saw a man coming across the parking lot with a big bundle in his arms. For a moment I thought it was Ronald, and I felt how good it would be to have him there with us on Christmas night. But as he drew nearer and passed beneath the window I saw it was a stranger, coming home most likely from a day with his family, his arms filled with presents. He cut through the lot and then went out onto the street to continue down the road, leaving little craters of footprints in the snow.

I took my tea into the bedroom and drank it slowly in the dark. There had been a few good times with Ronald, but I couldn't remember the events, only how they felt—friendly, that was what it had been like; mildly companionable.

When I lay down to go back to sleep, James's head was beside mine on the pillow. I started to drift off to sleep, but through his cold-clogged nose he was snoring, and the sound suddenly snapped me awake. A long time ago, I couldn't remember when, his father had made that same rattling sound in my ear. I rolled James over on his stomach and placed him at the opposite side of the bed from me, up against the wall. But in a few minutes I was lonely for him, and I pulled him back to my side.

The electricity and gas were shut off for ten days after Christmas, since I hadn't paid the bill. Finally, I swallowed my pride and asked Andy to lend me the $16 I needed to get them put back on.

When I paid him back, he said, "Do me a favor and keep it. Go out and get yourself something pretty, something cheerful, some beads, a scarf, some lipstick. You're a female; look like one."

I slipped the money into his pocket. "I get by, Andy, never you fear. I just don't want to come in here girlied up because I know what animals you all are. You'd ruin me." I fluttered what was left of my eyelashes.

But Andy was right. I looked in the mirror that night for the first time in ages to study myself. Ugh. I looked like Joan of Arc being dragged toward the stake. My brown hair was shorter than any man's at the Company. It kept falling out in fistfuls and breaking off until I'd have to cut it to even the scraggles. It was at least half white too. And my light blue eyes looked frantically possessed in their deep, always dark-circled sockets. I was gaunt, pale white with big-boned hollow cheeks and a skinny neck and flat chest. My hands had been chewed and bitten until they bled almost continuously.

Pat and George were getting married at the end of January, before leaving on his six months' research grant to Central America, and I began to think about the wedding. A party. A reception. I'd never been a bridesmaid.

She looked sort of embarrassed. "Well, I was only going to have one bridesmaid," she said, naming her oldest friend. "You don't want to do all that shit. If you're going to buy a dress, frankly, I'd rather see you buy something you could wear every day instead of those old rags. You can be one, if you want, of course, and you can get a dress for twenty or thirty dollars, probably. Go ahead. I don't care. But you are a little old to be a bridesmaid, don't you think? Twenty-seven? Wouldn't you be embarrassed?"

"No," I said, "I'd be proud, I really would." I didn't dare tell her that I badly craved that vote of confidence, that public endorsement.

"I think it's sort of poor taste, frankly, when you have James and all," one of her friends said, offering me a stinky-looking pink cigarette. She lit one, and the smoke made me start to cough. I hated almost all smokers, I decided. "Certainly, it will anger the family, won't it?"

"The family? A few aunts and uncles, and Grandfather—it doesn't know I exist," I said. "They won't see me. I can walk right past them and it's like I wasn't there."

"Well, that's my point. It will only anger them."

"Christ. My point," my sister shrieked, "is that the whole wedding is such a fucking heap of hypocrisy. George and I've been living together for six months. I hate it. I want to elope. I hate the whole white-dress bit and flowers and rounding up someone to 'give me away.' I wouldn't even be a bride except for Grandpa. And a bridesmaid—you have to be joking."

O.K. I backed down. But I'd bring James to the wedding. He was too young, please, now don't be this way. Finally, I agreed to come alone and to buy a new dress.

I looked all one Saturday morning, with James rolling around underneath the cubicles in half a dozen fitting rooms. Nothing made me look beautiful.

Finally, I found a crazy dress that made me roar with happy laughter. I couldn't quite see why, but I wasn't going to worry. It was past lunchtime. I liked it. It was dark blue with three intersecting red lines across the front. Twenty dollars. I wrote the check. When it bounced, my sister paid the missing dollar seventy-eight and the three-dollar fine. She was a brick.

When I put it on the afternoon of the wedding, I soon saw what had struck me as so amusing. The red lines, one just above the waist and two descending from the neck to the hem, formed a giant scarlet letter A. But I had to wear it. I had nothing else that fitted me.

I was late, arriving at the church two minutes before the service was to begin. One of the snotty ushers told me I'd have to go in and be seated as the wedding party was coming up the walk. He took me down and placed me conspicuously alone in a pew at the front, practically in the lap of the publisher of the paper that had fired me for being pregnant. I felt my red A blaze in the candlelit dusk of the late snowy afternoon. I kneeled to hide it from the eyes of the holy, not to pray. I would never wear that dress again. I threw it out when I got home.

At the reception, I stood in the kitchen doorway and talked to one of the students who was passing around trays of drinks and champagne. I got very drunk on two glasses of wine and had to leave without even trying to catch the bouquet. I called a taxi.

"My sister just got married," I said, leaning forward to the front seat of the cab to talk to the pimply young driver. "Now there's no one left, no one at all."

"How's that?"

"She was a friend, my last friend," I said. "She's run off with some stranger, forever."

Now there was no one to help with James. Now we were really on our own. Well, maybe not quite, I thought with a smile. George had pressed a ten-dollar bill into my hand when I'd told him I was drunk and going home.

"Here, better take a cab," he'd said, and his smile spread from one red cheek to the other.

I figured the taxi meter and a tip would eat up about $4.75 by the time I went to Trina's to get James and back to our house. We would have $5.25 left, and *then* we'd be on our own.

16

In February a Company project in Missouri got into trouble, and Andy went to its rescue, taking me to write a report for the Federal funding agency on the brilliancy of his salvage operations.

We were there three days, and Andy spent every night in Kansas City out on the town. He'd stumble into my motel room every morning around ten o'clock, all red-eyed and debilitated and in need of black coffee.

The last day I asked him how much of what he was doing he wanted in the report. This made him quite angry, and from that minute on, all afternoon as we drove home, he wouldn't speak to me.

In Colton he stopped to get some Valentine's Day candy for Flora and then took me out to Trina's house, where I'd left both James and my car.

"We'll see you soon at the Company," Andy said. "I don't know what you got out of it, but I was glad you could handle the paper work for me."

"My pleasure," I lied with a smile and got out of the car. "Give my best to Flora."

Andy's face suddenly reddened, and he pounded his hands on the steering wheel. "O.K., O.K., go off in a huff."

"I don't know what you're talking about," I told him, sticking my head back down near the window. "I just want to see James. I'm not in any huff. You're the one who hasn't said two words since last night."

"Look," he reached out and took my gloveless, chapped hand. "I read you, loud and clear. I know. But I just can't. Fucking you would be like putting it to sandpaper; you're all rough and hard It hurts just to think about how abrasive you are. I can't fuck a woman who hasn't got a soul. You hate people. You've got to learn to bend and bleed."

"You're right, Andy," I said, and walked into Trina's house.

His words, so totally unwarranted as far as I was concerned, felt like rape. For weeks they lingered inside me, humiliating me, frightening me, festering like the dreaded sperm of an undesired lover.

I had no desire for Andy Crummel. I had no desire for any man, unless it was for a strong back to carry a week's groceries up the stairs.

Sex had been fun, as I recalled, but it was easily forgotten nowadays in the rush and fatigue of life. When people like Dr. Novak or Franny Sprague suggested that I owed it to James to get myself a man, I told them I met no men. A lie, an utter lie. Men trooped in and out of the Company by the hundreds, and I never looked at them twice.

I was, after all, polluted by Ronald, or so I felt. When I showered, I'd keep my clothes on until the mirror was fogged to avoid any chance glimpse of my horribly ugly body. I studiously avoided glancing down at my genitals.

When I menstruated, the days were ones of insane fear that someone would know, would find out. I began to flow so heavily that I actually did bleed all over my office floor one day. After that, I stayed home until I could be seen at the hospital clinic.

The intern who examined me said the reason I was bleeding so heavily was that my body was not adjusting to the IUD.

"What?" I said.

"Intrauterine device. I'll just take it out and fit you for a diaphragm."

143

I had completely forgotten the IUD, the little white paper-clip contraption that had been inserted inside me at my six week postpartum checkup. I'd told the doctor then that the last thing I needed was a means of contraception. I'd scarcely spoken to a man for eleven months. Better be on the safe side, he'd said; you may change your mind and get back into circulation.

The intern handed me a pink box. My new diaphragm.

"Pink. Maybe this one only lets girl sperms in?" I said.

"We can't give you pills, not with your headaches. If you can't trust the diaphragm, come back in a few months and we'll try a different kind of IUD."

But of course I had no need for a diaphragm, even. And with the IUD out, the bleeding stopped; in fact, much to my relief, I didn't menstruate for almost a year.

But I had one vaginal infection after another. The hospital clinic kept telling me it was because of all the antibiotics I took but I knew better. It was the dirt, that incredible, invisible, inescapable dirt of Ronald inside me.

A routine checkup revealed a cervical erosion, a minor condition requiring cauterization. I demanded that they put me in the hospital and give me ether and remove all the womanly bags and pockets. The clinic doctors thought I was joking, but I wasn't. I lay there smiling with pleasure as they cauterized my cervix with hot needles that hissed and burned.

"Burn it all out," I said, knowing they couldn't even reach the seat of the filth.

In any case, one thing I had vowed: I would never be fucked again. If ever in this world I again parted my legs to receive a man, it would be in love long-standing and well-proved: love, not lust.

All this Andy read as my lack of soul, my abrasiveness.

I wished I *were* sandpaper inside, I thought as I drove James home, in the third snowstorm in four days; I'd get old Andy and put it to him, all right.

I began to cry. What an outrage it was. I'd never even thought of Andy in those terms, and he rejected and insulted me both at once. The long line of cars was stopped for a light, and when it started up again, my car would not start. The days in the snow outside Trina's had not helped it any. What's more, we were stopped on a little freight siding, a railroad track.

144

I made no effort to move. I decided I'd let everyone pass me by and then when a freight car lumbered up it would all be over for James and me.

I sobbed and then clicked my tongue. "Andy!"

"Click" came back to me.

"Click." I clicked my tongue again.

"Click," went James, squashing his fat tongue and then smiling up at me with the light of a halo in his eyes.

"Click."

"Click."

"Click, click."

"Click, click."

I picked him up and began to cry into the front of his snow suit. "My darling James," I said, "you're the love of my life."

I felt like a miner trapped for eleven months in a cave. Suddenly, I had heard the *click, click* of rescuers' shovels. All was not lost. Inside that beloved ball of sour milk and honey baby, inside that boring, exasperating, screaming animal, a human being with a mind was beginning to pick its way to the surface.

I put him back down and jumped out of the car.

"Hey," I called, waving my arms to a passing telephone-company truck. "Help me! My car's stuck on the train tracks."

It was a long time before I had to go back to the Company and face Andy, because I got the Hong Kong flu several days later and then complications set in.

I was in the final stages of the flu, I thought, lying in bed, waiting for the aspirin to knock down a last surge of fever just enough so I could warm up some supper for James, when the doorbell rang. I let it ring twice and then thought, as it rang a third time, I'd better try to answer it. It could be a neighbor or someone offering to get supplies.

Ronald stood in the blackness of the filthy hallway and grinned at me. "Say, I like your nightie."

I shut the door and took my coat out of the closet to hide the frayed gray flannel of the nightgown down to my ankles.

"What do you want?" I asked him when the coat was safely buttoned.

"I've been neglecting my duties as a father," he said, grinning

145

again. He pulled out a plastic, inflated duck and a transparent sort of ball with fish swimming inside it to show me.

He still grinned; he was like the horrible Cheshire Cat turned peddler, I had no doubt that he'd soon ask me if I wanted to buy some dirty pictures. He had that look.

"Those are very sweet," I said, pressing my hands into the throbbing of my temples, "but I'm sick and we can't have any visitors tonight."

He walked on in and threw the toys down on the nearest chair and began to unbutton his coat.

"Ronald, please. I mean it. Get out," I said, "I'll call the police."

"Look, for Christ's sake, all I want to do is have a little drink, see the baby—what's so bad about that? Jeez, you act like I've come here to rape you."

Ronald. You couldn't argue with him unless you had lots of time and lots of energy. He was easy to outwit, but too slow to know when he'd been bettered. I couldn't begin to argue with him when my temperature was 103 degrees. I sat down right next to the phone, just in case.

He drifted into the kitchen, and I heard him throwing ice in glasses. He was in for a surprise. I hadn't bought a bottle of liquor since I'd gotten pregnant. The surprise was mine: he'd brought his own. He emerged with two glasses of gin. I wouldn't let him get it near me; the thought of it nauseated me.

"Where's the baby?"

"In his bed," I said. I buried my head in my knees and was reeling back and away with the fever. It was all unreal, Ronald wasn't in my apartment, not after all that had happened, the paternity hearing.

He came out of the bedroom with James in his arms and began bouncing him up in the air, swinging him, "Wheee," and down, "Wheee!" then he devised a game where he'd throw James onto the couch and James would be terrified until he bounced on the cushions. In between such trips, Ronald would drink his drink and that finished, he began on mine.

My fever was breaking now, rivers of sweat were beginning to run down my legs inside the tent of my nightgown and coat.

"Gee, I'm sorry you're sick," Ronald said, coming over to rumple my greasy hair. "Can I get you some tissues, rub your back? Do you

146

need anything?" But he said it with that evil grin, as though he had some huge secret he was waiting to spring on me.

"You know what I need? I need so damn much, you couldn't begin to know. I'm so sick and tired, I need help with that child, I need money so desperately, I need someone to help me carry the load. Oh, shit, you don't even care!"

"Oh, but I do, I do," he grinned. "It's just that you look so competent, this place is so luxurious. . . . "

"It certainly is luxurious, isn't it? Is that why you've kept your coat on, the luxury of so much heat?"

"Look, what's so bad about no heat? You have a coat, don't you?"

He was trying to get me to fight with him, trying to get me upset so that he could move in. That was good old Ronald.

"You're right," I said. "I thought I was cold until I met a man who had no skin."

He looked at me quizzically for a moment and then finished my drink and went back after James.

James had pulled himself up to his feet on the couch and was gazing out the window at the light of the traffic.

"Want to do some more flying?" he asked James and threw him down on the couch.

The second time, something went wrong. I was fairly sure later that it was an accident, although I don't understand to this day how Ronald could have made such a miscalculation. He threw James up into the air and not at the couch at all, but at the bookcase, on a different wall entirely.

I watched in disbelief as James cracked against the bricks and tumbled down to the floor. He lay there for a moment and then began to howl. I picked him up; his head was cut, not badly—a little split in the scalp on the side—but it was bleeding mightily.

"Now will you get out?" I yelled at Ronald as I took James into the bathroom. I locked the door behind us.

James gradually stopped crying, and I held a cold cloth against his cut. The bleeding slowed, all but stopped. I made a bandage.

When we came out, Ronald was still there, leaning against the wall outside the bathroom. "All better?"

I didn't answer. I took James and put him into his crib. He began to cry again. "Just a minute, love, chicken noodle soup!" I told him.

147

Then Ronald's hands slipped around to try to find my pelvic bones in the thickness of my coat.

I jabbed back with my elbow. "What in the hell are you trying to do? Get out."

"It'll be all right," he grinned. "Gee, I wouldn't be that stupid twice, would I? Look!" He slipped something into my hand. I knew what it was, but I had to look. Poor Ronald. It was the cheapest kind of condom made, the kind that always breaks.

I put it into his lapel pocket. "Go on, out, right away," I said, in the tone of voice I used on James. "Hurry up, now, I'm sick and I have to get supper for James. But," I said, following him to the door, "if I were well, Ronald, it would still be no. Never again."

"Are you getting any?" he asked, not grinning for once.

"No, not since I got the clap a while back. Now, go on, beat it."

The toys—for the bathtub we could not use—were there on the floor. I took them into James in his crib. He squealed at the fish in the ball for a few minutes; then, comprehending it in his eleven-month-old way, tossed it to the floor beside the duck and went back to the bars of his crib, where he pulled himself up and leaned forward to see the parking-lot lights.

When James had eaten and was in bed for the night, I pushed the couch across the front door. That hook would snap if a baby leaned on it, and I was afraid, as my fever returned, that Ronald would come upon me in the darkness.

He did, but in a dream. I slept in the long-ago cottage at the lake, and my parents were alive. In fact, I was in a big bed with my mother and my sister, the three of us taking an afternoon nap together in our nightgowns. Ronald came tiptoeing in and began to fuck me. If I moved to protest, I'd waken my mother and sister; if I screamed, Stanton, who was walking back and forth on the lawn outside—I could see him through the little rectangle of light left by the partially drawn shade—would hear. None must know what was happening. When Ronald was through, I got up and went into the bathroom and vomited in disgust. Then I tried to wash his semen out of me. It was not semen, though, but yellow baby diarrhea that showed on the washcloth. I spread my legs on the toilet seat and let it flow—like scrambled eggs, out of my vagina. It wouldn't stop and it was all over me, my hands, my arms, my legs, even the bathroom floor.

148

"Mary, Mary," my father called, banging on the door. "Come out this instant!"

In the morning, I found that I had in fact thrown up in my sleep, but the neat little puddle on the pillow beside me was the only stain on the bed.

I called Trina. "I'm ill, will you help me? Will you come here and watch James while I go to the doctor's?"

"Sure. For a dollar and a quarter an hour?"

"Yes."

She came in the late afternoon, when her husband got through his classes and could watch Pammie. I took a taxi to Dr. Browning's and sat in the warm familiarity of his office. I couldn't stop crying, about the dream, the Company, how miserable I was, how sick the world was getting.

"Promise me you won't tell anyone?" I said. "If anyone knows how sick I am mentally, they'll take James away from me."

He laughed. "Let's have a look at you and get some X rays."

Later he showed me the films. "See, it's spread into the other lung too; you've got a really good case of old-fashioned pneumonia. No wonder your head's in a mess. This has been going on too long. We'll lick it now, though. You're going into the hospital tonight."

I went home and asked Trina if she'd keep James.

"Oh, sure," she said brightly. "How long you figure you'll be in?" Her face fell when I said only a few days.

My doctor said I could borrow the money for Trina, for anything Blue Cross didn't cover. "Listen to the radio; they're all dying to give you money for a good reason."

I put a toothbrush, comb, a notebook and pen in a paper bag. Then I began to get James's clothes together for Trina, who was on the telephone telling her husband the good news. "Maybe we can get the drapes?" I heard her say.

What would ever happen to James at Trina's? Sure, he'd stayed there before, but not this long. What if he got sick? What if he couldn't understand why I'd left him?

I picked up a little navy blue shirt of his and started crying into it. He'd looked so sweet in it, kicking in the dim sunlight on winter mornings. I had had so little of him, and almost nothing of him was saved in my memory. His first year had almost slipped by and I'd never sat down with him, gotten to know him, understood how his

149

mind worked, or seen the dimensions of his world. I had had a baby but I'd never had a chance to know him. James had always been secondary to the compulsive matter of our survival.

I put the shirt into my pocketbook; it would be a relic to hold onto during the nights at the hospital.

"Hey, Mary, you're getting some company," Trina shouted.

Ronald, I thought, in terror. I will murder him tonight, I really will. There was a heavy old brass doorstop; I picked it up, ready to crack it against his head as he came through the door.

But it was not Ronald. It was my own sweetest James walking like a newborn colt, swaying from side to side, carefully keeping his hands from the walls, as he wobbled into the room. He looked around for me, and then burst into a huge smile of victory.

I dropped the brass doorstop and scooped him up.

"You walked, James, you walked!" I cried "I'm so proud of you." I pulled away to see his face, and it was wrinkled up in imitation of mine. I smiled and he smiled. "So proud of you, darling," I said, trying not to cry any more.

Off he skittered across the room again, right for the lamp on the floor by my bed. He turned it on, and then off, and then on.

"Go show Trina how well you can walk," I said. "Go out there." I pointed. He smiled and walked toward the door, watching my finger all the way

In the hospital, as I lay there with molds or roots and berries or hormones, or whatever they were, dripping into me and being shot into my behind and handed me in little paper cups, I cried a lot more about James.

Things would be different from then on. I would know him before I knew anything else. I would stop work and go on welfare, if necessary. I have kept none of those vows, but I've never stopped making them. Every night I say, "Tomorrow I will be a mother." But I've yet to be little more than a part-time custodian, sometimes a tutor, or a sister too old for him to enjoy. And the loss is mine. I weep, for I have had a child and never known him.

"I could have loved you better, didn't mean to be unkind. You know that was the last thing on my mind"*—that was a song I thought of as I lay in the hospital.

* © 1964 United Artists Music Co., Inc., New York, N.Y. 10019. Used by permission.

I'd thought of it before, of singing it to lovers, but with them, there was always an out—I could have loved Alex better if he'd allowed me to, or Ronald if he'd been sober or decent; but with James, James was my baby, and in part, he'd become what I made him, and I'd made him nothing—nothing consciously. And he was always there; unlike a lover, who goes off to play tennis on a weekend, James was always there waiting for me to love him. And I wasn't sure that I'd loved him at all. He was a weed that had grown up without any care or guidance, a wild child.

Where had he come from? I had no sense of him as my flesh and blood. He had made himself from the very first, when one determined sperm had fought its way through diaphragm and spermicidal jelly to find an ovum. He had shaped himself by stealing what organic materials he needed from the body around him, which was, by accident or design, mine. And those materials were all of me that was in him. The calcium in his little finger bones may have been the quart of milk I gagged down during my sixth month of pregnancy. That was the sort of tie between us.

But what of genes? He had blue eyes like mine. And he had my smell. It had been a shock, smelling his head one hot summer day and recognizing the faintly metallic scent of my own skin. We both smelled like rusty plows left out in the hot sun of a hayfield.

Ronald. He had nothing of Ronald, I decided quickly. But then, I could remember very little of the Ronald I had liked a long time ago. What had I liked about him? He was slow, he was unimaginative, he couldn't conceptualize at all, he wasn't affectionate or good in bed, which meant I'd never much liked sex with him. Yes, there was one beautiful thing about Ronald—his posture, and James had it. From the first day that James had pulled himself onto his backside to sit, he had held his back as straight and strong and confidently as Ronald did, shoulders back with natural ease and grace.

Eyes, smell, posture—the rest he'd have to make for himself, or would he? Had it in some way been predestined, his ultimate remoteness? While he seemed very affectionate and gregarious, in essence he was alone and pleased, remote and at ease with himself. I could lie beside him at night, craving his warmth, dying to hug him, but he'd roll away in his sleep and lie sprawled out as though he were the only person in the world. At one year, he was this way. What would he be like at twenty? One thing I knew; he would not be in bed with me. He had, through maternal neglect, taught

151

himself to eat even soup from a bowl with a spoon—without help and with very few spills. He was working hard already, and what more could I ask?

As I thought about it, I decided the only thing in the world I believed in, without reservation, was work. Hard work. What kind didn't much matter. You found your level and you worked on it until you dropped. Then you picked yourself up and went home and did a different sort of work to unwind for the sleep you needed to work again. There were times in your life when your work went badly, or times when it made you despise yourself, as my work at the Company did, but then you had to look to the joy of having worked, rather than to the nature of the task. And James had worked very hard to bring himself up that first year. He'd roughed it, sleeping on the floor, eating lukewarm baby food, waiting out my infections and those asthma attacks I failed to forestall, craving the attention from Dr. Browning which they brought. He'd survived with a lot less sniveling and self-pity than I. He'd been the sunlight on the dark winter water. Like Alex, he had much that I admired.

Alex was my first lover, incredibly beautiful and blond and distant. He could look at you and listen to you and his mind would be a million miles away, seeing the way the sun would strike the front of the building he was sketching in his head. Even in bed he was remote, and his hands were cold and dry. After sleeping with him for almost two years, I got up enough courage to ask him why he had never kissed me. I was young, but I knew people kissed especially before they had sex.

"Kissing is something special," said Alex, and he brushed his hand down my cheek. "Sorry, but that's how it is with me."

He had just been divorced from a woman he said he loved deeply but could not live with any longer. I wrestled to understand that for a long time and finally gave up. It was beyond me, then. Today, I understand.

He was beginning to practice architecture, and he worked until two or three in the morning. Then he'd come bang on my window. The dinginess of my one basement room, all I could afford on a beginning reporter's salary of forty-five a week, overwhelmed him. So I'd dress, tripping over myself in fear that he'd grow weary of waiting for me and go home to sleep alone, and walk the block and a half to his empty white loft with the ceiling open to the night. Sometimes he'd be too busy in his head to speak. He'd roll onto me, and I'd lie there wondering if a passenger in a plane passing overhead might not be able to look in and observe my legs? Doubtful. Then he'd roll away, turn out the lights and reach for his cats. Long, white-haired Persians. I would run to the steam of the bathroom and the antihistamines I kept in his medicine chest. As I'd fall asleep from the pills, I'd hear him cooing to the cats, stroking them, caressing them, kissing them. Sometimes, I'd awake in the night to find one of them sitting on my chest and purring in harmony to my wheezes.

In the morning, when the traffic would wake us, he'd shake off the cats and come into me again. Then, sometimes, he'd smile, and it was like a ripple of sunshine broken through the clouds onto the cold gray sea. That meant that the day would be good for him. He would get up and cook breakfast for us.

I never had any sexual feelings for him, but I worshiped him, literally, calling upon his name to aid me in whatever task was at hand. When he got married and stopped rapping on my window, I began going to church. He never loved me. He made this very clear, regularly. He'd hold my hand and reaffirm it: "I do not love you." I would nod and cry, with him holding me, gently rocking back and forth until I stopped, and then we'd go back to our separate lives.

When I told him that he'd been my first lover, he shook his head, no. "No, don't say that—I should have been better to you." Tears came in his eyes. "Now it's too late."

"No one could have been better to me," I told him. "You were what I wanted. Exactly. Have a happy marriage."

When I sent him an announcement of James's birth, he wrote back; "Wonderful! Too much! Splendid! You always wanted a baby, didn't you? I'm so glad for you!"

I had wanted a baby, hadn't I? Hadn't that been what sorrowed me most about his not loving me? His insistence that there be no baby? I'd refused to use any birth control, and so, cursing, he took the precautions.

James's origins lay as much in Alex as they did in anyone. In what was the first satisfying relationship I had, in the one which set the tone of those to follow: remote and uninvolved, distant beneath the flesh.

153

I would take James to one of Alex's buildings, and I knew what he would do. Go wild with joy at so much light and open space—dancing out his appreciation—and then cuddle up in my lap for the trip home, remote from it all, as though nothing had happened.

Dr. Browning came and told me it had been ten days now. I could go home.

"I've realized I have to start living my own life," I told him.

"So, what else is new with you, hmmm?" he said. "Did you see our boys won the hockey game last night? Sudden death overtime?"

"No. I mean I've been through this big crisis about James. I'm going to get to know him, but most of all, I'm going to stop surviving and start moving. I've got to control my own life, and I will."

"You will," he said. "I thought you did. This first year has been a bad one for you, physically, but we'll keep things under control, keep you on some steroids for a while, get you on long-range antibiotic therapy.

"The first year is hard for any woman, with the first child particularly, and you've held down a job too, without any help to speak of. I think you deserve a lot of credit."

"James deserves the credit," I said. "I just lay there."

"And who made James into that bubbling, outgoing little hooligan? Most one-year-olds pale beside him."

"Trina helped, but he really did it himself."

"Trina, that girl I met at your house the night you came here? Come on, get serious. I doubt she said boo to him all year."

"Well, maybe I do deserve some credit," I said smiling. But it was short-lived. I was no mother. I just wanted to get home and hug James.

17

As the earth began to thaw with spring, I got rid of the old car and rode everywhere on my bicycle, rejoicing that I reached each day's destinations primarily through the strength of my own legs. Riding along in the chill April wind, with the sunlight splotching the pavement through the first feathery greenness on the trees, I felt moments of animal exuberance. In a flash, I'd know that I was free and alive and young.

But James was a problem. I had a Sears Pak-a-Poose carrier (economy model), and I took him in that to Trina's. Carrying him in it on a bicycle was dangerous; but worse, we were conspicuous.

I was being followed whenever I went out in public with James. I wasn't sure who or what was pursuring me, but I felt them gaining on us, gaining on us, until I'd break into a run of panic and race up the stairs to push the couch across the door.

I realized that this was a new insanity, possibly a symptom of serious emotional disorder, but if I told anyone, James would be taken from me. And what could I do? I certainly could not afford a psychiatrist.

The attack would come, I knew in my bones, only when we were together. They knew that alone, I could outwit them, outpedal them or if necessary roll them in the street and kick and bite. No one would dare attack me alone. And James, more glowing, more loving, more beautiful than the Christ child to me, no one would ever harm him.

But with James to protect, with James gently at my side, summoning up some sort of tender vulnerability of love in me even on my most wizened days, there would be no defense. It would all be over in seconds, the shapes of blackness crashing down on us, spilling our blood.

James had to go out on weekends. I found a high-school freshman, Melissa, whose father was a policeman. Nothing would happen to Melissa and James. She came on Saturday afternoons and took him in his little yellow corduroy jacket to the park, or, more often, to the shopping-center snack bar, where she met her classmates to consume French fries and Cokes. On Sundays, they walked.

James had his outings, but again I was not having my child. I'd have his supper ready when he got back; I'd have read a novel, or the Sunday paper. I wanted to be with my son sometimes. I had to make an effort, again.

I remembered how my father had begun to walk with Pat and me when I was six years old. He had been bedridden with his bad back for almost a year, trapped in a plaster cast like a giant turtle helpless on its back. Finally, my mother took Pat and me away with her, leaving him alone on their farm in Idaho and bringing us to Colton and her parents. That was when her father rented us the apartment in the old maids' building and hired a nurse for us. He and my mother then went off to the Caribbean to rest and decide whether or not she should get a divorce.

One day my father arrived in Colton in an ambulance. "I want to be with my children," he told us. A doctor removed the cast and substituted a brace, great armor around him, which he wore until he died ten years later. He began to walk again with two canes, at first just to the bathroom, and then out to the dining-room table, and then out to the courtyard in front, where he could watch the track team practicing. Finally, he announced that the time had come for him to do some serious walking. And I danced up and down, sensing his joy.

156

"Maureen," he said to the nurse, "when you're bringing the girls home in the afternoon after your walk, which route do you take?"

"How you mean 'route'? Which streets, you mean? We usually come down Westgate Road, and over to Spencer; then we've only this block here."

"Fine, I'll meet you at the end of Spencer and walk the last block with you. How would that be?"

Watches were synchronized, we were to meet at four fifteen sharp.

It was the longest afternoon I ever spent in the park, but finally four o'clock came, and we started walking home. "Not too fast now," Maureen kept saying, and "You be holding onto this carriage, you hear?"

It was almost dusk when we turned onto Spencer Street. In the distance, at the very end of the street, I saw my father getting out of a taxi, and then he stood alone on the corner, supporting his giant body on the two skinny black canes, painfully standing, waiting for us. I ran to hug his legs.

"No, careful," he laughed. "Keep ahold of the carriage."

And we walked the last block, so slowly the wheels of the carriage scarcely seemed to turn at all. When we were safely in the apartment, my father said Mount Everest had finally been conquered, and Maureen had a drink, and my sister and I had ginger ale with our oatmeal.

It seemed such a long block to me then, but years later, long after my father was dead, I happened to have to walk down it one afternoon. It wasn't a block at all, really. There were four tiny houses on each side of it, and room for perhaps six cars to park. When I thought of him, hiring the taxi to take him to the top of it and then his joy at walking it, I cried.

Now, twenty-one years later, I thought to follow my father's example and walk out to meet James and Melissa one afternoon as they started home from the park.

I met them at three, and they were still on the grass listening to the thudding of a rock concert in the distance. I sat beside them for a few minutes and began to get very twitchy. The grass was dirty anyway, littered with cigarette butts, old matches and tops of soda cans, but worse, I could feel my shoulder blades creeping up to prepare to meet the attack.

157

"Let's go," I said, and as we got up, I noticed James putting something in his mouth. Something bright red.

"What kind of candy did you get this afternoon?" I groaned at Melissa.

"None—we didn't get any candy," she said, proud of her abstinence.

I took a step before reacting. I pulled James's head back and took from the pink cradle of his tongue four red capsules, all soft and ready to be swallowed. Seconal, perhaps, or something worse, some homemade ticket to oblivion, pink fogs, or God knows what they'd thought of to get us with, for clearly now, if we were together, they'd use James to get to me.

I couldn't stop shaking.

"What's the matter," Melissa said, "Do you want me to call my father? Are you sick? I'm going to call Daddy."

"No, no," I said. "Look, you just go on, take James home. I'll go get a bus."

And I ran away, leaving her looking very puzzled. In the darkness of the bus shelter, I sat back and caught my breath. I was safe for the moment. James was safe. But something had to be done. I was not my father's daughter.

I borrowed still more money for a new car. I thought we could drive out on weekends, way up toward the lake, where we'd be safe. But we weren't. Once or twice I got James out of the car and actually onto the sand before I felt the shapes gathering behind us.

Fortunately, my sister and brother-in-law came back in July to house-sit for a huge mansion with a junglelike garden. On weekends we went there and were safe. No creature of darkness would dare invade the cheery yellow atmosphere my sister spun even inside the dark vault of the old house.

James crawled in and out its porch windows and through the weeds outside like a tiger, and then he'd race across the grass trying to reach the Frisbees my brother-in-law and his friends were tossing back and forth.

I'd sit on the kitchen counter, as my sister baked chickens and cakes for seven or eight hungry male graduate students, and try to hint to her something of what was happening. I never dared tell her about our pursuers, but I suggested that I felt uncomfortable even in the supermarket now with James.

"Leave him here with me," she'd say. "I love to have him."

But that wasn't really the issue.

"Stay for supper," she'd say. "Hugh isn't bad, did you see him? He's the one with the little pot belly. He's quite nice. He said the other day how brave he thought you were."

Once in a while I'd stay, silently chew my food and then leave. I had nothing to talk about with them; I knew little about the world of graduate schools. But James was all right now; there was a sanctuary for him on weekends.

One Sunday night when we were just coming in, Flora Crummel called. There was a big, open Women's Liberation meeting in ten minutes at the university.

"I don't have a baby-sitter," I told her. I couldn't take James back to my sister's; they hooted about the women's movement all the time.

"Bring him with you and Andy will keep him. Andy and the girls are driving me over."

That was safe enough, but when I pulled up alongside of the dented remains of their car, Andy shook his head. "Flora's crazy!" he said. "I promised the kids we'd go swimming at the lake. James is just too much for me to handle around the water. If you were really liberated, you'd take him with you."

Flora and James and I stood on the sidewalk.

"Don't ask me to explain, please," I asked her. "But will you hold James? You can say he's mine, if you want, but if you hold him, I'll feel safe about it."

"Come on, James," said Flora. "God, and I thought I was through with this wet stage."

As we walked into the lounge, a hairpin of a woman in white pajamas was leaping through the air in a karate demonstration, yelling "Heeyah!"

"Heeyah!" James yelled at her, and several dozen faces turned and smiled. "Heeyah!" James repeated, overjoyed at such an audience. He didn't stay on Flora's lap for more than a minute. He was running around the room pulling at all the different hair clasps he could see. When the wearer of a big tortoise-shell butterfly objected to his pulling it from her massive mountain of hair, he began to cry.

A woman who looked pretty much like Fidel Castro without the

159

beard got up in her army fatigues and suggested curtly that all those sisters who were here only for day-care purposes go caucus outside.

"We'll do no such thing," Flora shouted, leaping up. "Children are only one facet of our problem as women in today's society. We'll caucus later."

I wondered what would ever happen if she talked to Andy like that.

A soft-faced woman in a fuzzy white sweater and shorts stood up and told how she was just getting divorced. The trouble had begun, she said about five years before, when she and her husband had been at a cocktail party where everyone was ripping apart *The Feminine Mystique*. On the way home, she'd confessed to him that she saw a lot of truth in the book, although, of course, she was happy at home with their children. He'd been so enraged by her confession that he'd refused to have sex with her for almost a month.

"That was a long time ago, and now I'm going to get married again, and I'm going to have seven children instead of four to stay home with. But my new husband understands. He wants me to go to graduate school. But what I want to say here tonight is some of us want to change the world and the nuclear family and that's fine. That's something to be thought about. But there are others who just want a little more freedom to do our own thing. We have to love each other. Women have never been allowed to love each other. We have to stop being catty bitches and scratching at each other. We have to listen and understand and support one another in whatever steps we make."

"There can be no liberation of women until the nuclear family, ne cornerstone of the capitalist society, is destroyed," the Castro woman shouted.

At the end of the meeting, a sheet was passed around for names and addresses of any women who wanted to join small discussion groups. I signed. Flora was already in one.

"What will I do if they're all Bolsheviks and Lesbians?" I asked Flora.

"Call me immediately. I'll switch places with you."

When we got up to go, I realized James was asleep in my lap, sucking the hem of my slip. And nothing had attacked us. Perhaps we were safe inside the many-faceted bosom of Women's Liberation.

In the group to which I was assigned, there were a dozen women,

160

nine married—all with children—two engaged and me. There was no leader; we took turns moderating and talked around the room each week about anything we wanted to discuss. Most of us were amazed at how hard it was to talk openly to women and how uneasy it made us feel to miss a meeting and fear that the rest of the "girls" were catting about us the minute our back was turned.

Several women felt they couldn't speak at all—no one had ever wanted their opinion, seriously, on anything since they left college.

One woman, a thirty-five-year-old, baggy-looking wife of a professor, with three children and an unused degree in law, prefaced everything she said by, "Well, it doesn't matter what I think, but . . . " After a few months, she stopped that and began to speak in a loud tone that commanded the attention she felt even her most trivial comments deserved.

None of us had thought in terms of planning our own lives once we were out of college. Oh, there'd been vague stabs at it—the lawyer who'd never practiced, for instance, and one woman who had wanted to go on the stage and had started off for the London School of Dramatic Arts, only to be given a now-or-never ultimatum from her fiance.

As far as careers went, I was astronomically successful to them. Even the Company job which I scorned was unbelievably good fortune. "My God, how did you ever get such a good job? So much money? Do you realize I have a master's degree in mathematics and I've been a secretary for five years now?"

Most of the realization and awakening seemed to go on during the week between meetings. We'd all arrive with armfuls of examples of sexism we gleaned from magazines, newspapers and books, and heads full of ideas to pass along.

My story, what I'd encountered before James was born in trying to have a baby out of wedlock, seemed an extreme but fairly relevant example of what each of the others had gone through to discover what she wanted to do in life. There had just been no stepping out of line for any of us middle-class college girls. You got pinned, you got a ring, you got married. Then you had a baby, and another and another. Or you were selfish.

One woman who finished college at nineteen, graduating *magna cum laude* in mathematics and planning to go to graduate school, was forced by her boyfriend to have sex that summer or break the

161

engagement. She wasn't that averse to the idea of sex anyway, but she wanted to make sure she didn't get pregnant. He was an old man of twenty-seven and said he'd handle everything.

They were married several weeks after she would have entered graduate school, and her family was delirious about the coming baby. Only when they went to conceive a second child did her husband confess to her that her parents had been in on the whole thing with him from the beginning.

"This time it will be easy," he told her. "Your parents aren't standing in the corner cheering me on."

By the time I withdrew from the group, she'd left her family with a sitter and was busily studying for the Graduate Record hoping to get into graduate school the following year.

One night, one of the gentle, happy mothers in the group said to me how difficult it must have been for me, having no one to love me or help me at all with the baby.

I said, maybe, but never having done it any other way, I couldn't be sure.

"What is hard, though, and worries me," I said, my voice already beginning to quiver, "is the paranoia. I mean, I guess that has nothing to do with Women's Lib, but I know I'm cracking up. I'm so incredibly paranoid all the time. When it's over, when an attack is past, I see how silly it was, but at the time I just freeze. I can't really go anywhere with James. I feel we're being followed, people are going to stone us. It's just crazy."

"Good God, you'd be crazy if you didn't feel that way to some extent," said Becky. She'd dropped out of graduate school because her husband, a young businessman, wanted her home with dinner ready every night when he was done working.

"Of course, not too long ago you might have really been stoned. Now, you're just immoral, a fallen woman, a sad case, more to be pitied than censured. Everything you've done has put you outside of society. You willfully created a 'broken home.' And instead of cowering and asking forgiveness, you just thumb your nose. Good God, you really are outside the fold, and you can bet everyone wants to take shots at you in one way or another. If you went on welfare and acted helpless, asked every passing man to help you with your bags, you'd be much more acceptable, you know."

162

"Yes," another woman said, "I resent you because you make me feel how stupid I was to get married just because I was pregnant."

"I'm working very hard to save a marriage and you say to me, 'It's not worth saving,'" said another, bitterly.

I left the meeting in tears and spent a week or two thinking of myself in those terms: I was outside society, I had elected to leave the fold of people whose behavior conformed to moral standards. I felt very unhappy. I wanted to belong. I wanted to be a part of the good world. I should have had an abortion; I would have, if I'd thought of it in these terms. But then in the end I knew I was fooling myself. I'd never belonged anywhere. I'd always been outside the law, just off center if I aimed at the target, never at ease, always out of place. If I'd been in the fold, I would have had the abortion or given the baby up. That's what women in the fold did.

So I had always been different; there was nothing new about that. What was new was that now there were hundreds of other women, thousands across the country who, for many reasons, were also different from the legendary image of a woman, and they were trying to find their strengths rather than dwelling on their weaknesses. They came to like themselves.

And so it began to happen to me, as it did to each of us, the great rush of first self-love, an exhilarating, powerful joy, a triumph unlike any I had known except on the night after I had James. God damn it, I was a human being. I could make what I wanted to out of my own life. There was nothing shameful or bad about me. In fact, if you didn't judge me by Hollywood standards, I was beautiful—just like every other woman. Every one of us had a few varicose veins, stretch marks on our stomachs, corns on our toes.

By the end of summer my paranoia was gone. And I knew what I wanted in the immediate future. First, a decent apartment. I called the health and fire inspectors. They noted down numerous violations. I got copies of their check lists and sent them with a letter to the landlord.

A month later, the apartment was completely renovated. With an entirely new bathroom and kitchen installed, walls were replastered and floors sanded. My rent was not raised. A small rent strike was necessary, however—I organized the other tenants; there were five of them—to get the halls redone, security locks put on all the doors and the furnace fixed.

But most of all I wanted to get back to a newspaper, where I didn't have to pretend to be involved in solving, but could merely goad others into caring, into trying to solve. Each week I sent résumés to all the box numbers listed in the ads in the trade magazine *Editor and Publisher*. Sometimes I got a rejection letter, but usually not. When a tiny paper in a small Eastern town called to offer to fly me out for an interview and then canceled two days later, I asked why. They said they'd checked my employment record with the Colton paper and been told by the personnel office that I'd been fired for moral reasons, period. Intrigued, they'd persisted and finally called the city desk late at night. Apparently the tale of my sexual escapades, as related by the bored man on the desk, was as flamboyant as the city was dull that night.

John Philips contacted the Colton paper for me. The management was apologetic and promised to direct the personnel office to say, "Resigned at our request because of pregnancy." But there was little anyone could do about the stories boys spun at night.

It might take me a while to find a newspaper job. I went to Andy and told him I was sick of his poverty program.

"So are the Feds, I'm afraid," he said. "I've heard our contract probably won't be renewed. We may all be looking for work soon. But, Mary, you won't desert me, will you? You'll stick with me until the end?"

"I can't promise, Andy," I said, smiling at the power I felt, especially when he shook his head sadly.

Then, just after Christmas, a very Southern-sounding but rather deep woman's voice called me one evening. She said she was the personnel director of the *Dryden Clarion*, a medium-sized daily in the South whose blind ad I had apparently answered. The folks up there in Colton had good things to say about me. Would I fly down for an interview? I said I would after New Year's.

The day I left to fly to Dryden, it was snowing heavily. When the storm let up a bit, our plane got off the ground, but after an hour in the air the pilot announced that we'd have to detour to Washington, D.C., because of the turbulence. By the time we got to Washington, that airport had been closed, so we went north to Baltimore. Finally, the pilot told us we were coming down in New York City. My

164

fellow passengers hissed and booed, feeling angry and punchy after a nightmare of a flight. But I was pleased.

I turned down the airline's offer of a motel room and rushed off in the snow into the city, hoping to see my old college roommate. Unfortunately, there was no answer at her apartment, and when I called her husband's office, I was told they were in Puerto Rico on vacation.

I called the Dryden paper and explained that I was stuck in New York until I could get another flight out. The personnel director checked while I waited on the phone and suggested my taking the train down early the next morning. She would send her secretary right over to the station to pay for my ticket at their end of the line. Could I find some place to stay overnight?

"I think so," I said, getting a happy sort of brainstorm.

I telephoned Stanton's New York office.

"Just a minute, I'll see if he's in," his secretary said. "May I ask who's calling?"

He came right on the phone.

"Plenty of room, plenty of room. Whole apartment's empty. Go on over there now, my man will let you in."

"When are you coming home?"

"Right now, if you're going to be there."

As long as I wasn't going to have to pay for a room at the Y, I decided I would buy James a cement mixer he wanted. I asked Stanton to meet me at F. A. O. Schwarz, thinking it would clarify the fact that there had been no change in my motherhood.

I'd picked out the cement mixer, given the clerk the only check I had with me and was about to give her James's name and address when two hands cracked down on my shoulders.

"I remember these wonderful shoulders," Stanton said, looking embarrassed but pleased at his courageous greeting.

"So you're queer for hunched shoulders!" I said coldly and finished the purchase.

"You buy toys in here and you're dressed like a waif," Stanton said, taking my suitcase.

"Priorities, or maybe coming to Schwarz is an act of atonement. I always feel I shouldn't leave James."

"Do you have any clothes in here?" he asked, swinging the bag up in the air.

165

"A nightgown."

"I can't take you to dinner looking like that," he said. "Come on, let me buy you a dress."

"You don't communicate with me for a year, almost two, and now you're going to buy me a dress?"

"What did you call it?" he said, looking grayly ahead, clenching his old teeth. "Atonement?"

We went into Bonwit Teller and he shouted out "Dresses." He looked at me with amazement when I said I didn't know what size. I took off my coat, which was beginning to feel like a dead St. Bernard tied around my neck, and went into a fitting room.

The mousy little woman actually caught her breath when she saw my maternity slip, pinned together in back to lessen the fullness in the front, and held up to current skirt heights by a piece of string. She left me there, looking at my sour face and bony shoulders. When she came back, she had with her an armful of slips.

The dress Stanton sent in was the last sort of dress I would ever buy or wear on my own choosing. It was very bright and festive, a red and green Donald Brooks silk number. Jesus. I knew it would cost about five hundred dollars. I desperately wanted to ask him if I could get a cheaper one and a coat, a warm coat. Something I really needed. But it was all being done behind my back. I did walk out of the fitting room in the dress, over my black tights and wet loafers, to see if he liked it. Oh, yes. I wanted to stop the whole thing right then and go get a Greyhound bus back home.

But I didn't want to embarrass him in the store. His face was actually warm with color, and it was the most proud pleased thing I'd ever seen. His body was sprawled across the chair, as though he were born to such tasks as waiting for a woman to be fitted for a dress. There was just nothing rigid about him now. I shook my head at him in the mirror. I'd play along for a few minutes. It was sort of fun. Cinderella. I was being remade into a lady for Stánton. There were pantyhose and shoes. I carried the new things and made him carry my old coat to the store door, in the hope that it would inspire him to buy the one thing I wanted, but it didn't.

"Thank you," I said, as he took the packages and I put on my coat. We walked out of the store. "I don't know what I'll ever do with a dress like that, but it is pretty."

166

"Wear it when you have dinner with me," he said, and he put his arm around me.

Maybe some radical change had occurred in him. Maybe he'd gone into analysis which had paid off quickly.

He kept the apartment on East 71st Street because when he was in this country, he spent three or four nights a week in New York. He was tired of hotels, he said. And besides, this was convenient when foreign employees of his came here on company business. It was huge, and furnished in the same dark Oriental rugs and old furniture of every Montgomery dwelling. A black man in a white coat was in the kitchen, reading *The National Observer* at the table. He leaped up when Stanton and I came in.

"Freddie, would you see that the guest room and bath are in order?" Stanton said. "This is Mrs. Hanes, and she'll be staying tonight. I brought Freddie from Africa," he told me.

He handed me a glass with bourbon in it.

"Wait, don't drink yet," he said, and leaned forward and kissed me hard and dry and tight on the mouth. Maybe the analysis hadn't been a complete success after all.

"Come here," he said then and just hugged me. I shivered inside the wetness of my coat, and as the old feeling of comfort, of protection, welled up inside me, I began to cry.

"Don't cry," he said into my hair. "Don't cry. It's been hell for me too. I tried to telephone you so many times. You were just never home."

"I work all night, practically, during the week," I said. "You could have written."

"What could I say in a letter?"

"I don't think it would have mattered what you said."

He handed me back my drink. "Go take a bath, warm up—you're cold. I have to make a half-dozen calls, including a transatlantic, and then change. We'll eat late, all right?"

I lay in the hot bath, getting dizzy from the whisky and wondering if Stanton really meant for me to sleep in the guest room. Maybe he was just observing proprieties around Freddie. I couldn't much remember what sex was like, and I decided I really didn't want to find out again. What I felt for Stanton in this crazy afternoon of unreality was a long way from sex.

167

When I was dry, I put on my new slip and tiptoed out to the kitchen to find Freddie.

He quickly averted his eyes and went out, only to return with a bathrobe—one of Stanton's, I guessed.

"I'm sorry," I said, "I didn't think. I mean, I'm not really naked in this heavy slip . . . "

"Yes, miss."

"Will you do me a favor? Can you go out and buy me something?"

"Yes; tonight there is no dinner to cook. What may I get for you?"

"I want a plain red lipstick—there's that drugstore in the building next to this. Can you go there? Just plain red. No blue, no orange. O.K. Just tell the woman that. And I want some cologne."

There had been a big Guerlain display in the window as Stanton and I had walked by. What kind could I get? God, not Shalimar; every factory foreman's wife wore that on Mother's Day. What else did they make? Vol de Nuit. It probably wasn't unpleasant, although I couldn't remember having smelled it.

"Here," I told Freddie, "I'll write it down for you, because it's hard to pronounce." I wrote "Guerlain's Vol de Nuit" and "Red—not blue or orange—lipstick."

Freddie looked at the piece of the kitchen pad I handed him and at my kindergarten-neat letters.

"I am not an uneducated American Negro," he said. "I am attending the Columbia University School of General Studies. My people are proud. French, it is my second language. English is my third."

"I didn't think you were stupid, Freddie," I said, in horror at my racism. "I meant, I can't pronounce the French myself—'Vole der Nueet,' see? And I wrote the lipstick thing because I thought, well, it would be confusing for a man to buy a lipstick, that's all."

"You lie," he said, in the same dull voice. "But I will be your errand boy because I want Mr. Montgomery to be happy. He is my American father."

We ate dinner in a tiny restaurant decked with green trees and mirrors and music coming from a piano somewhere off in the shadows. We drank a lot of wine and talked and laughed a bit too loudly.

"The South? You?" Stanton said. "That's the funniest tning I've

168

heard all day! What would you find in Dryden, besides the Ku Klux Klan?"

"A job."

"You have a job! Why should you work so much anyway? If you want to work, I'll get you a job here or back home, which might be better. Just wait a few months, see what happens." He took my hand. "That's an order."

When we came out on the street the snow was fluttering away, and we walked home, happily childish from the wine, arms around each other, catching snowflakes on our tongues. In the apartment, a fire was burning in the living room.

"Freddie remembered the fire. Sometimes he's in such a rush he forgets. He visits his sister every night at eleven thirty, after the library closes. She likes to have coffee. She's way out at Sarah Lawrence too. They're very close."

"Apparently," I said, sitting down in front of the fire. "He goes all the way out to Bronxville at midnight every night to see a sister? Stanton, come on. He probably has a girl around the corner."

"I'd doubt that very much," Stanton said tightly. "He's a devout Christian, you know, even talks about divinity school after college. No, I wouldn't question Freddie's morals."

"Neither would I," I said.

We sat silently for a while, and then Stanton popped his head into my lap, as he had so many years before, but he was still quiet, smiling to himself a bit, looking happy. He hadn't clenched his teeth once all night, I thought.

"I'm falling asleep right here." He got up and took me by the hand.

Outside the guest-room door, he hugged me. "Welcome home, Mary," he said. "Sleep well. We'll have breakfast, and then you'll call that newspaper. Good night."

The coldness that had been rising slowly into my throat since I'd heard about Freddie's morals burst into a chill of fear.

"I'm scared," I whispered. "Let me sleep with you. Just sleep. I'm scared to be alone in this strange house."

Stanton tightened up in a second and pulled away. "For heaven's sake, what are you trying to do?" he said. "We've got to be careful. Good night, Mary."

169

I turned off the light in the guest room and then pulled open the curtains that Freddie had closed and made up the bed that he had turned down. I sat by the window for a long while, listening to the wind wailing through the canyon outside the window. It was the coldest, loneliest sound, I thought, I'd ever heard. Sometimes, in the orange-gray of the city night, I could see a snowflake in the wind, not very often.

At 3:45 I heard Freddie come in. His sister sure drank a lot of coffee, all right, after the library closed.

At 4:20, when I figured Freddie was safely asleep, I took off all my new clothes and folded them very neatly on the chair. I put back on my wet-footed tights and soggy loafers and the jersey and old gray skirt. I poured the Vol de Nuit down the sink in the bathroom and threw the bottle in my suitcase. I put the lipstick in the trash, and I left a quarter for Freddie on the dresser. A tip, that would fix him.

I couldn't take the clothes. What had I ever done for Stanton?

I had a couple of hours to wait for the train south. I wandered around Penn Station, read the newspaper and had some tea. In a phone booth, I wrote, "Lonely? Call Mary," and followed it by Stanton's phone number. It was a terrific idea. and I began to chuckle. I went from booth to booth then, writing, "Swedish massage, call Mary, after 6 P.M. Men only," or "Oral French, experienced teacher, pupils over twenty-one, call Mary." I particularly liked "Buxom blond wants to play ball with visitors to New York, Tuesday, Wednesday and Thursday nights. Call Mary." Each time Stanton's number was large and clear.

If Stanton had any good memories of me, the lascivious-voiced phone calls coming into his apartment with my name would destroy them, by confirming his worst suspicions about me. That way, the end would be easier for us both. At least, that was the way I rationalized my revenge.

Just before the train left, I spotted a bank of flashing lights, a computerlike machine: "the world famous Anavac" would do an electrographic personality analysis from my signature for just one dollar. I signed and handed over my dollar.

The results were given on a card which listed two columns of characteristics. For example: "Affable, friendly" was in a column opposite "Shy and reserved." The electrographic analysis was the

170

line that wandered between these columns, moving closest to those characteristics the signer had most strongly.

The line flickered around gregarious, courageous, artistic, emotionally mature, but veered almost off the page for three qualities I thought would amuse old Stanton: I was incredibly "Generous, considerate," "Attractive to the opposite sex," and "Interested in sports."

I mailed it to him and ran for the train.

18

The snow that had covered New York during the night had paralyzed Dryden. The train was delayed a half hour just outside of town, while men in checkered jackets ran about in the mist with unused shovels in their hands and shouted helplessly. A young black man in a three-piece tweed suit came down the aisle dispensing questionnaires from the U. S. Department of Transportation. The Feds wanted to know what we thought of the train trip and how we'd make this same voyage the next time.

"There will be no next time," I wrote irritably and handed it back to him.

Dryden, or the fifty feet of it which I could see through the heavy white fog, looked like the Klondike. Across from the dripping old green station, a couple of wooden buildings, one boarded up, hovered together blackly.

There were no cars on the street, which was covered in perhaps two inches of snow and topped with several inches of gritty yellow sand. When a taxi plowed up in front of the station, the driver told me he didn't know whether or not he could make it up the hill to the newspaper.

172

"Real bad, dangerous, cars piling up." He shook his head.

"Oh, for God's sake," I said, "Look, I'm from Colton, and this is nothing, just nothing. Let me drive."

That sent him scurrying back to the wheel.

I was sorry about the fog. I thought it obscured my view of the city; I saw only an occasional shoulder of a small brick building, or a corner of a sandy lot, poking through the heavy whiteness. Later I was to learn unhappily that the fog had obscured almost nothing. It was a very small city.

The newspaper's personnel director, Miss Tyrone, welcomed me into a striped-wallpapered office, festooned with Girl Scout slogans and citations.

As I was sitting down, she glanced at the application blank and said, "Oh, you're single. Still waiting for Prince Charming? Or do you believe in free love?"

"No love is free, Miss Tyrone." I glared at her big bosom and spent the next half hour turning her prying questions into such profound metaphysics.

"Well," she said finally, "all that remains is for you to meet the editors and take the psychological tests."

"No tests. Sorry," I said.

"Well, we've never hired anyone without them. Everyone takes them."

"Nope." I got up and took back the folder of yellowed clippings I'd given her. "Could your secretary get me on a plane this afternoon as early as possible?"

"But you have to have lunch—the editor is waiting," she said.

We walked up through the snow with the editor, Howard McKinley, to the only hotel in town. It was dark and oily-looking, with soiled pink fleur-de-lys-printed carpets. A couple of old men sat in the lobby, and I expected to see a great wooden fan revolving above our dining-room table.

On the way up, Howard, a small, tawny young man, was talking about how he'd spent the evening playing Ping-Pong in the snow with his sons. I could see them, leaping about like little springboks, sailing after a speck of whiteness in the fields of black and whiteness. I liked that. I liked him. I knew he'd never expect me to play Ping-Pong.

It was so late that the dining room was empty. Tyrone insisted

173

that I join all of them in a drink. I took two or three sips of a martini and knew I was drunk. It was that kind of day. I leaned back and let Howard grumble on to Tyrone about some problem of the day. I felt sorry for taking up their time. I ordered the cheapest thing on the menu to atone.

Tyrone was trying to sell me on Dryden. Whenever Howard would stop rumbling—it was just his voice; his words were not abrasive—Tyrone would slither in with: "—and we're only two hours by air from Washington," or, "William Faulkner spent the night here once."

As we left the building, Tyrone pointed to a church several doors down. "You like theater? That's our playhouse—the parish house," she said. "That's the cultural center of town."

"Terrific," I sneered.

"Come on, Tiny!" said Howard. "Let's get back."

Alone with Tyrone in her office, I again asked about my plane reservation.

"The first one we could get you on isn't until nine tonight," she said, looking truly grieved.

"Wonderful. You know there's been a death in the family, and now I'll miss the wake," I said.

"Anyone close?" She moved in to take my elbow.

"How close is 'close,' Miss Tyrone?" I asked, moving just outside her reach.

"Well, as long as you have so much time, you can take our tests now," she said. "Just one, then, the general intelligence?"

"O.K.," I sighed.

Her secretary locked me in a little green room with a telephone. "Call that number," she said, pointing to the sign on the wall, "if you finish before I come back. Don't worry. No one ever does finish."

After those sips of martini, I couldn't even read the instructions, let alone any of the questions. I kept seeing the green handwritten entries in the menu Stanton and I had read last night. It had been a strange menu, in green ink, with no prices.

The test. I picked up the pencil and went down the answers column marking the boxes in an artistic sort of pattern, skip one, check two, skip three, check four.

174

Then I called the number.

"Wow," the secretary said, and as she took my test, I thought I saw her swallow, but I couldn't be sure.

Howard got me into his office. There were half a dozen photographs of children romping around. A good Bible-reading family, I could tell. Wait until I hit him with my family!

"You don't want to come here, do you?" he asked.

"No. I don't," I said. Then I got worried; suppose they refused to fly me home? I only had about six or seven dollars with me and no checks. "Look, I think you've got a fine paper, from the little I saw of it. And I like you. The trouble is, I'm afraid of a certain sort of attitude: 'Do you believe in free love?' Miss Tyrone asked me that. I'm an unmarried mother, and that's all I need. I hate what I'm doing now, but at least no one bothers me about that." I pointed at his family. "I have a son, too!"

He blinked a half smile out of his frown. "Really? How old?" The amenity done with, he frowned us back to business. "I don't know about free love, but I can promise you, you'll be left alone here too," he said. "No one will care what you do once you leave this building."

He proceeded to tell me where I would sit and who my supervisor would be if I wanted to cover urban affairs. The city editor came in and took my hand. "Welcome aboard," he said; "Glad to have you on my team."

Finally I backed out of the room telling them I'd let them know. I really had to think it over, although the salary, $11,000, was probably adequate.

Tyrone took me to the hotel, where I could get a limousine to the airport, forty minutes away.

"Well, so you think you'll come? We'll make it real easy for you," she said, taking my elbow as we crossed the street.

I pulled my elbow free.

"Why didn't you tell me you have a child?" She was smiling.

"You didn't ask. I put it on the application. Why don't you read your own application?"

"Fair enough." Old Tyrone was a good sport—I could hear her fellow Girl Scout leaders saying it now.

"How easy will you make it?" I asked.

"Find you a place to live, get you set up, pay all your moving expenses. Come on, you know you want to come," she said with a kittenish grin.

My plane, on its way north from Miami, was two hours late arriving. Then there was more snow and some sort of turbulence in the air. By the time we left for home it was midnight, and would-be passengers were leaning against the terminal walls and dozing or staring blankly at the long-since-empty candy machines.

It was too late to get James. The heat was off in my apartment. I didn't even take off my coat. I just lay on my bed with a blanket over me and shivered from fatigue and all that had happened. Around five o'clock I got up and took a sleeping pill. On an all-night radio talk show, the jerky comic, a moderator, was still trying to telephone Fidel Castro in Cuba, a gimmick that had been going on for months.

I thought I would rather talk to Fidel Castro at that moment than any living person, certainly more than any living person I knew. He must know a lot about living. I would say, "Fidel, I'm coming down to lie on your beach and smell the sugar cane. When you and the boys get to revving the engines of those old 'fifty-two Chevies of yours, remember, you'll be disturbing me. We'll play some Ping-Pong on the sand when I'm rested, you hear?"

I was mad, but then maybe everyone was. Dryden? Colton? Havana? East 71st Street? It didn't matter. There was no one I cared about at all, when you got right down to the warm-in-the-skin level. Me? I was all I had to live with, wasn't I?

I called Howard in the morning and told him I'd come. He said he had the flu and that's why he wasn't jumping for joy around his office.

"I got fired by the other newspaper for being pregnant," I told him.

"I wondered why you weren't going back there. Listen, how soon can you start?"

When I hung up, I started to cry. I felt as though I'd just jumped out of an airplane only to decide halfway down that I didn't really want to die.

Andy was rather dazed when I went into his office to tell him I was leaving. He nodded vacantly, and then began rummaging

176

through the wastebasket and shaking his head. I went down the hall to tell the bookkeeper.

"You have another job?" she asked anxiously.

"Yes, in Dryden."

"You're lucky," she said. "Did Andy talk to you yet? Well, we've gone under. Two contracts canceled this month. We're out of business on February first. I'm starting to look everywhere for another job. I might even have to go to Dryden myself. There doesn't seem to be anything around here."

I was fairly sure that something would stop me from going to Dryden. Someone would save me, Stanton or Andy; someone would come up with an excuse for me to stay, I kept telling myself as I packed our belongings. After the movers had gone with the furniture, James and I slept in a sleeping bag on the floor for two uncomfortable nights, and I kept the phone by my ear. It never rang. We had to leave.

19

As we began the long drive down to Dryden, James sparkled around in the back of the car and laughed joyously as he pulled his clothes, piece by piece, from the laundry bag in which I'd stuffed them. It was as good a toy as any. But by the time we'd been on the road for two hours, he was vomiting. I took him into the front seat and let him throw up into a towel. When he was through, I pulled to the side of the road and threw the towel away. His forehead was burning, and his cheeks were red. It wasn't just carsickness. He lay with his head in my lap, and I rubbed his forehead with one hand.

"It's all right, James," I kept telling him. "Things will be all right from now on. You wait and see."

We slipped off the highway and down into the city of Dryden in the black dullness of the winter night. We passed lots covered with the rubble of urban renewal, and then endless rows of squat brick houses where every now and then a dim light burned. The streets were deserted. I found an open gas station and stopped to ask for directions. An old woman in leather bedroom slippers and a dark flannel bathrobe hobbled out to fill the tank of my car. Inside she looked at me nervously several times as she ironed my credit card onto the sales slip.

"No. Never heard of no such street," she said. "Map of the city? Never heard of such a thing."

I asked for change for a quarter so I could use the pay phone.

"No change here. Don't keep no money after dark," she said.

"I've got a sick child in the car; I've been driving for twelve hours and I'm going to report this to the main company."

"Damn niggers," she said, opening the cash drawer with the key she unpinned from her bathrobe hem. "Rob you blind. Like rats, they come out in the dark." She gestured at the windows. "Can't keep no money 'round the station. The niggers get it." I went outside to the pay phone and called the police for directions.

The house Tyrone had found was squat and brick, one identical link in a chain that seemed to spread across the city. It had a low-slung, brick-pillared porch like something out of a late-1940s movie. I could see Rita Hayworth in her padded shoulders leaning against one of the pillars watching her soldier lover go off to the war, dragging his duffle bag.

I left James sleeping in the car and went to the other half of the house and knocked on the door to get the key from the landlord's aunt, Miss Kelly.

"Oh, the movers were here about an hour ago," she said, through the three inches of open door space. "You weren't here, so they left. Said they had a load due in Florida tomorrow. They'll be back Tuesday."

She stood there trembling faintly, in her white old lady's skin. In the sliver of house I could see through her door, there were lace doilies and plastic geraniums on a table, and antimacassars on a fat maroon chair.

"What are you going to do?" she asked.

"I guess we camp out next door? If you'll give me the key?"

In the beam of the car flashlight I saw that the house was filled with dust, junk and old broken toys. The electricity was off, there was no heat, and the oil tank in the cellar was empty. The downstairs bathroom toilet was very unpleasantly clogged, and the entrance to the upstairs bathroom was blocked by an old mattress, splashed with a dark bloodlike stain.

179

The walls, pea-soup-colored in the glow of my dying flashlight batteries, were covered in hand prints, even big animal-paw prints, and grease was splattered all over the kitchen.

I rang Miss Kelly's bell again. "I won't stay in that house," I told her. "Have you seen it?"

She shook her head. "I don't go out much now—it just isn't safe. Why, just the other day, three of them jumped a woman up the street."

"What's your nephew's phone number?"

When Tyrone had called me up to describe two houses available in the city, she'd hinted at the dangers of the neighborhood. One house, she'd said, was really very charming. The rent was only two hundred dollars a month. The other was more than adequate to my needs, three bedrooms, one hundred thirty dollars a month, but it was in a mixed neighborhood.

"Mixed?" I asked naïvely. "You mean there are stores or factories?"

"No, there are some colored, one right out back of you."

"I wouldn't live in an 'unmixed' neighborhood," I said to shame her, unsuccessfully.

"Well, if you feel that way. They don't seem like bad sorts. I mean you're taking a risk, but I talked to the fellow out back. He might cut your grass in the summer if you give him a dollar."

The house would be fine once it was fixed up. She'd done well by me, Tyrone had. There was a yard. Unbelievable luxury. It was twice the size of the house.

I said good night to Miss Kelly and went back to the thruway and a motel.

I brought James into our room from the car. He was very hot, and he lay on the bed staring at me as I poked through the suitcase to find the thermometer. His temperature was only 104 degrees. Nothing for James. He'd survive. I gave him some aspirin and bathed him and put him into bed. Then I called the hospital to get the name of a pediatrician, just in case he got worse during the night.

"I want a doctor who is very kind and spends a lot of time talking to parents," I told the head nurse in pediatrics.

"Well, we don't recommend doctors," she said, "but the kindest one—I mean, if my little girl was sick, I'd go to Dr. Davidson. He's out near where you're staying too, I think."

180

I looked him up in the phone book and wrote down his number. It was well after eleven o'clock now. James was staring listlessly at the television, where Dean Martin was mouthing some drunken song. James was too sick to fight me for the sound.

I telephoned the landlord. "I've just been by to see the house, and it will have to be cleaned out and repainted before I move in," I told him.

"You wake me up to tell me that?" he said. "I just had it cleaned out and repainted before the last people moved in two years ago. I can't do it again."

"O.K., then I won't take it."

There was a silence.

"O.K. I want to be reasonable," he said. "I'll have some of my men out there in the morning. If it's as bad as you say, we'll make it nice for you. Honestly, I haven't had the place rented for the past year. I've been waiting for the right kind of tenant, if you know what I mean. Miss Tyrone, up to the paper, told me you were a fine lady."

"That's a long way from the truth," I said, "but I am white, and so's my little boy."

"Well, I couldn't rent to colored with my aunt right next door. My last tenants were fine people; they just got into some trouble at the end. Wife's still in the state hospital. Don't know what happened to the kids."

"You'll have some men out there in the morning?"

"There's a weekend coming up; tomorrow's Friday. I'll see what I can do."

By the time room service brought supper, James's fever had broken. He sat up and drank some milk while I ate.

"You were asleep in the car," I told him, "but the house where we're going to live has a big yard. You can play outside all by yourself."

He smiled, his mouth all red from the fever, and then curled up with his nest of nylon strips and went to sleep. He was almost two, and he'd developed a fetish about nylon. He would not go anywhere without dragging one of my slips or a pair of my underpants behind him, until I got a piece of nylon in a yard-goods store and cut it into strips or "sucks" for him. It had been embarrassing to be walking down the street and have some man come running after me, holding

181

an ancient slip or a pair of faded-gray underpants which James had just dropped.

In the morning his fever was only 102 degrees. His nose was running and he was beginning to cough. He had the flu, and it would pass without a doctor's help.

I called the telephone company. I could have a teleohone that very afternoon if I'd be in the house to show the serviceman where I wanted it. The oil company whose name had been stickered on the empty tank said a truck would be out immediately. Kelly was a big landlord in the city, I was discovering. But the gas and electric company said it would connect no utilities until I had made a twenty-dollar security deposit. If I mailed the check right away, it should be cleared by Tuesday, and they'd get things hooked up by Wednesday at the latest.

"The check won't clear that quickly, because it will be an out-of-state bank," I said, and was told that in that case, I'd better come downtown and pay in cash today.

I explained that I was alone in a motel with a sick child and I'd rather not take him out in the rain any more than was necessary. I'd never had to make a security deposit for electricity before.

"Look, miss you're a single woman, and you're in a high-risk neighborhood."

I asked to speak to the head of the credit department. Yes, he told me, there were certain areas of the city which they designated as high risk. The clerk I'd talked to had made one mistake, though. The fact that I was a woman was not important; they'd discontinued that policy.

I wrapped James in a motel blanket and drove to the house. There were two panel trucks parked in front, and a man in overalls let us in, opening the door before I even had a chance to take out the key.

"Come out to cheer us on?" he asked.

"No, just waiting for the phone company."

"Boys will be painting today," he said. "Kelly sent two niggers —one's in the kitchen, one's upstairs. I'm Pete, the plasterer."

I put James down on the floor by the fireplace and stood in front of him, waiting for Pete to go back to work.

"Well?" I said finally.

182

"Cute little girl," Pete smiled. "Could I pat your hair, honey?" He reached out toward James.

"He's a boy. Now, if you'll excuse us," I glared, making a cap for James's head quickly with my hands.

"You planning on getting some light? Awful hard to work in the dark."

"I'll go see about that now," I said.

I carried James back out through the rain to the car. It wouldn't start; in fact the engine wouldn't even turn over. I sat there, with the rain streaming down.

Pete's hand knocked on the window, right beside James's cheek. "Give you a push?" he shouted through the glass.

He nudged his truck up behind me and pushed the car out into the street. When we were rolling at about thirty miles an hour, I popped the clutch, the engine caught and we were on our way. I honked the horn to thank him, and just as I did, he crashed into the back of the car so hard that James was thrown against the dashboard.

I pulled over to the sidewalk and looked at James's lip. It was just a little tooth nick, and I began hugging him to quiet him down.

Pete came to my window this time. "Checked you out—you're O.K., not a dent," he said.

I felt that to let him see James's cut was to invite further contact with him, so I nodded and waited until he was gone before driving on. When I parked outside the power and light company, I saw that the rear bumper of the car was badly crinkled, in fact, even the hood over the engine was dented.

I made the twenty-dollar deposit and then from a lunch counter called the telephone company and asked them not to send the man out today after all. It was too late; he was already on his way. The next installation opening would be at the end of the following week, so we returned to the house.

"So soon?" asked Pete, again opening the door for us.

"Has the phone company been here?"

"No. Come on out in the kitchen. Bring your little girl—I want her to see what a good job the nigger's done."

A big black man in white coveralls was on top of a ladder, scrubbing the ceiling with a brush. The stove and cabinets were already spotless.

"That's very good," I said. "Thank you."

"Yes'm," he said from atop the ladder.

"You know," Pete said, leaning against the ladder, "that boy up there, he won't let me see his tail."

"What in the hell are you talking about?"

"I know. You Yankees don't hear nothing about it, but down here, we know, they got tails, just like monkeys. I see four of them in the service . . . they were truly a sight to see, tails all long and with this real kinky-like hair."

I sat down on the kitchen floor and held James tight against my stomach, waiting until Pete had left the kitchen to move, but he stood there, his baggy overalls right next to my face.

"You dented my car," I said, to Pete's leg. "What did you mean, not a dent? The back's knocked in." I looked up at him this time.

"You lying nigger lovers are all the same, and you're no better than them." He pointed up at the black man. "You and your little bastard there. Yeah, I know. Kelly told me. Well, I never touched your car." He shuffled off into the dark house.

"What's your name?" I asked the black man on the ladder.

"George, miss."

"You don't know any woman who'd like to baby-sit full-time for me? Starting next Monday, a week from this Monday, in the afternoon until eleven or twelve. That's when I'll be working."

"Might," he said, not looking down. "I'll have to ask around."

I sat on the floor, and James crawled around the base of the ladder for a few minutes and then came back and collapsed in my lap.

"He sick?" George asked.

"Yes."

"Hurts you to see them sick, don't it?" After a few minutes he said, "I ain't promising nothing, but if I was to find somebody that was willing, where'd she find you?"

I wrote down my name and the motel room number.

He slipped it into his pocket. "No promises. But I'll have me a look. Ralph, upstairs, he might know someone if I don't."

"It would be very nice of you to ask around for me."

He looked down, catching my eye for just a fraction of a second, and nodded.

It was four o'clock when the telephone-company man arrived. George and Ralph left in Kelly's truck, and then Pete came

184

downstairs. "I'll be in the other bedrooms tomorrow, fix them up for you." He grinned at James asleep on the floor by the fireplace.

"Bye-bye there, honey," he said and started over toward James.

"Don't touch him," I said quickly and added, "unless you want to get the flu."

I watched him plod down the walk and around and into his truck. It started with a great cloud of black smoke; then he tooted as he pulled out onto the road.

About twenty feet ahead of him, on the opposite sidewalk, a yellow cat started out onto the road. It stopped halfway into its lane and waited for the truck to pass. But the truck didn't pass; it veered sharply into the left-hand lane to hit the cat. I could hear its short scream through the window before the truck returned to the proper lane and moved on down the street into the dusk.

The cat was not quite dead when I got to it, but its rear legs were gone into a hot red pulp. The blood soaked into my skirt and then my thighs until the telephone man pulled me away.

"Come on," he said, his freckled face very pale. "You'll get hit too. Did you see the car that got it?"

I shook my head, too sick to become involved further.

As we drove back to the motel, I realized it was not just the horrors of the day that were making me shiver. My back and legs ached, and my head was cracking open. I too had the flu. We stopped at a drugstore, and I bought more baby aspirin and adult aspirin and Kleenex and cough syrup and six boxes of disposable diapers. We might be in for a long siege.

Sunday night I heard someone knocking on the motel-room door. A middle-aged black woman in a house dress under her open coat stood there, hopping up and down in the cold.

"I'm Ethel Winston," she said. "You know, George's sister."

"George?"

"The man that was out to clean your house."

"Come in," I said, holding my nightgown around me. James, far on the road to recovery, was crawling through a tunnel he'd made from two chairs and the wastebasket.

"That him?" Ethel said, laughing. "That the one you want me to sit for? Boy, I never seen nothing so white. Even his hair is white. Come here, boy!"

I asked her a few foggy questions--she'd worked before as a

185

cleaning woman, she'd finished high school, she'd been married going on thirty years. Yes, she'd raised five kids of her own, but they'd all left home now. No, her husband wouldn't mind her working at night.

She looked at me incredulously when I asked if forty dollars a week would be enough. "You say forty?"

"Well, I'd give you overtime too, and there won't be any housework, just his supper, and yours, of course."

"That'd be O.K., she said.

She'd be there next Monday at two. She waved as she climbed into an ancient Cadillac.

After she left, I realized I had forgotten to ask for her address and phone number, not to mention references. She might not even show up. I didn't know anything about her or her brother either.

Oh, hell, I thought in my sloppy feverish way, you never really know anyone in this world. You can know someone for years and have no idea what's inside. I figured I knew Ethel as well as I knew anyone. She'd work out O.K.

And she did, for a year. She was never late, she never missed a day. She left the house as neat as she found it. She said she loved James and James adored her. She cooked only soul food, and the house always smelled of hot lard when I got home at midnight, but I could be awfully persnickety about such things. I had no major complaints.

I did discover during the course of the year that she had looked at me incredulously when I offered her forty dollars because the going rate was twenty-five, and that the reason her husband didn't care about her working nights was that he was serving time in the county jail. He wouldn't be up for parole for another year.

"He'll do anything, that man, when he's drunk," Ethel said. "But he's stopped drinking."

"Now that he's in jail, you mean?"

"Yeah, since he's been in jail, he ain't had one single drink," she said solemnly. "He's been asking for the Lord's help, and I guess he's been getting it."

"Ethellllll," I shrieked. "Get serious."

She looked at me for a minute and then, seeing in a flash how she'd been had, doubled up with laughter.

"He always was a weasel!" she wailed.

186

20

The city room of the newspaper was as tight as an attic crawl space.
It had been painted an easy-on-the-pocketbook green sometime after
World War II, and the single small window was blocked up with
glass bricks; it was a room with a view of nothing but the production
of the next edition.

When I arrived the first day, a copy boy showed me where I was
to sit. I put my purse down on the shiny linoleum top of the desk
and looked around, wondering if I should tell anyone I'd arrived.

"What are you doing? You can't sit there," a mousy-looking man
began shouting at me as he came out of the locker room. "Not next
to me, you don't. No!"

The city editor appeared to investigate his distress.

"Sit right down there and keep your mouth shut," the city editor
yelled at me. I stopped biting my lip; at least I now knew what to do.

The city editor and the other man stood in the corner and shouted
at each other and pointed wildly like angry umpires. I missed their
dialogue because the man on the desk yelled at me to take an
obituary. I picked up the phone and started talking to the un-

dertaker. I did it pretty well, I guess, because he was soon yelling at me to take another. I was on my fourth when the man whose desk I was contaminating came over and began to empty the drawers, throwing old yellowed newsprint clippings and pencil stubs into manila envelopes. He was muttering to himself about how he was going to be damned. He left without looking at me and moved his junk into a desk on the other side of the room.

No one else noticed me the first day.

The second day, a black photographer took my picture to go on my press card and said it would never come out. It was impossible to photograph me because I had all this dead white stuff on my face.

"What is it?" I asked.

"Skin," he snarled, disappearing into the darkroom.

I spent the afternoons doing obituaries. At night, if the man on the desk thought he could spare me, I was allowed out to meetings in the black community. Urban affairs, it turned out, meant anything to do with race or poverty. I was told by several male reporters that I should refuse to go to these meetings. It wasn't safe on the streets at night for anyone, especially a woman, and I should make sure that I had someone walk me to my car after work. I thought it was ridiculous to be afraid in a small town like Dryden, but I did hold my shoulder blades together apprehensively as I walked quickly to my car the first few times. I remember thinking how appropriate it would be if I were knifed in the back on my return from a meeting in a waxy brown church where the only piece of news had been, "Sister Williams is up to the women's hospital having her womb removed, and would surely appreciate a card of remembrance from any of you good folks. . . . "

I had thought that working afternoons and evenings would be ideal, giving me a solid six hours with James and freeing me from the dreary evening hours I had spent locked to his cribside. But it didn't work. It was always two or three o'clock before I'd be unwound enough to fall asleep. And at six or sometimes seven, James would be chirping like a flock of goldfinches, flying all over the bed and cooing "Juuuice" in my ear. I'd clamp him in the vise of my knees, hand him the hem of my nylon nightgown and get fifteen or twenty minutes more sleep, but never enough to keep me from sagging all day.

By the time I got to work, I'd been on my feet running after James

188

for six or seven hours. My fatigue was accentuated by the pink, freshly shaven cheeks and minty-toothpaste smiles of my male colleagues, whose good wives kept the children out of Daddy's way.

Obituaries didn't do much to revive me. When there was no night meeting, I'd sit there and hear the male reporters being sent out to cover a fire or an attempted murder or a political meeting. One night when I was run down by a cold, I fell asleep at a community meeting. When I got back to the paper, the man on the desk asked me what kind of a story it was. "None," I replied. He smiled, "Good."

At least at the Company, I'd been needed.

Gradually, things improved. I discovered No-Doz, and after a month or so bitched to the city editor about the sexism in a newsroom where the most experienced reporter they had on nights sat doing obituaries while boys right out of school covered the news.

"My God, you're much too expensive to write obituaries," he said. "I kept meaning to ask you what you were doing. I haven't seen anything of yours in the paper."

At one of the dreary meetings, when the new black director of a community center said he wanted to get the power and light company to hire more blacks, I mentioned my "high-risk area" experience. The next day we both assumed fake names and addresses, mine being in an all-white neighborhood and his in one of the poorer black sections. He was categorically refused service until he made the entire deposit in cash, while I was given an apology for any inconvenience and the promise that a man would be out within the hour, with no mention of money at all.

It was a new story for this town, and it helped launch the black leader. He got the power and light company to change its "credit procedures" and helped defeat its request for a rate increase before the state Public Service Commission. He also got it to open an office in the black neighborhood and begin a program of hiring minority group members. And from there, he went on to force the downtown merchants, the banks and the hospital to hire more blacks.

They were fun stories to write. And there were others that I began to find. I could describe situations needing cure and try to prod those responsible. In contrast to those frightening, guilty days at Faraday, Brinks and Crummel, I was now supposed to cure nothing. What I was supposed to do and what I could do, I was

189

doing. My guilt was peacefully oblique, lying only in my privileged, white, middle-class background. I lost no sleep over that There might be better work, but none that I knew had the great fringe benefit of providing such a useful and satisfying and socially acceptable channel for one's anger and frustrations. When I began pouring into my work that vague but often desperate anger that besieged me as the first softness each morning began to harden, I was a freer soul.

Quite soon after we were settled in the house, James rode his tricycle downstairs headfirst. When he hit bottom, the house shook in the seconds of stillness before he cried. Miss Kelly called right away; was everything all right? I blocked my free ear and shouted that I'd let her know. I picked him up. Nothing major was broken; he was merely turning black and blue from head to toe on one side of his body. The next morning we were going to our first appointment with Dr. Davidson anyway, and he'd live until then. In the meantime, all toys with wheels went to live on the ground floor.

Dr. Davidson's office lay out the suburbs. To reach it we drove through miles of brick and white aluminum-sided pseudocolonial houses, with shaved yellow lawns and antiqued milk cans on their doorsteps. The waiting room was filled with nice neat little mothers in nice neat little pink blouses and tweed slacks. Their hair was immaculately cemented into ornate out-of-style beehives and bouffants.

Dr. Davidson was a handsome, swarthy young man who spoke with a faint German accent. He looked me up and down carefully, trying to decide, I was sure, whether I was safely on Medicaid or whether he'd end up taking me to magistrates' court to get his fee.

He read the history I'd filled out on James.

"The father's side, it is empty. Oh, I see, you are not married," he said matter-of-factly.

When he had finished examining James, he said he was a healthy child except for the bruises. Where had he gotten those? How had he managed to take such a bad fall down the stairs?

James was dressed, and I reached for my coat. But instead of letting us go, Dr. Davidson began to ask me about what I was doing in Dryden. What I had done before, in Colton? Was I in any

190

political movements? Women's Lib! Did I get bored and depressed cooped up alone with a two-year-old all day, all weekend? When I wasn't working? Did I ever feel angry, ever feel like hitting him?

"Sometimes," I said, "not very often."

"Yes, I can see you must spare the rod," Dr. Davidson said, nodding toward James, who had climbed up on top of his desk and was drawing with a red ball-point pen on the fresh white blotter. "And he got the bruises falling off the dining-room table? Oh, that's right, the stairs. Well, I have to take your word for it," he said. "Make sure it doesn't happen again. There are gates to go across the tops of stairs." He looked at me rather strangely as we finally left.

We were waiting for a green light, in a long line of chrome-and-walnut-paneled station wagons filled with cherubic suburban children and Irish setters, when I realized what Dr. Davidson had been getting at.

"Oh, of course! You know they've made a big thing about that here this year, child abuse," a fellow reporter told me, later that day. "Just passed a bill making it compulsory for a doctor to report even suspected cases."

For a week I waited each morning for the police, knowing they'd come with a warrant and take James away to a foster home, an orphanage, maybe a state hospital where they'd want to place him under observation to determine the extent of the psychological bruises. When the police failed to show, I decided I liked Dr. Davidson. At least he was willing to give me another chance, unlike others in the suburban world around him, where we didn't quite make it. In the supermarket James would run in joyous welcome to embrace children his own age. They'd retreat whimpering to cling to their mothers' legs, or stare blankly down from their mothers' shopping carts. We'd walk down the aisles chatting to each other, James still answering in gobbles and squawks, and I'd see a pair of mothers look at us and shake their heads.

The black family in back of us had three little boys, all under four years. They were foster children, the mother said, wards of the state. I asked if they could come over and play with James in our yard. No, that wouldn't be a good idea. I asked if James could go into her yard; I'd come and watch them. No, she said, they were just getting ready to go in for lunch. Several times I asked again. No. Some other time maybe, she'd say.

191

I found a white family with young children two blocks away. James played happily with them until one day their mother brought him home, holding both his hands tightly together. He'd thrown a stone at her little girl. He needed to learn more control, how to play with other children, before he came back to their house.

"James doesn't act like other children," I said to Dr. Davidson. "I see them in stores and places, and they're all quiet and different. I'm afraid he isn't normal or something."

"Of course he isn't normal," Dr. Davidson said. "He doesn't come from a normal home; how could he be?"

"Jesus Christ, spare me from your mediocre aluminum-sided normal people with their stuffed toy brats," I raged defensively, and stormed out of his office. I cried all the way home. I hated anything normal; of course I did. I wouldn't be normal if I could, but God damn it, James was going to be as normal as he could be.

I telephoned the doctor as soon as I got into the house. "O.K., what can I do to make him normal!"

"There's nothing you can do; you have to work. If you could stay home, lovely, but you can't."

"I wouldn't want to stay home with James all day," I said, expecting him to hang up.

"Exactly. Why should you? But don't expect your child to act like children whose mothers are always with them. Look, you think I'm being critical. I merely point this out to you so you will understand. None of the books apply to you. Your life is different. You are not other mothers. James is not other children. Look at me—I was born in Vienna. O.K., so I will never be at home here; I will always be a foreigner. I go to parties, I start to talk about politics, they look at me. What does he know, the foreigner? My children suffer; I cannot play baseball with them. The game has rules I never knew. They want their daddy in the Little League."

"I hate it here," I said. "Horizon-to-horizon suburbia. And you should too! How can you fit in? Why do you live here?"

"You can't have everything in this world," he said. "You will find this is a little oasis, a little garden in a country of cities and concrete. You should live in Dryden Farms if you want to be happy here. There are some freethinkers there."

I found out that Dryden Farms was a small incorporated town on the fringe of the suburbs, and if the state had any painters or writers or actors or musicians, any socially acceptable misfits, they lived there. James and I drove out to look at it. It was a bower of green even in early April. There were acres of open space where children could run without being hit by a car, and the shabby houses were hidden in the woods. One of the town fathers, I discovered, was my supervisor, the city editor at the paper.

"I want to live in Dryden Farms," I told him.

"So do a lot of other people, and not everyone can," he said sourly, ending the discussion permanently.

As Howard had said, people at the paper certainly did leave you alone. No one cared what you did once you left the building. Or what you did inside it either, for that matter. Everyone knew I was an unmarried mother, and no one seemed to care. In fact, a couple of people went out of their way to tell me that a relative of theirs had had a baby out of wedlock, or an abortion. These things happened in the state and no one got too upset; life went on.

What did upset people, however, was any talk of the women's movement. I wrote some articles on liberation and how its goals were to make life more pleasant for men as well as women. At home this would have been like writing about Christmas falling on December 25. Here, it brought the roof down. I began getting threatening phone calls at home, and hate letters. I went on a radio talk show, and practically all of the incoming calls had to be censored.

"You fucking Communist," one man yelled, and I found that amusing, especially as it got out over the air.

But there were other calls, things like "I feel sorry for that child of yours, growing up with a mother who doesn't want to stay home where she belongs and look after him." These hurt.

When we went back to Dr. Davidson in early April, I told him how I sat on my bed mornings, watching the rain fall on the ugliness of the city, and wanted to die. I liked my work, and so things were all right until I had a few hours with James and nothing to do, or until I was alone. Off the job, I hadn't talked with an adult since I'd last seen him. At home I'd feel insanity creeping up the stairs of the house after me, just as it had for the prevous occupant. The funny house for me. What would become of James? I was a terrible mother. I got so bored.

"You must structure your time even more closely. Plan what you are going to do with him as much as you can. Maybe it will just be watching a TV show that you'll both like, or going to walk in the wildlife preserve. I tell you this; plan, always plan, or you both go crazy. Maybe you should get some help for yourself, some psychiatric help? You ever think of that?"

"No," I said. "Besides, I can't afford it."

"Well, there are clinics," he said. "I just suggest it for what it's worth. It seems to me you must have a lot of things to talk about with someone."

I had nothing to talk about with anyone, so I would not take that suggestion, but I did begin to make a schedule. We wrote it out each day at lunch for the following day. While I cleaned, made the beds and got the laundry together, James would watch "Sesame Street." Then we'd read until the market opened. If it was raining—and it always was—we'd crayon on the kitchen floor while I fixed lunch. Then we'd run, rain or shine, for at least a half hour before eating.

There was a small park in the neighborhood, maybe four acres, and it was always deserted while school was in session. It had a stream running through rock- and leaf-covered shoulders, and old weeping willows. James could run on the paths beneath the trees for at least twenty minutes without having to be stopped. There had been nothing like this in the city of Colton. James was free. And as I trudged along behind him, I knew no one was watching me. No one cared. No one knew us, or wanted to. I was free too.

On my days off we went up into the area around the preserve, in the gentle hills where James's running took us along the riverbank, beneath the drooping trees, and then along the edges of rocky bluffs where mice and small rabbits would tunnel before us through the grass and where, in the darkness of the woods, owls hooted, even by day.

We drove south into a region of large farms or plantations, where muddy fields spread out with a flatness that frightened me, and skinny ante-bellum houses towered over gray and yellow fields and buzzards circled in the pale sky.

We had no place in the white middle-class world of suburban Dryden and no place in the small black city, where our neighbors were too shy, or hostile, or proud to accept us. But slowly we began to make our own life, just the two of us, James and I.

194

21

A great barking sound was echoing through the quietness of the city as I left the newspaper on a chilly April midnight. Police dogs, I thought, tracking down some poor black kids who had stood on a street corner too long. The newspaper's doors were all locked after 5 P.M., and I was too tired to walk around the building and go through the hassle of proving I wasn't a thief just to learn exactly what the barking was about. I'd call the city desk when I got home and find out what the police radios were saying.

When I got home, however, the same barking filled the streets almost a mile away. Ethel was sitting on the floor to watch Johnny Carson. She had the Sony earplugs in because it was a big thrill for her to hear what no one else in the house could. No, she said, pulling one plug out for a second, she didn't hear no dogs. She took a big bite out of the last piece of cake left over from James's second birthday.

As she was putting on her coat to go home during the commercial, she had second thoughts. "I know what you was talking about! I heard all these dogs barking away as I was coming down the stairs with the TV. Seemed like an awful lot."

I walked out to her car with her. The moon was up and the sky was shining navy blue. Everything was very quiet. "I heard them way downtown," I said. "How could there be so many dogs all over the city?"

"You know what I think; I think it's just that season, Mary. Everything's all stirred up; I know I sure is."

Yes, I'd noticed the new wig, shiny black clumps like Pekingese ears, and the new red fingernails, and the switch from detective magazines to love comics. Maybe she was right. I'd better not call the newspaper, I thought as I washed the cake plate.

I had on my nightgown and was washing my face when I heard it again. I leaned out the window and looked down the empty street. Nothing. However, as I pulled my head in, I saw a long waving V of birds. Canada geese, flying northward home to breed, and singing or barking as they went. The city was ringing with their rejoicing.

Across the street, one window was lighted, the upstairs bedroom, Tommy's. Tommy was a twenty-three-year-old paraplegic, wounded in Vietnam, now kept alive by month-long visits to the veterans' hospital and the daily visits of nurses when he was home. His mother worked in the five-and-ten downtown, and before she left for the store each morning, the nurse would help her get him up—by a special hoist, Miss Kelly said—and into a reclining wheelchair.

During the mornings, I could see him sitting on their glassed-in porch, by the orange glow of a space heater. He was watching the rain and the cars splashing past on their way downtown. Daytime TV bored him; he was a bright boy, had planned on being an osteopath, Miss Kelly said, and music still depressed him, so he didn't have much to do but watch the cars. It takes a long time to get adjusted, Miss Kelly told me. Music depressed him because he'd played the trombone in a dance band, just on the weekends. Nothing special—church dances lots of times, a club once in a while.

On my mornings of agony, he was an itch on the sole of my foot, underneath the callus where I couldn't quite reach it. As I sat on my bed and cried because I was trapped and alone, I'd see him. He snould have made me feel better by contrast, but he didn't. He

196

illustrated my condition so vividly that he made me feel worse, almost hysterical.

Sometimes excitement and eagerness for life rose up inside me like the aching of an amputated limb. I could no more throw myself into it, flying off to seek adventure, than Tommy could. I couldn't even go to a movie. I was just beginning to get enough out of debt to buy red meat. There was certainly no money for recreational baby-sitters, and if there had been, I probably wouldn't have spent it. I felt guilty enough about just wanting to leave James on the two nights a week I had at home with him.

I hoped that Tommy hadn't heard the geese.

Lying in bed that night, I began to plan how I would spend my income-tax refund on some clothes, for me first and then for James. I hadn't had a new dress since my sister's wedding. I was sick of wearing belts on my old maternity bags. I was twenty-eight years old; soon it would be too late for me ever to have been an attractive woman —as if it mattered.

I got the tax refund, but by then I owed it all to a dentist. I kept fifty dollars and bought half a dozen pieces of cloth to make dresses. They were clumsy bags no better than the maternity sacks, but they were nice colors, deep pink and blues and purples. It was unlike me to wear colors, but I felt pretty in them.

The dentist kept me from my five-hundred-dollar wardrobe, but in a sense, he gave me Joseph, and later I came to look upon my two overpriced root canals with some affection.

The pain, a thunderstorm in my jaw, began on a Friday night. The few hours' sleep I got that evening were the last I had for three days. There was no one in Dryden who could do anything about a toothache on a weekend. If I went to the hospital emergency ward and waited for three or four hours, they'd give me something for the pain. Forget it. I couldn't go around doped up when I was taking care of James.

Monday morning I found a dentist who promised to fit me in. He took a quick X ray at eight o'clock and said I had two abcessed teeth next to each other. He shot me full of novocaine so I would wait docilely for a longer opening in his schedule.

I sat on his orange-and-brown Danish Modern couch and tried to read *Arizona Highways.* But now that I was free of pain, I kept drifting off to sleep. I'd see two painted deserts, and then two boxes of plastic philodendrons at my knee, and then there'd be a moment of bliss before I would remember where I was and jerk awake. I had been well conditioned: only derelicts and babies sleep in public.

Each time I'd wake, I'd see a very dour-looking banker in a three-piece suit, staring at me over his copy of *The Wall Street Journal.* I'd glare at him and reach for another copy of *Arizona Highways.* I'd try valiantly to read it, but the next thing I'd know, it would have slipped to the floor.

I began to get quite annoyed by the man's staring. I knew he was affronted by my swollen face, unwashed that morning, and my tangled hair. My brown-flannel maternity dress looked like a nightgown in its old age. I was messy and ugly; I'd just thrown James in the car, dropped him at Ethel's and sped to the dentist's.

"Maybe you'd find these more interesting," the man suddenly said to me, and stood up to hand me two pamphlets from the table beside him. One was on root-canal therapy and the other was answers to questions most frequently asked about endodontics.

"Very funny," I said, putting them down on the couch and going back to *Arizona Highways.* When I looked up he was smiling to himself.

"What's so God-damned funny?" I snapped.

"You. You look awful. I was right where you are a month ago. I'm just patting myself on the back for having lived through it all."

"That's really funny," I said, and tried to read again.

"You know, you could just give in and let yourself sleep," he said, as I picked the magazine and my purse up off the floor. "Either the tooth or Dr. Sullivan will wake you up eventually."

"Christ, if I go to sleep here in this horrible suburban dentist office, I'll probably wake up to find I've been subdivided and made into three split levels. Besides, how can I sleep with you staring at me?" I was picking pennies, a lipstick and two soggy Kleenexes out of the shag of the carpet.

"It's taking a lot of work for you to stay awake! Where do you live? Not in the suburbs, I take it."

"In the city."

"Aren't you afraid? Most of the women I know won't even to in town to shop any more, thanks to our National Guard episode."

"You obviously know the wrong women," I said hostilely. "I

198

figure there's about one chance in eighty thousand that I'll be murdered in the coming year, and I'd never be that lucky."

"Where are you from?" He'd folded up *The Wall Street Journal* and was apparently planning on helping me stay awake.

I went back to the magazine. Then, feeling I couldn't be quite that rude, I said, "Colton," without looking up. "You've heard of it?"

"I went to college there and stuck around to get a couple of graduate degrees. What are you doing here?"

"Here! What am I doing here?" I waved my hand around and picked up a snarl of dirty hair. "I'm just sitting here hoping to get my hair done." Suddenly the absolutely irrational anger in my voice struck me as absurd, and I started to laugh. "I'm sorry," I said. "I'm working for the newspaper, and I don't know why you're making me so cross. I guess I don't like being stared at. What do you do? Clip coupons?"

"Among other things," he said, opening his briefcase and pulling out some typewritten papers. "Sometimes I try to tame savage beasts." He looked at me over the top of his glasses, and his eyes were sparkling.

"Dr. Cooper," the receptionist said, opening the door and ushering out a teen-age boy, "Dr. Sullivan will see you now."

"I'm right in the middle of reading this paper," he said. "Could you take someone else first? I'd like to get it finished now."

"Lucky you!" the receptionist said, beckoning to me.

The dentist was reaching up to raise the volume of the Muzak as I came in.

"Who's that man out there in your waiting room?" I asked him.

"Man? Who could that be?" he wondered out loud.

"Cooper!" I shouted as he came at me with a rubber dam.

"All right now, Mary, we're going to give you some more novocaine and open both of these babies up today. We'll want to put you on an antibiotic. I'm fairly confident we can save both teeth, but it will cost you, roughly, two hundred dollars apiece, without the fillings. You realize a bridge would be about the same?"

I nodded bleakly.

"Interesting man, Dr. Cooper," the dentist said into my face. He'd been tippling the Lavoris. "One of these liberal types, you know, but a very religious man. He was telling me last time about—what was it—oh, something about how if we understand

199

each other and love each other, then there's hope for the problems of the world. I told him, 'I don't know about you, Doc, but I don't want to love you. I prefer broads, myself.'" He winked at his assistant, whose pale-blue uniform matched his shirt. Both matched the color of the light overhead.

"So you're interested in old Cooper? How about that!"

I shook my head violently.

"All right, now, Mary, if you'll just hold still, I think we're done with this baby. He teaches American history over in Babcock, at the state university. Ought to tell you, he's an ex-con, though. Served time in jail in Mississippi a few years ago. Something to do with civil rights. Didn't teach him a thing, though—he's still in there. Sent one of them to me this year—must have pulled him out of some pool hall. But he paid the bills for him, so I didn't complain. He goes into Babcock all the time and talks with these guys. Me, I won't even go there during the day any more. They'll stick a knife in your ribs any chance they get. Doesn't bother him, though."

"You must be a very good dentist if people come all the way over from Babcock to see you," I said after I'd gone through all the rinsing and spitting.

"Cooper, you mean? No, he lives about ten minutes from here, up into the farm country. I am a good dentist, of course."

Dr. Cooper was sitting where I'd left him, reading *Arizona Highways.*

"Watch out, you'll fall asleep!" I told him.

He got up and took my raincoat off the hook and held it up for me. My arm went into a hole in the lining, and I pulled it out to try again.

"It's stopped raining; why don't you carry it?" he said. His eyes were light gray and sparkling.

I suddenly felt very naked, and I quickly put the coat on and buttoned it all the way down.

"You have a car?"

I nodded.

"Well, then drive carefully and get some sleep. You'll feel much better in a day or two. It's been a pleasure," he said, stepping out onto the sidewalk with me and watching me slouch off.

As I got in the car, I saw how my face was all red. I was blushing. And I'd been so embarrassed that I'd forgotten to thank him for

200

letting me go ahead of him. Good. He was obviously some kind of a nut, staring at me and all.

About a month later I was sitting on a plane, hoping to get to Washington for the day and fuming because it was taking us too long to leave the crummy airport, when I saw Joseph Cooper again. He was tall and muscular, standing out in a long string of men coming down the aisle. A young black man in a Calypso hat was holding his sleeve and muttering at him.

"I hear you, I hear you," Cooper said gently.

In the dentist's office I had failed to notice how extraordinarily strong and competent-looking a man he was. He was suntanned and appeared to be very athletic and healthy, confident and relaxed.

A strange thing happened. The ghost of Catherine of Russia stood up inside me. "That one!" she said, pointing at Joseph Cooper. "I want that one. Bring him to me." I looked up at him as he passed my seat and smiled as best I remembered how.

"We'll work it out," he said to his companion and walked on down the aisle. He had on dark glasses, and I couldn't tell if he'd seen me. He wouldn't remember me anyway.

I'd looked him up in the newspaper morgue. There'd been a couple of wire-service stories about "University Professor Jailed in Mississippi Leads Hunger Strike." He'd gone down with some of his students and ended up spending several months in jail, refusing to post bail when he was arrested along with a group for disrupting the peace, parading without a permit and other minor charges.

The plane had been airborne for a half hour when he sat down in the seat beside me, sliding over until his arm touched mine. Then he took off his dark glasses.

"That's better," he said. "And now, what is Mistress Mary's pleasure this morning?"

"I wanted to thank you for letting me go ahead of you at the dentist's. Will that do?"

"Fine. I was afraid you were going to write one of your hostile articles about how I took blacks to the back of the plane."

"I will write a story about it," I said, "unless, of course, you're willing to make some sort of deal."

"Name your terms."

"Well, I really don't think this is the time or place to discuss such things, do you?" I asked primly.

201

"Friday night—you don't work Friday night. I'll take you to dinner."

"God, you've found out a lot about me."

"I have spies everywhere in the city. I even know where you live. I'll pick you up at seven thirty. Will that give you time to get the little prince in bed?"

All day as I rushed about in Washington, I smiled to myself about my great conquest. But by the time I got back to Dryden I was feeling very foolish. God what a stupid thing to have done. Maybe he'd forget about Friday. He'd probably want me to go to bed with him or something awful. That was sort of, well, exactly what I'd had in mind. Jesus, what a mess. Then I looked at myself in the mirror, my pinched, cross-lined face, hopelessly ugly. Repulsive. There was nothing to worry about as far as his having any sexual designs on me. How pathetic of me to have wanted him. It was quite simple. I'd just go home, leave town forever, in the morning.

In the morning, I felt it was a bit extreme to flee back to Colton just because I'd flirted with a man on a plane. Obviously he wasn't interested in me, except as a vehicle for publicity. He'd even mentioned the possibility that I might write about him.

Ethel couldn't baby-sit Friday night; her brother and sister-in-law were coming over to play cards. O.K., she'd keep James at her house, if I brought him over—just for a few hours, maybe two, while we had dinner.

At seven I took James over to her in his pajamas, with his teddy bear and nylon sucks. When I got home, I sat in the living room watching through the windows for Joseph to arrive.

At seven thirty-five I knew he'd forgotten, and what a relief. I opened the door to start down to get James, but Joseph was coming up the walk with his arms filled with daisies.

"I guess you can see how I spent the afternoon," he said, holding his arm out for me to take the flowers. "Out in the meadows picking daisies for Mary. It was ridiculous. I couldn't do any work all week anyway, waiting to see you. You'll have to stop working nights so I can see you when I want to."

"That's why I won't stop working nights," I said. "'Mary and Joseph' is almost too much—under the circumstances—for one evening. For more than one, it's an impossible joke."

202

I found a galvanized bucket under the sink and put the daisies in it. It was the only container in the house big enough to hold them all, and I lugged it to the fireplace. He came and stood beside me as I poked the stray flowers down into the water.

When I stood up, I saw that he was looking at all the junk I'd put on the mantelpiece. There were two turtles, put up there to escape the unintentional cruelty of a two-year-old. There were the insides of an old water meter I'd picked up in an alley in Colton years before and kept because of the patterns of the bronze gears; a dozen plastic pigs the size of a little fingernail which had come inside an Easter egg I'd bought for James, who would only have eaten them; a walnut-sized pebble.

"What's this?" Joseph asked, holding up the stone.

"Some old stone I found in the street."

"When?"

"When I was walking to the hospital to have James. I picked it up to pinch with my hand, to take my mind off the pain, and it was a lucky stone—see the ring around it? So I saved it."

There was a hand-carved Russian bear of plain white wood which my sister had gotten for James for Christmas. Joseph held it up and pulled its string, and its arms and legs leaped up as though it were giving a great ferocious roar of attack.

He laid it down. "Just like Mary, isn't he? You touch the bear and he growls and attacks you." He put his hand on my cheek and kissed me very softly on the mouth. "See," he said, "that's better. You don't need to growl. I'm not going to hurt you."

We rode to dinner in a battered gray pickup truck. "In case you were really nasty, I was going to make you sit out in the back," he said.

He lived on a farm, and they needed the truck. He was using it tonight because his son had come home from college unexpectedly and demanded the car. He had to have it to impress some older woman in the graduate school. There was also a daughter of sixteen, three years younger, at boarding school.

"You must have gotten married quite young," I said.

"Twenty. Elise was only eighteen."

"Where's Elise now, down on the farm watching TV?"

"Not a bad guess," he said. "She did seem to do a lot of that. Actually, she died five years ago."

203

"I'm sorry," I lied.

"I'm sorry she had to smoke cigarettes in bed, although it wasn't a terribly painful death; she wasn't burned, she just suffocated. It seemed terrible at the time, of course."

"Why haven't you remarried? Because you're still mourning her?"

"Maybe. I guess I haven't seen the need. I have a housekeeper, the children are seldom home, I like being alone."

"If you have a housekeeper, you don't need a wife. That's what marriage is, being a housekeeper. A free servant. That's why I'll never get married."

"That's a part of marriage for women," he said. "But the other part is real commitment. You have to have a lot of confidence for that."

"Confidence in someone else, blind confidence, so that you put your destiny in his hands," I said, "and stupidity."

"Maybe. Confidence in yourself, certainly, as being able to handle the commitment and endow it with some significance."

"Blind confidence in yourself as the kind of a person someone wants to be with day and night for years to come."

"Confidence in yourself so that you know he's willing to put up with your bad weeks and months to get to the good ones again."

"That sounds awfully nice," I said bitterly, "but it would make me uncomfortable to know that someone was there with me just because he had to be, or because he couldn't find an excuse to stay out that night."

He looked over at me. "Why do you think I'm with you?"

"I thought about that, and I figured you wanted publicity. Then when I saw the flowers—if they're a PR gift you're either awfully clever or awfully cheap—when I saw the flowers, I didn't know. I guess I thought you wanted something else."

"I guess you thought right the second time," he said. "Something else."

"Wait a minute," I said, to cover up my embarrassment. "It works two ways. I don't want to be with anyone all the time. I even resent having to come home to James, my little boy, all the time."

"Sure, that's normal. But you don't resent him as much as you love him and need him."

"I think you're wrong. I resent him more than I need him."

"Don't argue with me about my revelations," he said.

204

I sat there in the restaurant and scowled at him during dinner. It was a small Italian place, and the heavy air conditioning, combined with the smell of cigarettes and garlic, made me feel queasy. Who was this horrible man who was trying to take control of me, leading me on to tell me what my weaknesses were? I thought about excusing myself to go to the bathroom and leaving him in the restaurant. But it was a long walk to Ethel's and a longer walk back to my house. Besides, as I looked at him I changed my mind. His face was really quite lovely, with fine lines and well-set ears. I wanted to touch them, and I wanted to smell that smoky tea smell of his skin again, as I had when he'd kissed me, and I even wanted to make love again, just once before I was too old. Of course I never would, however. Never.

When James was in bed at home, Joseph took my hands and pulled me up to stand beside him. "Time for us to go to bed too," he said, as though we'd been going to bed together every night for a thousand years.

"I don't know, I don't know. I don't think so."

"What don't you think?" he asked, starting up the stairs.

I had to go through with it.

"Oh, all right," I said, pulling my hands back to cover my face. "All right. I'll go to bed with you, but I'll keep my shoes on."

I was sitting on the edge of the bed, very slowly taking off my dress, sort of stretching it over my head, glad it was a tent to hide me, when I felt Joseph take off my shoes.

"There!" he said, tossing them across the room to the doorway. "One! Two! They're right there, see? Pointing out and ready to leave whenever you are." And it was only then I realized what I'd said in my nervousness.

He pulled the dress off my head and then put his hands on my shoulders.

"Don't leave for a little while," he whispered. "Promise?"

22

At dusk the air was heavy with the smells of honeysuckle and cut hay as we would walk with James up through the meadows near Joseph's farm to look for ferns and mushrooms in the woods, before going home to bed. As we drove down to the city, the back roads were always sparkling with fireflies. It was a beautiful time, those first few months with Joseph. And as I look back it is easy to remember only the joy of being in touch, in love with another human after such a long time alone, and how, out of that pleasure shared, that expansion, the man I would come to love began to take shape.

It is easy to forget that terror also would come upon me in icy waves, incapacitating me for hours. In the midst of the closest happiness, I would freeze and pull away to plan my escape. Once I even made plane reservations to New York and drove with James asleep in the back seat all the way to the airport at one A.M., only to miss the plane by being unable to find a satisfactory parking space, one close enough to the terminal I planned never to see again.

I didn't try to run away any more because Joseph seemed to know intuitively when to come to me and how and when to leave me alone. But equally, I had begun to sense through my years with James that if I wasn't in control of my own life, it didn't much matter. I probably was, but if not, hell, I'd be dead some day anyway. I might as well relax and enjoy the fading of the light.

Three days after our first evening together, the telephone rang at nine ten in the morning. "Miss Hanes, will you hold for Dr. Cooper?"

Joseph said in a very gruff voice that he was coming into Dryden just for a few minutes, and he had to talk to me before I went to work. Would I be at home around one thirty?

I knew from the tone of his voice what had happened. It explained why he had not come to see me on Sunday, the day before. He was obviously not a casual seducer; he might have had one affair since his wife's death, but I somehow doubted it. Now he'd realized how foolish he had been to get himself in a potentially hazardous position with an ugly, stupid, neurotic woman like me. He would try to end things gracefully before they began.

James spent the morning running back and forth under the shower of the sprinkler in the back yard. He was yelping and filling old milk cartons with water and grass cuttings as I mowed the lawn and weeded my lettuce. When I was through, I sat on the steps in the shadow of the house and watched him. Sometimes, I'd get up and wet my hands and press them against my eyes, where the headache was starting in lights gliding past like white mosquitoes.

I would be very calm and mature: "There was no need to go to all this trouble to tell me . . . I knew, but thank you for coming in." That was all I had to say.

Late noon James had to eat. I made him a sandwich and went upstairs and got a towel and dry clothes for him.

"Come in now—lunch," I called, too tired to distract him indoors with a ploy such as his dump truck. I ended up pulling him inside, screaming and kicking every inch of the way. I was drying him off as he snuffled out his last tear when Joseph walked in through the screen door.

"How's Mary this beautiful May Monday?" he asked.

I didn't look up at him. "Fine. How are you? I'll just be a minute," I said, "I want to get James dressed."

As I pulled James's clothes on to his damp little body, I could see

207

the tips of Joseph's immaculate shined shoes, incongruous against the shreds of my rug.

"O.K. Go get your lunch," I told James. He ran off, and I sat where I was on the floor and folded the damp towel very neatly to go in the linen closet, and then, realizing what I'd done, unfolded it.

"I'll just go put this on the clothesline," I said, wondering when he was going to get up enough courage to tell me. As I stood up, I saw that his face was absolutely gleaming with feeling at me.

"Do that later," he said. "Come sit beside me now and talk to me. I've got to be downtown in fifteen minutes for lunch. I have a dozen errands I should be doing, but I just had to see Mary."

And so there were hours of security and hours of longing when he was still amorphous enough in my mind and strongly felt enough in my body to go everywhere with me in the comfortable safety of my imagination. I couldn't think about making love with him because it totally unnerved me, as though I were the heroine of some Victorian novel. One afternoon as I was driving to work I happened to think how in maybe ten hours he would be pushing, thrusting, sliding into me, and my car threw itself uncontrollably around a telephone pole in downtown Dryden.

I would walk down the street talking in my mind to Joseph Cooper, telling him things he'd never want to hear. I guess it was all part of the process of discarding much more than my shoes.

I walked one Sunday morning with James on my shoulders through the preserve, down the deserted trails to the banks and slowly back up through the woods, crawling eventually under James's weight. As I climbed, I wept out a hundred hurts and lonelinesses to Joseph, who was miles away from me, listening to a sermon in a dreary Unitarian church. And I laughed to him about the good things I'd been unable to share, little things James had done, things which no one, not even Joseph, would ever rejoice in as I had. Like the way James would pedal his tiny feet softly into my thigh as I lay on my side to nurse him. Or how, on those numb summer mornings over Mrs. Peck's garage, I'd awaken to the sound of his voice, bubbling and chirping as he watched the crows flapping to and from their nest outside our window. Or how, when he was just five weeks old, I stood over his basket and cried because I was sure he would die from his first cold, and he suddenly really looked at me for the first time and his flushed little face cracked into an enormous smile.

We sat in a clearing to rest, and I watched the shiny black carcass of a muskrat, white teeth shining against the rotted flesh, with the insects hovering over it as they did over the Beast in *Lord of the Flies*. I'd never seen a creature so perfectly swollen and black.

"There are so many things inside me that are rotted away, just from wanting to give life, from giving life, I've lost the ability to love, if I ever had it; to feel, if I ever dared feel. I'm so corseted. All I can give is my hardness. 'Yes, but I'll keep my shoes on.' I can't love you, Joseph. I can't love anyone. I have nothing to give but the anger and sadness inside me. Nothing to share but a quick game of sex."

James was running around in circles on the path up ahead to chase a small white butterfly.

"Fy, fy, fy," he squealed in delight. "Hurt?" he said to me, when he saw my wet face.

"Yes," I laughed, hugging him, "and feeling sorry for myself."

When we got home I wrote all that I'd spoken to Joseph in a long, wet letter, but when he came late that afternoon, I left it in the desk. I still have it, locked in a metal box of souvenirs—one of James's baby nightgowns, a steel ring I stole from a merry-go-round one enchanted summer when I was away from home at sixteen, and a boring detective story, the worst of James Bond, which Alex gave me when I had the flu. I saved it because it was the only tangible gift I ever got from him, and he wrote in the front of it, "For M. with L. from A."

In his own calm and balanced way, Joseph found it as hard to love again as I did. And sometimes he'd tell me things, and I knew that what he was really wanting to tell me, he couldn't put into words.

He'd put his head in my lap and smoke a long, skinny cigar after supper and tease me by blowing the smoke in my face.

"Go away," he'd say, grabbing onto my wrist to hold me . . . "I wanted to have a farm, and I bought one. I wanted to be a farmer, but I'm not. Other things seemed more important to me in my twenties and thirties. I'm not so sure now. I regret having never learned to work with the land, having to hire other men to do it for me, men who humor me by letting me ride around on the tractor on

Sunday. What is more important, really, than the land? What have other things gained for anyone?

"I regret having inherited just enough money to make me soft and my life easy, just enough so I've never had to worry, but not enough to be able to help people in any but a very minor way. I've really done so very little for people, or for myself. And I regret being too shy as a boy to enjoy females. I met Elise, she wanted to get married, and we did, after my sophomore year in college. I was a child."

"You don't regret going to jail, do you?"

"Yes. Sometimes. Maybe I should have fought it. If I'd gotten out, Elise might not have died. At least, she wouldn't have been smoking in bed. I'd made her give up cigarettes, and she only smoked when I was away. Do you ever wish you'd had an abortion?"

"Sometimes. Not when I think of James, at least not when I think of James on his good days. But I don't think there's any similarity between jail and a baby. I was very unhappy until I had him, always running away from things."

"You still are, aren't you? At least, you spend a fair amount of time telling me your travel plans. At dinner, you told me you were moving to New York in the fall. Friday, you were going to take your life savings and go to Greece. I seem to remember similar plans to visit Africa, Chicago and Boston. Several times you've been going back to Colton. I just want you to stay close to me."

I was genuinely shocked. "I do, don't I?" I said. "God, how strange! I did try to go to Atlanta when you went to San Francisco and forgot to tell me. But I'm not going anywhere, really, and I know it! How strange."

"Mary has to keep some sense of control over the relationship, doesn't she? Some sense of equality. But poor Mary doesn't know! She already has it."

"I love to think about your arriving here and finding the house all dark and empty. I've gone forever without even leaving you a forwarding address," I said.

"I'd be very, very upset if that happened. And it worries me to hear your travel plans. I just miss falling into your trap and begging you not to go, each time. I need and I want you."

"You shouldn't," I said, and got up and went outside to walk

210

around the block in the darkness for a while. I could feel my skin, all smooth and tight and warm from a day in the sun. No one could get inside it. I could so easily pack up and leave Joseph in a minute. Someday I would. I'd show him how wrong he was to believe in people, to trust them.

He was really a fool that way, always acting toward people with love and trust, even toward people who'd hurt him quite badly. And he never got bitter, oh, no, not Joseph. He was much too good. He was so God-damned kind and compassionate, he even put up with me. He was so impossibly good, a saint.

I hated him for a few minutes as I walked around. And then I remembered how a priest had once told me at a Rotary lunch I was covering for the newspaper in Colton that for him the hardest sin of all to overcome was the sin of pride.

To describe it to me, the priest had said, "I'm called to go out to the rest home down the road in the middle of the night to give the last rites to some poor old soul. And all the way over I'm telling myself what a good man I am to be leaving my warm bed to do the good Lord's work. Now in telling myself that, I'm sinning just as much as I'd be if I was home in my bed, denying the call."

That was Joseph, congratulating himself, taking enormous pride in the fact that he was always behaving more humanely, more rationally, and of course more peaceably than other people. That was the pride of all humanists, Quakers, Unitarians. They all believe in their own goodness before God's.

For some reason I had no desire to point this fault of his out to him. I just kept my knowledge inside me, and when he was acting so insufferably good, I'd think about it and feel superior—and less annoyed with him. He was quite human after all, and dear; in fact, lovable in a childish sort of way in his monstrous pride.

When I went back to the house I sat in the chair across the room from him and began to read *Newsweek*. After a while, I said, "I don't need you. But I do enjoy sex with you. I mean, I don't much like sex. But it beats Indian wrestling, just by a hair, when it comes to kicks." I would still feel him glowing inside me, in that strange place which only James had ever opened up before, and my skin smelled of his on the warm night, and my hair of his hair.

In the darkness, when he was asleep, I'd draw my knees up to my stomach and wait for the fear to pass.

211

Heavy splashes of rain began to fall on the roof outside my bedroom window. Joseph stirred.

"You're cold," he said, running his finger down the wetness of my back. "Don't always be so far away." He curled his body around mine, drawing his knees up into the backs of mine. "Don't always be so far away."

My voice shook, but I wouldn't cry in front of him. "You know, Joseph, sometimes I feel the world is going to end any minute. It's just that terrible."

"I do too," he said, "but this wouldn't be a bad time, would it, as far as a time for the end of the world goes? I'll wait with you. I like to listen to the rain; I like to hold Mary, even when she is a cold little knot."

But he'd always fall asleep again, leaving me to wait alone.

His sleep was a wondrous thing to me, and when my fear was passed, I'd turn and watch him in the light of the street lamp. I decided people slept in the style in which they lived. James thrashed about energetically all night when we were in the same bed, chasing me from one side to the next. I'd groggily fall off, catching myself in time to stand and stumble over to the other side. In his crib, he was like a dodge 'em car in an amusement-park rink. He'd head for the nearest side of the crib, or its head or foot, and crash into it; then he'd back off and, scratching his sucks under him, into him like fuel, head for the next side.

Joseph asleep was gentle and peaceful. He'd rarely move unless it was with a purpose. And he was so quiet, I often thought he was awake. "Joseph?" I'd whisper. "What time do you want to wake up?"

"Maybe seven? I have to be in Babcock at eight thirty."

I'd set the alarm and then reach over and kiss him, and he'd jump—only then waking up. Even in his sleep, he was able to respond to those around him. Afraid to disturb him, I'd creep slowly toward him, inching up just close enough to lie in the comforting margin of his warmth without touching him.

As I began to know him, to sense what was in the warmth he let flow toward me, the fear stopped. And instead, I'd be a thousand miles away as soon as we'd made love. Suddenly, I'd be floating up through the trees like a bird, gliding through the green, the infinite

212

green leafiness of the woods. I was free and at peace, miles from everyone.

Then I'd feel his body against mine, I'd hear his voice but be too far away to answer him, and then I'd be too far away to even touch him any more. And finally, into my mind would come the idea that I was in bed with Ronald. I'd try to scream, to pull away, to hit him. But I couldn't move or make a sound.

"Wake up," Joseph would shake me. "You're having a nightmare. You're crying. What's the matter?"

I got the idea that by sleeping with the light on, I could avoid what must be a nightmare. When it began, I'd snap myself awake and pull on the light. "I just wanted to see you," I'd say to the squints of Joseph's eyes.

"I'm here," he'd say.

"Why, why?" I asked once, wanting him gone from my bed, wanting to be done with nightmares, with touching and smelling and feeling.

He put his hand over his eyes and laughed. "Because nowhere else can a man have a hundred watts hit him in the eyes at three A.M."

I threw my arms around his neck and then reached back and turned out the light.

"Now, that you've attacked me, don't turn the light off," he said, rolling over on top of me and putting the light back on.

James went with us very happily during the summer. He didn't much notice Joseph, somehow, although he'd run along the beach with him or go out to buy wine with him before dinner. I still felt guilty about leaving James and said I could not afford baby-sitters. I was too proud—no, no—to let Joseph pay.

In October, I decided it was not just James that kept us always at my house. James could sleep anywhere. I asked Joseph why he'd never taken us to his house, only to walk in the woods almost a mile away.

"I guess in the summer it was because the children were there on and off. Now they're away. I don't know. Maybe I'm afraid you'll have another anxiety crisis, thinking I'm trying to make you into a housewife."

"I wouldn't unless you were," I said. "But I might as well be—all I have left is my legal freedom, cooking dinner for you every night,

213

working days to please you, rushing home to get just the perfect meal for my man. Ick!"

"O.K., we'll go there for the weekend, and I really will do some of the cooking. I promise. I'll even send the housekeeper away."

"God, you don't need to pay a servant when you'll have Mary," I snapped, trying to sound as though I were joking.

"I'll send her away so we can have privacy! Just for that, I'll do all the cooking."

The housekeeper left, but of course Joseph never got within ten feet of the stove, although he did take some of the food out of the cupboard the first night.

In the first weeks of our relationship, there had been a long battle about cooking. After seeing the light in Women's Liberation, I had vowed that the only man I'd ever cook for was James, and for him only until he was seven or eight years old. I'd spent years perfecting all sorts of exotic dishes just to win men. No more. I would not cook to be loved. No.

Alas, Joseph had to eat or he got very crabby, worse than a child. I stubbornly refused to let him pay for baby-sitters, so we could go out to eat. We could have dry cereal if he had to eat, I said. And I was dead serious.

"Well, I'm a fine cook," he said. "It doesn't bother me because I'm smart enough to know that cooking has nothing to do with sex." It was eight o'clock, and he was badly in need of food. He stormed out to market.

He came back a half hour later and dropped two shopping bags of food down on the sink.

"I'll help you," he said, modifying his original position only slightly. "Fifty-fifty. How's that?"

Grudgingly I agreed and began to unwrap a steak.

"Damn, I forgot to call Marion to find out what time her plane gets in tomorrow," he said. "She'll be off for the evening in a minute."

He went to the kitchen phone and made a credit-card call to some island in a lake near the Canadian border.

"Aunt Margaret? Joseph. Listen, where's my daughter? I have to talk to her. Oh, way down there? Hah! Could you send one of the boys after her? No, no, I'll wait."

For twenty minutes he chatted with his aunt about sailing; she'd almost gone over in a sneak gust of wind that afternoon, and the blueberries were really good this year! And Marion was feeling fine.

I stood there incredulously. How could Joseph, who was so wise and mature, pull such a sneaky trick on me? It was totally childish. Worse than his continual nagging that I work days, a demand I'd finally yielded to with much anxiety.

For the first ten minutes I stood glaring at him across the kitchen. Then, I decided I'd be as devious as he. I cooked him a meal, all right. Beautiful two-inch steak gray in the middle, peas still frozen, unwashed mushrooms boiled with the withered ends still on their stems.

He looked at his plate with genuine grief. "I've never seen such a heap of garbage," he said, shaking his head and looking at me very sadly. "How could you have ruined *my* supper?"

"How could you have welshed out on your agreement to cook it all by yourself, and then to do half? You didn't have to make that phone call right then! Or you could have asked old Aunt Margaret what time she was driving Marion to the plane."

"I didn't think you were this silly," he said. "I meant, I'd cook half the time. Not that I'd cook tonight necessarily." He shoved his plate away and left the table.

But the next night, he said he couldn't possibly cook in my cast-iron French pans; he had to have heavy aluminum. He went in to read the paper. I put two frozen vegetables on to cook and left them there for a half hour. I ran the chicken under the broiler for a minute, just enough to deaden the skin, and then scraped the charcoal vegetables onto his plate.

"Now, look," he said, pushing the food away. "I have a bone to pick with you. I don't like to see good food ruined. Do you really not know how to cook, or are you playing games with me? Because either you and I cook together or you let me pay for a baby-sitter so we can eat out. I've lost five pounds since Friday, just thinking about that feast. Another five will go after this. I'm going to have to have all my clothes altered."

It was the only time I have ever heard him even begin to raise his voice. I was frightened; I'd lost him forever. I began to cry. "I'm sorry, it's just that I'm so insecure about these things."

"Get over it."

215

I did. The next time he was there, I spent two hours, swimming like mad against the tide of my instincts, to turn out an absurd banquet of homemade consommé, asparagus with hollandaise sauce, lamb chops and warm baba au rhum.

It cost ten times what a sitter would have, but it was worth every penny of it to see Joseph's shock.

"Of course, cooking doesn't have anything to do with sex," I said, rolling my eyes at him.

"It doesn't. This asparagus is just perfect!"

Hell, I did like to cook, but I never admitted it to him. That way I always had my great sacrifice ready to cite, as he was cutting into a lobster tail Bordelaise or floating his spoon in the perfect frothiness of a soufflé Grand Marnier.

Besides, I figured, with him paying for the food, sometimes I came out ahead. Well, maybe not ahead, when I counted the time and energy and nerves I expended preparing his meals. Besides, if I did all the cooking, he said, it gave him time to read my articles in the evening paper and appreciate my mind. But because cooking had nothing to do with sex, I didn't feel too far behind, unless I was premenstrual. Or unless he was in one of his picky moods, when nothing was right. The soup was too hot. I'd forgotten to heat the platter. Where were the salad forks? What had I done with this butter? Left it in the oven? It was sliding all over his roll. On those nights I actually managed to keep quiet, biting my tongue and congratulating myself for being so wonderfully patient.

When we went to his house for the first time, he was supposed to pick us up around six, but it was almost eight when he arrived. I had put James to bed and was sitting next to the radio, planning how indifferent I would be when the news of Joseph's death in a car accident was broadcast.

"Let's go, let's go," he said. "Where's James?" He ran up the stairs to pull him out of bed. When he came down I turned away, but he saw. He put James down on the couch.

"Poor Mary, you were worried! I was all ready to shout back at you. I'm sorry, I should have called. I was in the library just checking on some references and I forgot the time, really. I just got sidetracked."

216

"I never should have mentioned going to your house," I said. "It's just that it makes me feel you're ashamed of me or something, keeping the unmarried mother and her bastard away from your door."

"Don't be silly; it's just selfishness on my part. James will love it, cows and horses and chickens, won't you, James?"

The farm was down the hill from the house, which stood in a woods. We parked at the farm and walked up a dirt path through the trees.

"Don't have too many formal parties, do you? No ladies in high heels on the path," I said, my breath steaming out in the cold, for the first time that year.

"The kids have had some parties. I had some of my students here for a weekend several times. I guess that's it."

In the darkness, I didn't realize at first that the house was made almost entirely of glass. Inside, when the lights came on, all I could see at first were the yellow and brown of the leaves against the night black of the glass walls. The kitchen, bathrooms and closets were banked in the center of the house, and the rooms coming out from them were entirely glass, with curtains that could be drawn between them. The housekeeper lived in a cottage down back, with her dogs. Joseph said, adding defensively, "She's white—and she wanted to live in a normal house. No one but a Cooper would live in a house without walls."

"Look," he said, showing me his daughter's room. "Even my Marion is getting rebellious. She needs more wall space." She had taped zodiac posters on the glass. "That's plenty of wall space, don't you think?" He pointed to the six-inch strips between the bathroom door and the closet, the closet and the hall doors.

The furniture in each room had been built to the same height, just above the knee, and stained dark. Against the dark rugs and the dark wood floor, you didn't notice it.

"Look, to prove I wanted you both," he said, smiling and leading us into the guest room. "There." Aluminum sides had been slipped under the mattress of the guest bed to keep James in.

"I went out to lunch yesterday and bought these. One of my students saw me driving up with them on top of the car and asked me if I was getting so old that I fell out of bed at night."

I put James to bed, and when I came out, Joseph was standing in the kitchen looking in the cabinets. He skipped the can of sardines across the counter at me.

"I'm doing the cooking, but you can open these and put them on a plate with some lemon, which I'll get."

He built a fire, and we sat on the floor in front of it and ate the sardines with some salt crackers and three bottles of cold ale which we shared. Some cooking.

"After Elise died, I felt I had to move out of our house, which was on the opposite end of the property. I had it torn down and immediately regretted it because someone could have lived there. It hadn't been hurt at all, just some wallpaper burned in the bedroom. But I thought I could smell smoke everywhere in the house, and I wanted to build a new one—start again, I guess. The architect asked me what I wanted, and I said, 'No clutter, something flexible, open, undefined.' He came back with drawings for this. I was sold from the first.

"You still feel uncomfortable. I think most people do. I use that as an excuse for not entertaining. You wait—after a few days, you'll find it hard to go back to walls. When I first stayed in your house, I had to tell myself it was cozy, like being in the womb. It made me very nervous. Being in a womb with a woman who I felt didn't care about me at all."

"It was awful at first, wasn't it?"

"I didn't think so then. Anyway, you wait—when you go home, the walls will make you nervous. They'll seem like just that—walls, boundaries, divisions between people.

"A friend of mine, a builder, came out to see the house when it was finished. He took one look at it, stuck his cigar back in his mouth and hopped into his Lincoln. 'I'll give it to you straight, Joe, you're a sick man. Walls give people a sense of being. You're trying to destroy yourself because of Elise,' he said. Maybe he was right."

We took a bath together, washing each other's bodies with the soft suds.

"You were right about the walls," I said as I dried off. "Now I have to get out of this bathroom. It's like a trap—I can't breathe."

"Good, I want you to get out. I don't want you to see me. I'm embarrassed." He was wrapping the towel around his waist to hide his erection.

When we were lying under the sheets together, I said, "You shouldn't be embarrassed about having an erection. You never were before."

"Not in your house; that's the normal condition there. I'm more embarrassed here because it's something that doesn't usually happen. But I'm always slightly embarrassed. It's so ungainly."

"Ungainly in the classroom, perhaps. But I think if I saw my teacher like that I'd clap my hands and bob up and down in my seat. It's really a terrific compliment, isn't it? When I see you like that I feel like shouting 'Yippee.' You just think it is embarrassing now because you don't see any signs on me, but they're there. Lord! I spent an hour fixing my hair and getting my clothes just right. Putting on the make-up I never wear. That's one obvious sign of wanting you. I don't do it when I'm going to work or sitting around with James."

I felt very sad, for some reason.

"There's so much wrong between men and women," I said. "I don't like to see it, at all, because I know how it can hurt.

"James was part of it—not James himself, but what I had to go through because of a child." I leaned over and kissed him. "God, I wish I had had your baby. I wish James, my James, could have grown out of a feeling shared. It must be a good thing—isn't it?"

"I don't know. I don't think anyone ever mattered to me before, certainly not so totally, and certainly not sexually—to my surprise."

I was quiet for a while, trying to decide whether to ask him about Elise or not. No, not now. I went back to my thoughts about babies. "If you want a child, it probably doesn't make any difference whether it was conceived in love or not. At least it probably doesn't matter once the child is born and lying there screaming in the corner," I said.

"Probably not," he said, and he kicked the covers back and brushed up over me and onto me. "Let's find out," he said.

"No. No more babies for me. Never. There are so many other things I want to do with you. But we could pretend."

"Just for now, you want me," he said later. "You'll go on and leave me; you'll go on to better things and places."

"I might," I said, running my hands down the slope of his arms. "But right now, I can't."

Perhaps he went to sleep. After a while, I pulled the covers up over him and kissed his face for a while, and then I fell asleep.

I remember waking during the night to see the room filled with moonlight. Outside, Joseph, naked as Adam in the cold night, was coming out of the trees. He pulled the glass open and slipped inside. For a few minutes, he chilled the bed. Then he shivered a bit, and then pulled the bedspread up around his shoulders. He lay there looking at me, not speaking, for a long time, before he put first his hand and then his cheek on my breast.

Monday morning he put on his three-piece dark gray suit and drove James and me home. He had to go back to the library to finish what he'd started Friday.

In the front hall of my house, James grabbed his legs, "Joz, Joz, don't go."

I picked him up. "Come on, darling," I said. "I have to go to work. Ethel will be here in a minute."

Joseph kissed James's fuzzy hair, and then he kissed me very solemnly on the cheek for a long time. "I do love Mary," he said, and kissed me playfully on the mouth. "I do love you."

23

A few days before Thanksgiving, I took James back to Colton, ostensibly to visit my sister and brother-in-law, who had produced a tiny, soft-eyed baby girl. She lay in her fluffy pink bassinette and blinked, closed her eyes and fell asleep as grandparents swooned over her.

"You weren't like that," I told James, holding him up to see the baby. "You came into the world singing at the top of your old lungs and you've never stopped, have you?"

James ran around the nursery floor happily screaming out his confusion about the baby. We went back to our room, far from the surprised faces, and sat on the floor playing with a yellow school bus filled with peg boys and girls. After two or three minutes, I was bored and picked up my book. Before I knew it, James had slipped out and run back down to inspect the baby. I found him patting the baby's head and making cooing noises.

"Mustn't touch baby!" The baby's grandmother smiled firmly.

So we spent a lot of time walking, exploring the shops near the university. The whole time I was hoping to run into Ronald, but I didn't, and finally I had to telephone him on the last night.

I arranged to meet him three hours before our plane was to leave. I had to see him, although I'm not sure why. Perhaps I was hoping that the sight of him would awaken in me some feeling which would enable me to turn my back on Joseph and the threat his caring posed to me.

We packed Friday morning and said good-bye to everyone. As we started down the path to the street, my sister broke away from her in-laws and came running after us in her nightgown and bare feet. She threw her arms around me, and I saw that she was crying.

"Postpartum blues, I guess," she said, turning so that the others could not see. "I love my baby, I love my husband, don't I? It's just not what I thought it would be—is it?"

"No, the baby's different once it's outside, breathing for itself," I said. "She'll be more lovable when she's older."

"I don't know—maybe I should go back and finish my thesis in January; then I could teach."

"Yes, definitely. Just remember, even that won't be what you thought it would be."

She smiled a little and ran back to the house, waving.

As James and I walked downtown, the sun was coming out a bit, but it was still very cold. I shivered inside my old coat, but he ran ahead of the cloud of his own breath, his yellow head shining in the morning dimness.

We went into a foreign-language bookstore and picked up a parcel that Joseph had ordered, and as we were coming out, I felt someone pulling at my elbow. I looked for seconds before I realized it was Ronald.

"I thought you weren't going to speak to me," he said. "Have I changed that much?"

"No, you look exactly as I remember. I just didn't see you, somehow. No, you're just as tall and dangerous and degenerate as ever. Same old bargain-discount model of Vincent Price."

"I see you haven't lost your tongue," he said, obviously pleased at being compared to a movie star.

I picked James up and carried him to keep him from running on ahead of us too far. Ronald was jabbering about a party he'd been to the previous weekend.

222

James was struggling against being held, and he began to cry and pull at my hair.

"We'd better go on to the airport," I said to Ronald. "It was nice to see you."

"Oh, you can't go, let me buy some ice cream for John."

"Oh, God," I said, starting to correct him but then realizing it was pointless: James or John, it didn't matter to him. "It's much too early in the morning and too cold for ice cream," I said finally.

"Oh, come on," he said. "You want some ice cream, don't you?" he asked James, guiding him into an ice-cream parlor.

"Ice cream!" James screamed with rapture.

Ronald ordered a big mound of vanilla ice cream, covered in blood-red strawberries, and then marshmallow and nuts.

James took one look at it. "Don't want it."

"Could you give us a tablespoon of ice cream—literally just a tablespoon—of vanilla on a saucer?" I asked the clerk.

There was a big conference with the manager. "Have to charge you half price." I nodded.

Ronald was sitting at a tiny toadstool of a table and was halfway through the sundae he had wanted all along.

"What's the matter with him? Doesn't he like ice cream?"

I had forgotten how he giggled with everything he said. God, it was annoying.

"I'm sure he'd love that," I said pointing to what was left of the sundae. "But when you said ice cream, you set his mind on this—ice cream to him."

Ronald looked at the sliver of yellow ice cream on the brown plate and giggled. "If he thinks that's ice cream you're bringing him up culturally deprived."

James finished his ice cream and then ran off to crawl through the metal hearts of the wire chair backs.

"He isn't very interested in me, is he?" Ronald asked, smiling.

"No, he's interested in physical activity right now. So, I gather work isn't too bad?"

"No, listen. Keep this under your hat, but there's a good chance I may get to go to Washington next month. Things are really opening up now, you know."

I didn't really listen. I was feeling sorry for him. He was so boring and stupid. How would I ever tell James what his father was like

223

when I didn't know myself? James would ask some day. What could I say—that I couldn't remember what the good things about him were, but there must have been something besides his posture? Maybe I should stay in Colton and spend some time with Ronald, and find out what it was in him I had found enjoyable. No, I decided, I couldn't take it. I'd die of boredom. The search for Ronald would be up to James if he cared to make it, and perhaps James would find his father behind that smirking face, behind the gibberish about the life of a would-be-more but very lazy news-paperman.

"So I was on my third martini, and this girl came up—man, she was fabulous," Ronald was saying.

"Excuse me, sir, is this your boy?" the clean-up girl asked, leading James by the hand. "You'll have to keep him out of the candy."

"Not mine," said Ronald. "Hers."

"Come on, James," I said, pulling him up on my lap. "You certainly did find the candy. God, I'll have to eat these chocolate hands!"

"Say, I was wondering. Do you ever see anything of Stanton Montgomery? James looks just like him, you know."

We walked out, leaving Ronald sitting there with a sticky silver dish in front of him and a stinky old rope of a cigar in his yellow fingers. We stopped on the sidewalk while I put Joseph's package of books in our little suitcase, and then we went to the bus. That swaying ride was to James the high point of the trip, the airplane being still beyond his comprehension.

We drove directly to Joseph's house from the airport, without even bothering to let him know we were coming. It was dark and close to suppertime when we got there, and I saw his son's new car parked beside his. Of course—the children were still home on Thanksgiving Friday. I left the suitcase in the car, and James and I walked up the dirt path through the trees.

I slid the glass door open and called, "Joseph?"

He jumped up from the living-room floor right away and came out.

"Bad time to drop by?"

"No, no," he said stiffly. "We're just lying here recuperating. The grandparents were here until about a half hour ago. Come in and meet the kids."

224

Fred was lying on the floor next to where Joseph had been, by the fire. He got up and shook my hand very shyly and formally; his eyes were twinkling.

"I'm going to go finish this chapter in my room, Dad, if you don't mind," Fred said, and smiled at me. "Nice to meet you, Mary."

"Marion's upset because I won't let her go a hundred miles out of the state to a party tomorrow night. She doesn't even have a place to stay!"

Marion Cooper, red-eyed and red-faced, was sitting on a stool at the kitchen sink, helping the housekeeper peel potatoes.

"This is Miss Hanes, and James is somewhere. Do we have enough food for one-and-a-tablespoon more people?"

"You mean for him, the tablespoon?" the housekeeper asked. "He's already eating. He knows his way around, that one."

James was sitting on the floor in front of an open cabinet eating crackers from a box he'd pulled out.

Joseph poured some sherry into glasses and then went back to the living room to finish the paper he'd been reading, without even taking his. I carried it to him, and he smiled and thanked me without looking up from the poorly typed page.

I sat on the floor across from him and tried to send him brain waves to stop reading and come talk to me. It didn't work. He was obviously embarrassed about my barging in, and it was stupid of me. I should have called or something.

"Joseph. I think we'll go before dinner," I said.

His legs shot out and he clamped my knees with his feet. "Go where?" he said without looking up from the paper.

"I don't know. Back to Colton, maybe."

"Give me a few more minutes. I'm scheming about how to keep you here tonight and how to get away with you—alone—in the morning. But, first, more important, I'm trying to figure out whether or not Fred is watching your legs through the curtain, because if he isn't, I'm going to come kiss you."

"I'm so awful," I said. "It just comes over me, a great attack of doubt. I don't want to hurt you or disrupt things, though."

He pushed himself up on his hand and landed on top of me, and began tickling me. "You don't want to disrupt things, do you?"

The door in back of us slid open and Fred stuck his head in. He was trying not to smile. "Christ, Dad, you told me not to fight with girls." The door closed.

225

"The new generation," Joseph said. "I forget. To them sex is like eating or sleeping."

"Not quite, is it?"

"Maybe I should let Marion go to her party?"

"She could lose her virginity?"

"No, she lost that a long time ago, I think. At least I've been paying for pills for her for a year or so."

"When is she supposed to go?"

"Tomorrow morning."

"Make witty old Fred drive her up, and he can make sure there aren't any dope peddlers on the corner."

"O.K. That solves the weekend. What about tonight?"

"Tonight we'll go home."

"No. We'll just put James to bed in the guest room, and say good night when the time comes. They probably won't even be interested enough to look through the curtains."

As it turned out, by the time we were ready for bed, Fred had gone to the movies and Marion had gone to her room to wash her three feet of shiny brown hair.

In the morning, when we got up, James was already dressed and sitting at the kitchen table, where he was trying to cut little gingerbread men out of a sheet of cookie dough.

"God love him," the housekeeper said. "He's a little angel, just like my own Timmy."

"Her only son was killed in Vietnam," Joseph said as we ate breakfast. "Tim, that was his name. No problem. We'll leave James with her. I want to fly to New York for the rest of the weekend and look at all the little girls."

"Hey—I just got back from a long trip, remember?" I said. "You go—I'll stay here. Have a good time. In Colton, no one is wearing a bra. So New York should be even wilder."

"I want to see the legs, including yours," he said. "And I want to see a friend of mine, Colin Bernadi. He's a sculptor—you'll like him. I'll call him and tell him we're coming."

Joseph had always told me he was a leg man, but I'd long suspected it was a lie he'd made up to help him over his embarrassment at my flat chest, and I think it was his own disappointment in my lack of bosom that made him bend over backwards to tell me I had nothing to be ashamed of.

226

"I know," I'd say, again and again. "I had big breasts when I was pregnant. They got in the way. I'd reach over to get a teacup and hit myself. It was very unpleasant. They got in the way."

In New York, I sat watching him observe the jiggle in sweaters and blouses and never once look down at a leg. He was talking to Colin Bernadi in the half light of the restaurant, and his eyes would glance at a passing bounce and then back to Colin. I sat there going around in my head happily from the wine and thinking how he really did love me to make up such a leg fetish. He really cared about keeping things easy between us, and through some miracle, I was not running; for the first time in my life I was not scared. In fact, I loved him because he loved me.

In the peach-colored mirror of the Ladies' Room, Laura Bernadi looked at me, sharply.

"I've known Joseph about six months, maybe seven," I told her.

"Colin and I, we just love him to death. He's such a sweetie. He's been through hell, you know" she told me, and stopped to put the white-pearl lipstick on her mouth. "Elise, his wife, was a saint, a living saint. She put up with his radical behavior and the prison term. She was there with bail, of course, the second he was arrested. When he refused, she simply turned around and came back. She'd wait for him, whatever he had to do that he felt was right. It killed her, though; she came up here and cried for days. She simply couldn't imagine how any man in his right mind would elect to stay in a putrid steaming hot cell all summer. Then she died in that freak accident. It wasn't his fault. He meant well by nagging her about smoking. But she just made up for it when he was away. And—it killed her, you know?"

"Yes, I know," I said. "I think he shares your verdict—that he is guilty."

"I didn't say that. Don't put words in my mouth." She snapped her small satin purse together. At the door she turned around. "I just wanted you to know that he is not alone, that there are people who care deeply for him and would do anything to keep him from being hurt again."

"Yes, I met his children." I smiled angelically.

When we were alone in our hotel room, I told Joseph that Laura Bernadi had told me what a saint Elise was and warned me not to hurt him.

227

"She went to boarding school with Elise. That's how I met Colin, years ago. Laura's impossible. She used to call Elise and plant ideas in her head about Communist plots that I was involved in, and diseases I'd get in Mississippi. Yaws was one of them. Absurd."

"Did you talk to Elise a lot?"

"Of course. But she was very much absorbed in the children. She didn't even read newspapers. So I didn't talk about the kinds of things I talk to you about. She wasn't interested in them."

"Didn't she even get involved in the League of Women Voters or the PTA?" I asked, trying to keep the pleasure out of my voice.

"She played cards once or twice a week during the day, and she visited newcomers to the Episcopal Church. If I was making an important speech, or when I got an honorary degree, she'd come."

"She wouldn't go to church with you?"

"No, she was just like you," he said, glad to get into my game and take away my lead for a minute. "She thought if she went to a service in an open, light church everyone would stare at her. She said her stomach would growl. She said she liked to sing hymns and kneel to hide in the dark behind the pews, just like you."

"I'll go to church with you," I lied. "Any time you want. We'll do exactly the same thing we did with cooking. We'll share our religions fifty-fifty. One week church and the next nothing."

"We'll go here, tomorrow morning," he said seriously, unbuttoning his shirt.

"Oh, damn, Joseph. I can't go tomorrow. I didn't bring anything to wear." We were lying a mile apart in our little twin beds, and I asked him if he still missed Elise.

"No—no, I don't. Except when I see the children and how well they're doing, and think how much of herself she gave to them. I wish she could see how well they're turning out, what a good job she did. Sometimes I wish I'd given her more. I wish she could have enjoyed sex, just once. I'd like to go back and make love to her again. Maybe she did, maybe I just remember things as I want to."

"But she had other things, didn't she? She understood her children, she was absorbed by them, she could communicate with them."

"Just the way you do with James."

"No, I don't. I love him sometimes. And we communicate in a

warm, fleshy sort of way. But I can't get inside his world. I can't see things as he does. And I don't want to."

"I don't want to talk about all these serious things," Joseph said. He got up, moved the bedside table out to the other end of the room and then pushed his bed up to mine.

I lay awake most of the night, watching the minutes roll past as numbers on the IBM building and worrying about James. I never made cookies with him. He'd never sit still for me the way he did for Joseph's housekeeper. Elise and her millions of sisters across the country had something I lacked. If I had a million dollars, I wouldn't stay home. I wasn't even like the Flora Crummels, who griped about their children and built day-care centers but felt ultimately that they'd been put on this earth to bear children.

There was a great nervous energy inside me, an angry sort of force, most of the time. It couldn't be satisfied in any way by a child.

Children were nice, children were pretty, children were even lovable, at times. But I would be glad when James was grown up, when we could play tennis together or argue about politics, or anything.

Elise was a saint. Jesus, she probably even put Joseph's needs in front of her own, made sure his shirts were clean and pressed as he wanted them. I could do that, just as I could be a mother, for maybe an hour or two a day.

24

One night late in January, I went upstairs to get a sweater from my room and found James lying across my bed. In his hand was the empty bottle that had held my sleeping capsules. I tried to wake him, but I couldn't.

As I waited for Dr. Davidson's answering service to reach him, I looked under the bed and found a lot of the pills that had been in the bottle, but figured from counting them that he had swallowed at least five, perhaps ten. It had been a new prescription which I'd just gotten from the pharmacy that afternoon. The bottle had been inside my purse, zippered shut, in the top drawer of my bureau. I saw how he must have climbed up on a lower drawer that was not completely in and how he had taken my purse to my bed to unpack it. He had had a thing about pills since his first orange-flavored baby aspirin.

By the time Dr. Davidson told me I could go home from the hospital, James could roll his eyes when I spoke to him and move his mouth as though trying to speak before falling asleep again.

I went home and made myself some tea. As I drank it I thought how, with James safe in the hospital, I could do anything I wanted. I would go to a movie. I looked up at the clock. Ten thirty.

"God damn it," I said aloud. "The first free night I have in three years, and it's too late to go to a movie." Then I realized that was only half of the annoyance of the whole episode. I was supposed to be in the state capital early the next afternoon to cover a meeting I really was interested in, a power-and-light-company hearing. Now, thanks to James, I would be late for it. I had to meet Dr. Davidson at the hospital at eight thirty and wait around to see if James could be discharged. If he could, I'd have to take him home, and I'd be even later. Ethel was just not up to coping with such things as white doctors and nurses and parking-lot attendants.

I was in the bathtub when Joseph called. He'd just gotten in from a faculty meeting. We chatted for a few minutes about out plans for the following night, and then he asked how James was. James had been going through a difficult time, perhaps the beginnings of some oedipal period or something, but he suddenly, bitterly resented Joseph and was very upset whenever he saw us even smiling at one another. When we'd try to talk, he would sing or yell at the top of his lungs to break up even mental contact between us.

"Not too well," I said. "He ate five or ten Nembutals tonight and I had to take him to the hospital and they pumped out his stomach and finally roused him with stimulants. When I left, he was waking up a little."

"Poor Mary, how awful, and I wasn't even home. I'll come in now," Joseph said.

"No, don't be silly. I'm all ready for bed, exhausted."

"You sound so upset, I don't blame you. I'll come in for a while. You shouldn't be all alone."

"I'm not upset," I said, and then noticed that my hands were shaking, and my voice was all trembling as I said, "I wasn't upset until I started telling you. Now, I can see how he looked, lying on my bed with the back elastic in his pajamas all drooping. I was sure he was going to die, but I never let on—I just sat there in the emergency ward, very calmly reading a *Good Housekeeping* from last June. Now we can have Grapenut Jello-O salad with tutti frutti dressing for supper."

I was crying. "Don't come in, I'm better alone. I need to sleep right now, as a matter of fact. I'll see you tomorrow."

231

In the morning, Dr. Davidson said he wanted to keep him through the day anyway.

I called the paper. I couldn't go to the hearing. I went home and got James's nylon sucks for him and called Ethel to tell her not to come. I sat in the hospital by his crib as he slept, and when he woke up at lunchtime, I held him in my lap for a few minutes. But I didn't want to touch him. I put the sucks in his bed and left him, standing at the railing and yowling.

"I'll be back in a little while," I told him. I went to the local mental health clinic and waited for an hour and a half until a social worker was free to talk to me.

She looked like Whistler's Mother, gentle and soft, gray-toned, but when she opened her mouth words came out hard and firm and as straight to the point as machine-gun bullets.

"O.K.," she said, "I'm Mrs. Drummond. What seems to be the problem?"

"I have a little boy, he'll be three in two months, and I don't love him. I hate him sometimes. I've never been married, but I don't think that has anything to do with it. I'm afraid I'll hurt him. He's in the hospital now, because last night I left sleeping pills in my bureau drawer and he ate them. When he comes home, I'll probably murder him some other way. I want you to take him and put him in a foster home with two parents, a mother who will love him and take care of him all day."

I wasn't just crying, I was choking, absolutely drowning in it all.

"That can be arranged very easily. When will he be able to leave the hospital?"

"Maybe tonight."

"Could they keep him until tomorrow? We can have a foster home by tomorrow morning. Will that be soon enough?"

"I guess so—I could keep him at home for one night, to say good-bye and everything," I said . . . "No, I don't want to put him in a foster home, he's my baby. I'd go crazy without him, I'd be so lonely."

"That's what I thought," she said, smiling. "I was worried there for a minute that you were going to take me up on that foster home. I was trying to think where I could put him. I'd have had to take him home with me for the night, just until you changed your mind."

I laughed at the cleverness of her trap.

232

"You're very depressed," she said. "You've been through an ordeal, having a child almost die. I'm going to see if I can get some medication for you, then we'll talk some more. And you shouldn't be taking Nembutal anyway."

She came back with some pills. I was afraid to take them; they might put me to sleep or anything. Who would get James out of the hospital? She glared at me until I swallowed them.

"I feel so guilty," I told her. "When I was pregnant, everyone kept telling me I couldn't be a mother, I couldn't raise a normal child, and they were right. I know he's retarded."

"We'll find out," she said. "If you're really worried, bring him in here and we'll test him. Why do you take sleeping pills?"

"Because otherwise I think and have terrible nightmares. Nembutal cuts down the terrors."

"What kind of terrors?"

"About what a mistake I've made with James, how I'm ruining him. I want to leave him all the time. I want to work. I wouldn't even stay home if I could."

"Who takes care of him while you work?" She asked a lot of questions about Ethel. When I said I didn't know what they did all day, she snapped that I'd better find out.

"I think you should get rid of that baby-sitter. She doesn't sound at all satisfactory to me. He should be with children his own age now anyway."

"I can't get rid of Ethel—she'd never get another job. Her husband has just gotten out on parole and they need the money badly. He's only working part-time in a filling station."

"Whose well-being are you most concerned with here, anyway? The baby-sitter's or your son's?"

"She loves James, though."

"Ask her if she'll work for ten dollars a week less and you'll see how much she loves him. I'll see you again in a week; bring the boy in with you. No more Nembutal. Do you promise?"

When I got home, I telephoned Ethel and asked her what she did all day with James.

"He watches the TV."

"What? What else does he do?"

"He has his lunch. Then he watches the afternoon TV."

"I thought I told you no television, Ethel."

"You told me it was all right for him to watch 'Sesame Street' and the cartoons."

"Yes, but the cartoons are all over by ten thirty."

"Not on UHF; they go all day."

"I'm very disappointed," I told her. "I assumed you understood what I meant. That it was bad for a child to watch more than an hour or two of television in one eight-hour period. Haven't you been taking him outdoors?"

"You didn't tell me to take him out when it was raining or snowing, in the winter."

"Well, I think we'll have to have a serious talk tomorrow. He does have a coat and boots and mittens. He should be out every day unless there's a very bad storm. He has to have exercise."

Maybe it wasn't just Joseph's presence that had been keeping James awake until all hours of the night, running back and forth in his room up and downstairs and anywhere he could get before I caught him. He hadn't had any exercise during the day.

When I went to the hospital to get him at five o'clock, Dr. Davidson said basically he was fine. He would cough a lot for the next few days, as his lungs were congested from throwing off the pills.

"You look very well, too," Dr. Davidson smiled. "You got some rest."

"No, I spent all day crying at the mental health clinic. They gave me some pills. I guess I do feel rather bright."

"I'm glad you went," he said. "Only whatever you do, keep the pills under lock and key. You hear?"

Joseph spent about an hour bouncing around on the floor with James before dinner, singing "We all live in a yellow submarine."

I could never do that with James, I thought, and took another pill.

"If you don't want to fire her, and I wouldn't think twice about it—I'd have had her out of here the minute she said 'Watch TV'—you could make out a schedule for her to follow with James like a schoolteacher's lesson book. He could save his drawings to show you every afternoon, and that sort of thing."

I tried that, and Ethel seemed very enthusiastic the first day, but James had in the evening the same red-eyed glazed look he always had. She said she'd forgotten to save his drawings.

234

I sewed a single thread across his jacket armholes so I could tell by whether it was broken or not if he'd been out.

"Did you take James out this afternoon? It was nice and sunny."

"Oh, yes, we went for a long walk."

"Did he wear his jacket?" I held it up. It had been on the hook by the door where I'd left it.

"Yes."

The threads were unbroken. "Listen, Ethel, I'm going to have to let you go if things don't improve dramatically right away. I know you're lying about taking James out."

The next day I came home in the middle of the afternoon to find James glued to the television while Ethel laughed into the telephone.

"Two weeks. I'm giving you two weeks' notice," I said.

"You can't do this to me after all I done for you." She threw herself on the couch. "With Buddy just come home, and money gone, he's sure to go back to crime, I know it well as I know my own name."

Then she sat up and shook her fist at me. "You just doing what the white man always done, blame his failings on the black. James took them pills you left lying there and you want me to take the blame."

"You might be right," I said, very calmly. "That might be why I'm so vehement about this schedule business. But the fact is, I felt so guilty and upset that I went to the mental health clinic, and they asked me about how James spent his day. I didn't know, so I asked you. The clinic thinks it's important for him to go to school now anyway, to be with other children. So, I'm going to fire you. He'll be in school."

But the next day her husband, who had been out all night drinking, came after her at my house. When she wouldn't let him in, he broke down the door and beat her up.

I picked James up at the police station. "Mumum!" he whispered into my breast, climbing out of the arms of the policeman.

Ethel was in the intensive care unit of the Dryden hospital with a fractured skull. Her condition was fair. She survived, and I tried to get her another job. I drove her to half a dozen interviews because she said she was scared to go alone. She turned down two jobs, one in a training program at a day-care center. In March, she called to say she was going home to Mississippi to live with her daughter.

James was dazed and very withdrawn for several days after the

235

beating. He stayed out at Joseph's with the housekeeper, and after playing quietly in the kitchen with her for two days, he suddenly began babbling incessantly about "meeceman" and imitating their sirens and showing me how he'd imagined they shot their guns, *boom! boom!* He never mentioned Ethel or Buddy or anything to do with the beating, which had been loud enough that Tommy across the street had called the police on his special telephone.

I got James into a private school which cost half what Ethel had cost, and within two weeks he was a different child, running across the schoolroom to meet me every evening, telling me what he'd had for lunch and what a long nap he'd taken, and how the babies upstairs cried when they were hungry.

I went back to see Mrs. Drummond. "You should get more angry at him," she said. "You should smack his little bottom good when he steps out of line."

I called Dr. Davidson. "I spank my children," he said, "but it's up to you what you do."

"I spanked Fred a couple of times, but I always felt that I'd failed when I did," Joseph said.

I'd already failed.

So I tried it: a quick slap on the rear, and James stood right up and obeyed. It seemed as though he liked to have it as a gauge for his behavior. He began to enjoy being "a good boy," a term he learned in school.

"I goodboy!" he'd say.

"Yes, you're a good boy most of the time, but sometimes you're naughty. Everyone is. But I love you even when you're naughty."

I couldn't bear to think he'd feel unloved.

"That's because no one loved you when you were a child," Mrs. Drummond said. "It's just written all over you; you were made to feel so awful and ashamed of yourself, unworthy and unlovable."

"Ahhk! So what?" I said.

"You're going to have to face these things."

"I have, I have, I have. It doesn't do any good. I'm just ambivalent about being a mother."

"You've built up an image of what a mother should be. Mothers are people. They get bored and angry, but they take care of their children when it's their responsibility, and they see that their needs are met. You're doing that. You've made some mistakes. Nobody's perfect. You think I didn't make mistakes? Let me tell you, I raised two sons alone and I used to get so mad at them. Today they're married, have five children all together and are very independent. No thanks to me, I'll tell you."

"I never should have kept James," I said, "All those social workers were right. He needs a father."

"Well, get him one."

"Yes, but I don't believe in marriage."

"That's very interesting. Tell me more about that one."

"Uh, hell, I can give you a hundred rational reasons, most of them having to do with women's liberation—you are exploited in marriage—"

"Only if you want to be!" she shot at me.

"O.K., let me finish. You may be exploited, but to be honest, I have to admit that when it gets right down to it, I'm too scared. I've always just panicked at the first mention of it."

"You think you're so unlovable that anyone will walk out on you. The minute you depend on someone, he'll be gone."

"I agree. But what do I do?"

"Time. Maybe you shouldn't get married. I don't see any reason why you should. You don't want to, do you?"

"No. I don't see any reason to at all."

She handed me another slip of paper with another appointment for a month from then.

"I'm not going to let you get away from me," she said. "I really like you. If I'd had a daughter, I'd want her to be just like you. Now, what you have to try to do is to think of yourself as a mother, but not with all the bad associations you have in your mind about becoming a mother. You really got off on the wrong foot, you had such a negative image built up in your little head about Mary the Bad Mother."

I walked back to work in the rain. I knew what she was trying to do, telling me she'd like to have a daughter just like me. She didn't even know me. But maybe she was right, I did expect to fail as a mother at least partly because I'd been told I would.

James was a lovely child. Of course, we'd see what he'd be like in ten years, or twenty years, how much of his outgoingness and trust he retained or how much of my disease he'd caught.

But I had made some progress, a lot of progress, in the nearly

237

three years I'd had him. I was close to someone now, wasn't I? I wasn't walled off at all any more. I'd never be the way my father had been, sitting alone in the dark of the early morning, unable to speak out his miserable isolation.

During my last two years at Miss Seymour's, I'd often set my alarm for three thirty or four in the morning and get up to do my homework in the peace and quiet. Most mornings when I went down to get some cereal, I'd find my father at the kitchen table. When I'd touch his shoulder, it would be as hard as stone, and his back was locked in the brace.

"No, no." He'd shake his head. "Go back to bed, sweetie." He'd light a cigarette.

I'd lie awake wondering how much longer he could survive without cracking open to an embrace, a tear, a face. Every day, I expected the telephone to ring and a strange voice to announce that he'd died of a heart attack in the street. In the end, he died of lung cancer in six pain-filled silent months. And he went without sharing a word about what was happening to him. In my sleep now he comes to me, and cries out, "Mary, I'm dying. Help me!" and I hold him to me, as I hold James.

In the spring, in April, James blossomed even more; his jealousy of Joseph disappeared to a great extent after a crisis one night at the end of March.

When James had been screaming and throwing things in his room all evening, and we were having trouble getting to sleep because of it at eleven P.M., Joseph got up, put his shorts on and went into James's room without saying anything to me.

I expected to hear great crashes and increased moanings, which had happened every time I'd been in, but suddenly, there was silence; and Joseph came back to bed with James in his arms. I could hear James hiccoughing with the end of his tears, and then he was quiet, and his hands were exploring Joseph's face.

"Get sucks, Mumum!"

I got up and got his nylon sucks from his bed and brought them to him in Joseph's arms. He fell asleep cradled between us, and it was breakfast time before any of us awoke.

I expected him to be back at our bedside, sucks in hand, the next night. But when bedtime came, he said good night to Joseph and went happily upstairs. After that, he came into the room at night

238

only a few times when he was sick and wanted me to put his seat on the toilet for him.

Evidently, once James was shown that he could share in whatever went on between Joseph and me if he wanted to, he decided that, in that case, he really had better things to do, like play with his flashlight or listen to his radio.

Then he began to fall in love with Joseph; and in some ways, I think it was only then that I really began to fall in love with James. We had something to share, the two of us: our love and our need for another person.

Whenever anything happened, he would announce to me he was going to tell Joseph. Usually, I didn't mind: the car got a flat tire and I changed it all by myself; or there was a birthday party in school; or the rain came in the back door and the thunder boomed. Sometimes, it was awkward. Joseph didn't have to know, I thought, when I burned six eggs in the morning, or when I didn't answer the telephone because I had to finish reading the end of the book before I got distracted with Joseph and dinner plans.

Much more than I did, James acknowledged Joseph as the head of the house. To Joseph were all things due, and he was responsible for everything.

James and I watched in horror as the toilet overflowed. "Jozev, Jozev," James screamed, putting his hands over his mouth.

"Ssh! I can take care of it," I said, and ran for the plunger and newspapers.

When we'd get to Joseph's house, James would sing the whole way and run up the hill shouting "Jozev" so loud that the dogs on the farm would begin barking.

At the end of May, Joseph went away for two weeks. He had to give a commencement address at a prep school on the West Coast, and he wanted to do some climbing in Wyoming for a few days with Colin.

Every night, James ran up and down on the front walk watching for his car.

"I go find Jozev," he'd say, kicking at me and crying when I went to bring him in for his bath. "I want my Jozev." I'd pick him up and carry him inside. "I going to tell Jozev you hurt me."

"You'll have to wait to tell him until next week," I'd say. "He's on vacation."

239

"No 'cation!"

"Yes, vacation. I wish it were no vacation too, I miss him terribly. Won't it be nice when he's back?"

"He come back?" James said, smiling happily.

"Yes, I think so. I hope he'll be back."

25

It is a hot July dusk and we are moving slowly in the swampy green flow of the Lowland River. Wood ducks and kingfishers and a family of blue herons flutter up into the trees to wait until the canoe has passed, leaving a thin dark trail in the pollen-dusted water.

The green of the trees is all around, hanging down to brush our heads, and we lift the branches to pass. The greenness is the green of the dream I used to have after Joseph I and made love, but now I can reach back, way back, stretching over James, and just touch Joseph's hand, and I can speak to him; but I am too sleepy from the heat, and too happy and peaceful from having him there guiding the canoe, moving us with the strength of his back. My paddle pulls in and out of the water, but when I stop and turn around to save James from the spider that has just fallen into his lap, the canoe keeps right on moving. It is Joseph who is carrying our weight.

I bump clumsily down onto the floor of the canoe as we pass beneath a tree fallen across the stream, and as I pull myself back up, I see Joseph meet the same trunk with all the grace of a dancer. He bends to the side, and back around and up again. He smiles at me.

James points to a big log coming up through the green water. "Look, Jozev, hippo!" and at another branch fallen half into the water, "Craw-dile."

We pull the canoe up onto the scrubby bank and start to walk up the hill. The roughness scratches James's leg and he whimpers.

"Stop that!" I say. "It doesn't hurt." But Joseph picks him up and lifts him onto his shoulders.

I wait until they catch up with me. "You're taller than a giraffe!" I say to James, and putting the bag of our supper under one arm for a minute, I press my hand into the small of Joseph's back to let the humming of my palms pass into his skin.

"What? Come on," he says, crabby from hunger. But he pats my behind.

We picnic sitting on the porch of an old shell of a cabin, overlooking the river. The wine is still cold. I fill James's plastic cup with ginger ale.

"Cheers!" he says, and holds up his cup to repeat the toast after almost every swallow.

We eat chicken and artichokes and hot-red strawberries, and James's voice is the only one against the twittering of the woods in the sunset until we are finished.

As I am packing up, James says "Pee." Joseph and James walk around to the back of the porch and I hear first one and then another splashing, and great yelps of glee from James.

We walk back to the water the long way, down through a mountain laurel grove, and Joseph stops to finger the shiny leaves, black in the dusk. "So pretty," he says. "I keep meaning to plant some outside the dining room where the lilac died."

In the car, going back to Joseph's, James falls asleep with his head in my lap.

Joseph and I swim in the pond below his house, with the fireflies around us and the stars above. I am surprised to find no leeches on my legs when I get out, and we walk back up the hill hand in hand, agreeing that it has been a rare sort of day, perfect, and wishing that I did not have to leave in the morning for the NAACP convention in Minneapolis.

"Work! Mary and her work! Why is the paper sending you? Look." He stops. "Here, don't you think mountain laurel would be nice here?"

242

"Yes, it would—I think I should dislike it, but I don't."

I start telling him about how when I was four months pregnant, my grandfather took me out into his garden so we could confer privately. It was all arranged, he said, I was going to have a Caesarean abortion. It wouldn't leave a big scar, just a sexy little scratch, he said, pointing to his own groin. He kept mentioning the scar, as though it were only fear of that which was keeping me from destroying the life within me.

He began to complain about how pointless his own life had been, about how all life came to nothing, life itself was cheap, and, how above all, one had to think of the family.

He pointed to a brown mountain laurel bush sitting on the other side of the garden wall in the sunburnt autumn field. My grandmother was buried under that bush, he said, telling me something that rather sickened me, she had been so neatly cremated and the ashes forgotten. Above all, I must think of her. He was in tears.

I said I was thinking more of the baby these days, the baby who would, by the way, be her great-grandchild. I laughed bitterly.

"I know you've always felt yourself outside the family, alone and unloved," he said. "But all this will change, believe me. I have let you down. Just because you were on your own and so independent didn't mean you had no need of love or guidance. I realize that."

When I got out of the hospital, he said, with my kissable little scar, I would come right back to his house. I should forget about being a newspaper reporter; that had been no job for a woman anyway. When I was ready, I could go to graduate school, or whatever I thought was best. But one thing was certain, I would have love and a family. Why, I might even be married in a few months. The scar would be nothing. It might even be possible, although he couldn't promise, for the small incision to be made low enough down to be covered later with pubic hair.

Would I think it over, reasonably, in the next few days, and let him know? He was confident I would make the right decision, he said, despite the reluctance I was expressing. If I didn't do as he suggested, it was clear he'd have nothing further to do with me.

I went back to my apartment and thought about it until I fell asleep. Yes, I decided in the morning, I'll do it, I'll have the abortion.

"Only I realized I had less reason to trust him then than I had had

243

in the previous twenty-five years, when most of my antisocial behavior had been unknown to him. I called him up to tell him my decision, but he'd already left for his winter house in the Caribbean. I was so shocked—and hurt. I began to cry. His secretary said she'd be glad to pass on a message when she talked to him the following week.

"That's what mountain laurel makes me think about. I remember looking at that dying bush and thinking how truly unhappy and lonely I had been until I'd found out I was pregnant. Later on all the social workers and people told me I was just keeping the baby so I would have a family. It turns out now they were right."

"There's nothing wrong with that," Joseph says. "Everyone is supposed to want to have children, to have a family. That's normal."

"Yes, and you're supposed to want to have enough money, but not by robbing a bank."

"But you didn't take anything that belongs to anyone else. You didn't hurt anyone."

"Ronald—"

"Oh, by all means, let's all weep for Ronald."

"Maybe it will hurt James."

"Yes, and maybe I'll hurt Fred or Marion. But it seems rather doubtful."

"Anyway, right or wrong, hook or crook, I do have a family now, don't I? That makes me feel so happy. Incredible, but I never thought of it in those terms until now, just now. James is my family, and you."

Joseph is standing in the wedge of light from the refrigerator door and drinking milk out of the carton.

"But I'm not part of your family and you're not part of mine," he says, frightening me. "I'm just the boyfriend until you're ready to make a commitment to me and our life together."

"You mean by marriage."

"Of course. Maybe if my children were older, married, independent, I wouldn't care." He gets down on his knees to pull out a box of crackers. "Hell, they have nothing to do with it. They'd probably say, 'Who needs a piece of paper?' just as you do. But I do. Damn it, I want you and James living here in my house, and I am too middle-class to have it week in, week out, without being married to you."

244

"You just want to own me. You want a guarantee that I won't run away."

"Yes, exactly. I want to be as sure as anyone can be in this life."

"If I ever got married, you know, I wouldn't wear a ring and I would keep my own name for all purposes," I say childishly.

"You make the initial decision, and we'll work those things out. As long as you have your own house, you're just playing a game. You can always go home, and you do half the time. If you didn't need to remind yourself how independent and secure you are all by yourself, then you would really be independent and secure. And when you are, you won't be afraid of your little piece of paper."

I get off the stool and start to leave the kitchen.

"Think about it this week when you're off in Minneapolis. Think about what would be so awful about admitting that you depend on someone. God, Mary—I depend on you."

In bed, I turn my back on him angrily. "You're just like my grandfather. You are asking me to throw away the happiness I've found in exchange for a promise."

"It's not a promise of anything you don't already have. You know what it is. You have it, you thrive on it."

"No, people change, people grow. How do I know what I'll be like in a year or two? Or in ten or in fifty years? It makes me sick, Joseph, really sick with fear, just thinking about it."

"That's something we can work out together, if you don't turn your back on me," he says, pulling me over in the darkness. "Sweet one," he says, "You were afraid to take off your shoes in the beginning. Now you've got two and a half pairs littering my closet."

The hotel in Minneapolis is a rambling ark with warped floors and flocks of cantankerous old women residents sitting on the lobby chairs and shaking their heads to one another about the invasion of colored people. And it is an invasion. The city is suddenly packed with black faces.

It is midnight before I can get to my room. It is stuffy with old air conditioning, which I turn off. I open the window and put a musty pillow over my head to drown out the sound of the preconvention gaiety.

I sleep very restlessly that first night. Almost immediately, I dream that the woman who is taking James to school and staying

245

with him at night has taught him how to go to the supermarket and prepare for himself the food he buys. I shout at her, furious that, thanks to her, he has no further need for me.

And later, I dream that Joseph is making love to me and, near the end, pulls away suddenly, leaving me ready to come and aching.

I wake up and the room is hot. The parties continue on all sides. It is four in the morning. I take a bath, get dressed and start to write a story to telephone in to the newspaper for the afternoon edition. At six thirty the dining room opens and I go down to breakfast.

During the day, I am too busy to think about James or Joseph. I do not sit down until six o'clock in the evening, when I call in a story for the morning paper and rush out to get some food before the evening meeting begins. However, that night when I get into bed at one o'clock I miss them, and I fall asleep to dream that Christian Barnard saves me with a heart transplant.

After he removes my black, diseased heart, he realizes that the replacement heart donated for me has been given to another patient. We discuss whether I should accept death gracefully or have an artificial heart put in my body. I elect the latter course, and he fits the metal, breastplatelike heart device around my chest, where it presses down on me, making it hard for me to breathe.

"You'll be out of this device soon," he tells me in his South African Dutch accent. "We will scour Cape Town to find another donor. In the meantime, your troubles are over. You are adapting well. There will be no rejection crisis now. You can live in this forever, if you wish. Believe me, it is all downhill for you now."

After that night, the convention is in full swing. I am too tired even to dream. I refuse invitations to parties and crawl back to my room to sleep for a few hours before breakfast. One of the Dryden delegates asks me if I am staying away from the parties because I don't mix with black people. I shake my head, too tired to care whether he believes me or not.

The last night I am there, Leon Sullivan, founder of Opportunities Industrialization Center, Inc., the first black member of the General Motors Board of Directors and a Philadelphia minister, delivers a speech in a black preacher's fiery tongue of incitement.

Middle-aged delegates—schoolteachers, lawyers, doctors, other members of the black middle class—begin yelling "Amen" and cheering to the rhythm of his words. The convention hall sweats and rocks. His voice is like an opera singer's, the loudest and most powerful sound I've ever heard rise out of a human chest, and I am caught up in the excitement he is generating, and the sense of pride and love and power.

I have an advance copy of his speech which has been released to the press. I stay only long enough to make sure he will follow his text and will indeed call for an end to apartheid in South Africa.

As I am leaving the hall, Sullivan is bellowing, "I want to see the black man, and the brown man and the red man, able to make his own way in the world, and stand on his own feet. . . . "

The hall is shaking with shouts of "Right on" and "Amen" and "Yes, brother, take your time now!"

Before I call the newspaper, I call Joseph. It is just after midnight at home, and I wake him up to tell him what time my plane will be landing the following night.

I say good-bye to the Dryden delegates the next afternoon and go to my room and wash my hair. I sit brushing it dry in front of the open window, looking over the blandness of the Minneapolis street, and plan what I will do when Joseph is not at the airport, as he has promised to be.

On the plane, I think how after that second night it was easy being away. It would be only occasionally discomforting to go through life living in one empty hotel room after another, moving from strange city to strange city. When I get to the airport, I will check into a motel and leave on another plane in the morning. The anonymity of such aloneness will be soothing. James and Joseph will not care for long, and they will be better off. The newspaper will survive, very easily.

As the plane pulls up at the gate of the terminal, I look away from the window. If Joseph is there, I do not want to see him. As I walk up the ramp, I read the airlines magazine very carefully. When I peek up, I see his eyes sparkling. He's kissing me.

"The tap water is so soft, you don't even need much soap—it just bubbles up," I chatter away compulsively, as we drive through the darkness. I have not talked to anyone in almost a week. "And they gave us real crab meat in our salads on the plane! And pot roast. It was quite good."

He puts his hand on my knee. "Just be still," he says. "It's all right."

247

And I am still. I smell the honeysuckle in the night air again, and I wonder what that sweetness and Joseph, and Minneapolis, and James asleep off somewhere in Dryden, and the NAACP and the whole world, the entire universe, have to do with me. I feel nothing for any of it. Nothing whatsoever. No.

Joseph's house is dark and cool. He doesn't turn on any lights, just a record, a new recording of a Mozart piano concerto he loves. I stand in the dark listening to the tinkling, and I clutch my elbows.

"Are you home yet? Will you come to bed?" He opens my arms.

I let my clothes fall indifferently on the floor and I lie down, prepared to go through the motions of sex. But when he comes inside me, it is he; it is my Joseph gently pushing me, prodding me to open, and I tremble and burst to receive him, to take all that life, flowing to build a channel between us. And then I lie quietly, wondering at what wonders flow between us in that almost placental closeness.

"I want to grow inside you, I want to extend myself into you, so much," he says and we talk again, as we seem to talk almost weekly now, about a child.

"You'd have to stay with me in the delivery room, the whole time," I say. "You put it in, you take it out. But I don't want to have a baby, not rationally. It is the last thing I want. No, never. But I do want it, I feel you there and I want you to just keep on growing—but it wouldn't be like that. Would it?"

"You want to find out as much as I do. We'll have a baby some day, and it will be a girl. I have it on indisputable revelation." And he falls asleep with hand on my belly.

In the morning, I am menstruating. Fortunately, he is up first and does not see the sheet. I am ashamed. In more than a year, I have hidden this from him successfully until now. When I hear the shower, I remove the sheet quickly and remake the bed. I roll the soiled sheet up and stuff it in the back of the closet.

"Why are you making the bed?" he asks, sticking his head out of the bathroom and shouting over the sound of his razor.

"We needed clean sheets."

"You didn't have to get them."

I am in the bathroom when he knocks on the door. He hands me the rolled-up sheet. "That should soak, otherwise it will stain," he says.

248

For a minute I think I am going to throw up. I am glad the mirror is steamed so I do not have to see even my own reflection. I know I heard disgust and hatred in his voice.

I scrub the stain savagely in cold water until it is faded enough so that when it is dry, the housekeeper at least will see nothing.

Joseph is reading *Scientific American* when I come into the dining room. He drops it quickly and pours himself some more coffee before picking up the Dryden paper, which contains the last of my articles on the convention. He has finished eating.

The housekeeper brings me some juice, but I am too tired, even after nine hours' sleep, and too upset to drink it.

"Come on, then," Joseph says. "I'm late. Are you going to work?"

I shake my head.

"Well, then, you'll have to drop me off at my office and drive yourself home. I'll take the bus over tonight and you can meet me."

I think I am going to cry as we drive back to Babcock. "I am empty inside," I say into his shoulder. "There's nothing there. I am so lonely."

"That's part of being a woman, don't you think?" he says. He is already talking to the new group of summer students, I can tell. He has on his omniscient-professor look, and he is leaning very seriously against the dais, and peering up over the tops of his glasses. "We will be dealing this term with the history of American peace. Think about it. Peace, not war," he is saying.

"You're not mad about the sheet?"

"Look, after you drop me off, go to your house and go back to bed. I won't be through until five or so. I'll call home and say we'll all be there for supper. I have a wooden hippopotamus for James—I meant to take it in to him the other night."

He gets out of the car, and I slide over into his seat and pull it forward. He stands there, hesitating to go in to the history building after all the rushing. "Did you think about what I asked you to?"

"Yes and no. I want to see James before I talk about it any more."

"Get some rest. I'll call you before I leave."

I pay the baby-sitter and clean the house. Then I lie down and try to sleep, but I am too keyed up. At two, I can wait no longer and I rush over to school in my car.

All the children are lying on their cots for their afternoon nap, so I have to go around to the back of the building, where the teachers sit at the kitchen table drinking coffee.

"Oh, I'm so glad you're back," one of them says. "James really missed you, acted very quiet and strange. I'll go wake him up—he's downstairs."

One of the aides is complaining about the mayor's refusal to attend a city council meeting that night to explain why he's endorsed a drug-treatment center for her neighborhood.

"You know, they're already coming in—the streets just aren't safe any more. And now, he's going to bring a lot of addicts in. You know, two of them got the lady down the street just the other afternoon, knocked her down and took her purse."

I had forgotten about all this hate while I was in the black, intelligent, optimistic atmosphere of the NAACP. I want to get back to work. I want to get at these women's prejudice and anger, and at my own.

James stands blinking in the doorway, all matted and foggy from sleep.

I am crying as I pick him up.

"I missed you so badly." I mean to lie, but realize as I say it that it is no lie at all. He is crying too. He hides his face in my neck, and I carry him to the car.

James loves to have me recite our schedule.

"Go home, have a long talk, play in the yard, watch 'Mister Rogers,' meet Joseph at the bus, go to Joseph's house, have supper, take a bath, go to bed."

He throws his arms around my neck, nearly forcing us off the road.

"Joseph has a present for you and so do I, a motorcycle policeman . . . James," I say, as we start up a hill toward our house, "Are you happy as things are now? Would you like to stay the way we are? Or live at Joseph's house all the time?" Then I think of a third intriguing possibility. "Or would you like to go away with me to a new country to live?"

"Huh?" he says. "Huh? Go home, watch 'Misrog,' get Jozev, take bath, go bed."

"Just think, James! A new city, a new country, with real hippos and crocodiles and lions, tigers, giraffes. South Africa, James, Cape Town! How about it?"

250

"Huh?" he says. "Huh?"

We are stopped for a red light, and he climbs into my lap.

"Go home, get Jozev. . . . "

I squeeze him. "You're my home, you nut cake. You're my home."

"You nut cake," he laughs, "you nut cake!"